# TESTIMONIALS

**Matt Holland, former Ipswich Town and Ireland captain**
'Values, integrity, ambition and a real connection with supporters aren't things that happen by accident. They come from the tone set at the top, and David always ensured that Ipswich Town was run in a way that players, staff and fans alike could be proud of. It was a special era for all of us who had the privilege to wear the shirt, with moments that stay with you forever.'

**George Burley, former Ipswich Town manager**
'David was an Ipswich supporter and a Suffolk man who was in it for the right reasons, and he brought vision and lots of enthusiasm. We enjoyed an immediate rapport, and our ambitions were aligned from day one.'

**Martin Glenn, former Football Association chief executive**
'David's determination to open up the FA to best practices from other countries and sports has massively helped our national team's competitiveness, and St George's Park has made this vision a concrete reality.'

**Henry Winter, football journalist and podcaster**
'Insightful reflections from a man at the heart of an extraordinary era in English football.'

**Terry Butcher, former Ipswich Town and England captain**
'David Sheepshanks is the football fan who got the chance to run the club he loves, guiding Ipswich through a very special time in the club's proud history.'

**Joe Royle, former Ipswich Town manager**
'I was extremely lucky to work with David, who was a big reason for me taking the job in the first place. I look back on my time with him, and service to the club, with great pride. His calm authority, integrity and deep understanding of the game, club and its DNA gave everyone a sense of stability, purpose and belonging. David truly cared about Ipswich Town, the supporters, the community in Suffolk, and he always carried himself with a dignity that earned enormous respect throughout the game nationally. I always felt that English football would have been extremely fortunate to have had him as Chairman of the FA, he possessed the judgement, balance, and long-term vision that the role demands.'

**Richard Scudamore, former Premier League chief executive**
'I worked closely with David to help him deliver his vision for improving the EFL and FA. He has always been a force for good, whose enthusiasm for football, and for life, has never dimmed.'

**Frank Dick, former UK Athletics coach**
'David lives a learning culture – curious, hungry to improve, and able to connect insights from all fields. His world is football, but that hunger has sought experience and expertise from other sports, professions and the business world.'

**Damian Hughes, author and podcaster**
'I have always admired David's thoughtful leadership and quiet determination to leave any situation better than he inherits it. His persistence and refusal to accept the status quo brought St George's Park to life. He has certainly left English football in a better place.'

**Lord Michael Barber, cabinet adviser and chairman of Somerset CCC**
'David Sheepshanks combines the urgency and ambition on which change depends with a deep human sensitivity to those responsible for making it happen.'

**Jim Magilton, former Ipswich Town manager**
'David's determination to succeed was one of the main reasons I joined Ipswich. His "one team, one dream" approach resonated throughout the dressing room and amongst the supporters and it helped drive us all towards that glorious day at Wembley. I will always be grateful to him for believing in me. His support and advice are things that I will never forget. He is a true Ipswich legend and a gentleman.'

**Colonel Lucy Giles, former commander Royal Military Academy Sandhurst**
'David's calm, inclusive leadership is both inspiring and deeply human. His passion and kindness bring out the very best in people.'

**Kevin Beeston, former Ipswich Town and Premier League director**
'David is an exceptional leader, visionary, driven, empathetic and fun. Genuinely authentic and passionate, he inspires belief and delivers.'

**Matthew Syed, journalist and author**
'David Sheepshanks has made a visionary contribution to English football. This is a scintillating account of that journey.'

# MAN ON A
# MISSION

# The  Report

**Love great sportswriting? So do we.**

Every month, Pitch Publishing brings together the best of our world through our monthly newsletter — a space for readers, writers and fans to connect over the books, people and moments that make sport so captivating.

You'll find previews of new releases, extracts from our latest titles, behind-the-scenes interviews with authors and the occasional giveaway or competition thrown in for good measure.

We also dip into our back catalogue to unearth forgotten gems and celebrate timeless tales that shaped sporting culture.

Scan the QR code and join the growing Pitch Publishing reader community today.

# MAN ON A
# MISSION

## DAVID SHEEPSHANKS

The Agony and Ecstasy
of a Life in Football

First published by Pitch Publishing, 2026

1

Pitch Publishing
9 Donnington Park, 85 Birdham Road
Chichester, West Sussex, PO20 7AJ
www.pitchpublishing.co.uk
info@pitchpublishing.co.uk

© 2026, David Sheepshanks

The moral right of the author and illustrator has been asserted in accordance with the Copyright, Designs and Patents Act 1988

Every effort has been made to trace the copyright.
Any oversight will be rectified in future editions at the
earliest opportunity by the publisher.

No part of this book may be used or reproduced in any manner for the purpose of training artificial intelligence technologies or systems. In accordance with Article 4(3) of the DSM Directive 2019/790, Pitch Publishing expressly reserves this work from the text and data mining exception.

Set in Adobe Caslon Pro

Typeset by Pitch Publishing

Cover design by Olner Design

Printed and bound by TJ Books, UK

The authorised representative in the EEA is Easy Access System Europe OÜ, Mustamäe tee 50, 10621 Tallinn, Estonia gpsr.requests@easproject.com

A CIP catalogue record for this book is available from the British Library

ISBN 978-1-83680-471-0

Papers used by Pitch Publishing are from
well-managed forests and other responsible sources

*For Mona, Sophie and Tom*
*with thanks from the bottom of my heart for your love*
*and support that has fortified me throughout this journey*

*and to Richard Bastin*
*for his invaluable editorial support*

## Mountain People and Valley People

THERE ARE two types of people in this world, valley people and mountain people. Valley people seek the calm and comfortable ground of shelter, safety and security. They may talk about change but do not want to be involved in it, especially if this means breaking from the routine of what has worked okay up until now. Their concept of achievement is not losing, so playing for the draw to them is all that's needed. Their concept of fitness is being fit to survive. They are the people you meet whose sentences begin with: 'I would have', 'I could have' or 'I should have'. They are the almost people, who have many explanations for not making it themselves but only one for those who have – <u>luck</u>. They talk about the risk of losing and yet they are losers – they just do not know it.

Mountain people have decided that valley life is not for them and seek to test ambition on the toughest climbs. They know that there is a rich satisfaction in reaching the top and the fight that's needed to get there. They live for the test of change and enjoy the resilience required to bounce back from the bumps and bruises that come with the mountain territory. They not only talk about change, they deliver it. They take the risk of winning because to them there is no such thing of a risk of losing. People can lose without training or practice, it comes quite naturally, so where is the risk in that? They know achievement is not always reflected in a gold medal but is always measured by the excitement of knowing just how much further their best shot takes them, when they take the risk of winning. Achievement is balanced on the finest of edges, but they know that. Whatever the outcome of the contest, they are always accountable for the result.

—Frank Dick, *Winning*

# Contents

Introduction ..................................................................................... 13

**Part One**

1. 2000 Memories – the Most Valuable Game in Football ............................ 18
2. A Rather Privileged Childhood – Early Beginnings from Another Age ...... 23
3. Boarding School ................................................................................ 31
4. Growing Up Down Under ................................................................... 37
5. My Informal Apprenticeship and Learning to Work, 1972 to 1978 ............ 43
6. Early Businesses – from Prawn Star to Mayo Man .................................. 54

**Part Two**

7. Bobby Robson – Glory Days ................................................................ 62
8. The Players that Made It Happen .......................................................... 74
9. Life Without Robson … and a Lunch Invitation ..................................... 81
10. John Duncan Arrives: Adventures Behind the Iron Curtain ..................... 93
11. New Arrivals: the John Lyall Era ......................................................... 103
12. Discontent – and an Unexpected Elevation .......................................... 112

**Part Three**

13. 1995/96: Setting Out as Chairman ...................................................... 120
14. 1996/97: So Near, Yet So Far .............................................................. 126
15. A Day in the Year 1997 ..................................................................... 131
16. 1997/98: the Same Old Questions ...................................................... 138
17. 1998/99: Third Time Unlucky ............................................................ 146
18. 1999/2000: on the Brink ................................................................... 155

**Part Four**

19. A Scandalous Decision on Television Rights and an Unexpected Appointment ........................................... 164
20. Chairman of the Football League! ........................................... 170
21. Candidacy for FA Chairman ........................................... 186

**Part Five**

22. The Wembley Showdown ........................................... 196
23. 2000/01: Even More than We Could Have Hoped For ........................................... 202
24. 2001/02: the Pros and Cons of Europe ........................................... 211
25. 2002/03: a Perfect Storm ........................................... 221
26. 2003/04: Joe Wheels and Deals ........................................... 230

**Part Six**

27. 2004/05: Punching Above Our Weight ........................................... 238
28. 2005/06: Living Within Our Means ........................................... 244
29. 2006/07: Jim's First Year – Learning on the Job ........................................... 255
30. 2007/08: Under New Ownership ........................................... 264
31. 2008/09: End of an Era ........................................... 280

**Part Seven**

32. Meanwhile, Back at the FA ........................................... 286
33. Branching Out ........................................... 294

**Part Eight**

34. The National Football Centre: A Long-Postponed Necessity ........................................... 306
35. Designing the Dream ........................................... 319
36. Costs ... and Values ........................................... 337

**Part Nine**

37. Manager, Chairman ... and Now Coach ........................................... 352

**Part Ten**

38. Reflections ........................................... 368

Acknowledgements ........................................... 373
Appendix: Statistics while Chairman at ITFC ........................................... 381

# Introduction

I HAVE been repeatedly asked in recent years when I would write a book and, despite some innate reticence, here it is! It's not intended as an autobiography, and doesn't aspire to be anything comprehensive, but is instead a collection of memories, aided by the diaries and notes that I have kept, with varying degrees of diligence, throughout my career.

Not that I wrote everything down at the time, of course, so at some points I have had to rely on memory, and that inevitably means I may not have got everything quite right. So I offer apologies not only to anybody who may feel wronged, but also to those who, for one reason or another, might have been slighted by not getting a mention, or the recognition that they deserve. My only defence is that – while I may at times be candidly objective – I have never approached this, or anything else I have done, with a sense of malice or vengeance. Gossip sells, of course, but creating a kiss-and-tell would have gone completely against the grain, and just wouldn't be my style. That said, a bit of radical candour about certain individuals is included.

Looking back, I was thrust into positions of leadership from a very early juncture, and, at just 22, I found myself being sent to Dubai to manage a frozen shrimp company. Progressing through the seafood industry and learning on the job (what we now call 'experientially') gave me a terrific grounding for what would come next, with success in my own firms, and prepare me for everything I subsequently encountered in leadership roles, some of them very public, in sport, charity and business.

All these positions have involved dreams. Not just flights of fancy, but visions distilled into a clear picture of what I was trying to achieve, and once I had that end – so, my goal – in mind, then it was always a case of trying to turn those dreams into reality.

Needless to say, getting to that point is rarely straightforward. Fortunately I was brought up as a 'can do' person, and from an early age had been imbued with perseverance; indeed the Latin *perseverando* is my family motto, which probably dates back to the 1700s when the Sheepshanks were wool merchants in Yorkshire. It's just as Winston Churchill said, 'Never give in, never, never, never!'

However, it didn't take me very long to learn that no matter how hard you fight, you can't do it all on your own. I am thus doubly fortunate in that I have also always enjoyed campaigning and rallying others to the cause, seeking out the help and support of people who know more than I do across a range of skills – and to whom I am deeply indebted.

I have also been repeatedly asked who exactly I am writing the book for. Well, as a signed-up and utterly devoted Tractor Boy since the age of 13, I hope I can say there will be plenty to interest Ipswich fans, and indeed hopefully all lovers of football, and England in particular. My three most significant roles were chairing Ipswich Town, the Football League and the Football Association project to build the new St George's Park national training centre. I also had a very brief spell as joint acting chairman of the FA, all of which came at a time when the juggernaut that is the Premier League was moving into the financial stratosphere and rapidly losing commonality and connection with the football pyramid below. So while loving Ipswich's time in the Premier League, and always being one to aspire to greater things, my roots and values are actually much more closely connected with the Football League and the amateur game below it – in fact I am proud still to be the president of the Suffolk FA.

I am a great believer in the lessons that the commercial world can learn from sport, and vice versa, and have to confess that I am also something of a business book junkie. So there should be things to interest people of a similar mindset, given what I have learnt about leadership, team building and resilience from being on the sharp end of the ecstatic highs and gut-wrenching lows of a life in professional football.

Largely as a result of my Ipswich experiences (as a director, and then chairman, for 24 years, 1987–2011), I have become a convert to the power of coaching: simply put, that is helping anyone that wants to be the best that they can be (and sometimes even better than they thought they could be!). Like all of us, I have had my share of ups and downs in life; however, it's what we learn as a result of those experiences that really shapes us, and I wish I'd had the benefit of a career coach much earlier in life (which might have stopped me falling into quite a few heffalump traps!).

One of the things that good coaching helps us avoid is too much destructive dwelling on what might have been. But, given the chance, I can honestly say that there are two people in particular who I would like to have met, and learnt from, much earlier.

The first is Frank Dick, the former UK Athletics supremo who has been a major influence on me for over three decades now, galvanising my self-belief and ability to keep going through whatever life threw at me. Frank, who I consider the veritable godfather of British coaching, believes in being better today than you were yesterday by actively seeking out tough challenges. 'You don't learn to climb mountains by going round them,' he likes to say. Things rarely turn out quite how you expect, and I have accumulated plenty of bumps and bruises along the way, knock-downs even. But that is what comes with the mountain territory described in the quote that begins this book, words that have proved an inspiration ever since I first heard them 30 years ago.

The second is former national table tennis champion Matthew Syed (although having him on board from the outset really would have been wishful thinking, as he is considerably younger than me!). I first came across him when I read his wonderfully motivational book, *Bounce*, which works through dozens of examples to build on Malcolm Gladwell's 10,000 hours concept and shows how much we can achieve if we commit the necessary time and effort. His later work *Rebel Ideas* gives me an honourable mention for the FA peer group that we worked on together. I consider Matthew to be one of the great thought leaders of our time.

Although there have been lots of honourable exceptions, especially in my earlier years in the game, I saw too many footballers fritter away their talents and failing to make the sacrifices required to excel. That convinced me of the need for a revolution in coaching, and a move away from 'command and tell' and towards 'pedagogy', so teaching and engaging young people to *own* their development. This is an approach that has been embraced and championed by Gareth Southgate, of whom I am a great admirer. First as U21 coach, and then as the senior England team manager, Gareth played a really important role at St George's Park – supporting both the project and my efforts to the hilt – at a time when we were pushing the boundaries of the presiding culture and creating a facility that has become a magnificent base for our international sides. It was also designed to be a focal point for coaching and lifelong learning, or so I hoped; however, this aspect is still very much work in progress.

I actually became such an ardent advocate of the coaching style of leadership – which focuses on unlocking potential rather than barking instructions from the sideline – that for the past decade I have worked as a performance coach for businesses. That same enthusiasm for empowerment has also spilled over into another big part of my life – philanthropy and the charity sector, where I have always encouraged people to support and engage with the causes that most matter to them, especially local, place-based philanthropy.

There has been plenty of laughter and tears along the way, and indescribable stress that I would never have survived without our many friends and the resolute love and support of my ultra-precious family, particularly my younger brother Rick, my (now very adult) children Sophie and Tom, and most of all my wife, Mona … and, of course, our dogs!

# PART ONE

# Chapter 1
# 2000 Memories – the Most Valuable Game in Football

'NAYLOR ... HE'S stabbed it through. Reuser is ... onside ... Reuser. Premiership! Done and dusted for George Burley. Nails bitten to the quick, but elevation now surely, assured.'

Some things just send a shiver down your spine every time you hear them. For me it's the words of ITV commentator Peter Drury. That won't come as much surprise to many people reading this, as they probably do the same for you too.

With everything we had gone through, how could it be otherwise?

The 2000 play-off final at Wembley that put Ipswich Town back in the Premier League was the culmination of a gigantic team effort, after years of what had seemed like far more than our fair share of crushing, last-gasp defeats. They had been years of heartache and constant struggles against self-doubt and the nagging feeling that somehow it was not meant to be.

It felt as if we had climbed the mountain so many times, catching glimpses of the promised land beyond, only to lose our footing right at the end, and see the prize snatched from us. So now, finally standing on the summit and admiring the view, the feeling of relief, of release, of pure ecstatic joy was unparalleled. Indescribable. Extraordinary.

From up there we couldn't just see the big time, we were in it!

\*\*\*

That Wembley match may have been the sweetest moment of my ITFC journey, but it wasn't actually the most significant fixture I ever went to. And again, I probably have a lot in common with other fans in saying that would have to be my first-ever game. In retrospect you could say it was a kind of baptism. A rite of passage. Or a first date that quickly turned to love and eventually marriage ... with all its ups and downs.

In my case, I was invited by three men employed on the farm run by my father, who was no fan of football, or any other sport for that matter. A strict military man, he demanded 'Whatever for?' when I told him they wanted to take me to a game. But go I did, and things were never to be the same again.

It was 11 April 1966.

Most fans start their journeys going with parents and even grandparents who have loved their club and had it ingrained in them for years. Not so me. How lucky I was that Bill Dickey, Don Howard and Mr Bilham took me under their wing. I went with them to all my early games, learning the ropes of being a supporter and experiencing the thrill of the crowd, the buzz and the palpable excitement.

It didn't take long for me to get completely hooked after that (since you are no doubt interested, it was a 3-2 victory over Leyton Orient with Ray Crawford getting two and Gerry Baker the other ... I wonder how many people reading this were there too). Danny Hegan quickly became my favourite player, and a few months later the young teenage me found himself looking across to the new side of the ground and asking who got to sit in what turned out to be the directors' box, apparently declaring, 'I would like to sit there one day ...'

And after a fairly roundabout route, one day 20 or so years later that would indeed be me.

By 1968/69 I had passed my motorcycle test, and would regularly go with my friend Charlie Croll (and sometimes his sister Caroline!) and take our place standing in the North Stand, joining in all the chants. I had also learnt to drive on an old Hillman Husky I had inherited from my father's aunt. It was no longer roadworthy, but so devoted to the Town was I by that stage that I painted it blue and white and tormented the farm workers as I careered around the place.

I became a director in the mid-1980s, which was not a time that evokes many happy memories among the Tractor Boys of an age to remember it. After over a decade at the very pinnacle of the English – and indeed European – game, the departure of the late, great Sir Bobby Robson to manage England had triggered a long, slow decline. There was a brief resurgence in the early 90s with John Lyall at the helm, but the trend was distinctly downward, and by 1995 there was no hiding the fact that we were in trouble. And not just on the pitch. As well as the perennial financial problems, there was also a tangible, widening (and distinctly alarming) gap between the club as an institution and the supporters who are, and always will be, its very lifeblood. So, I like to think, it was partially because at heart I was, and still am, an ardent fan who bleeds blue and white – with all the joy and pain that comes with it – that I was called upon to step up and become chairman. The invitation came as a wonderful surprise to me, although I would soon feel that the rest of the board were making a statement of intent by going for young blood and vigour.

There were plenty of sceptics, of course. Everybody seemed to be asking who the new chairman was and, more importantly, how much money I had to put in. The answer was, of course, none to speak of. But I had a deep love for the club and a clear idea as to the energy and business organisation needed to turn things around. Not that saying so cut much mustard with the critics. We were going to have to walk our talk!

Even before things came to a head during the disastrous 1994/95 season, I already had a fairly good idea of what exactly that walk, and that talk, should actually involve. I had, after all, done an eight-year apprenticeship as director dealing with club affairs. Plus I had spent lots of time with sponsors and supporters – including on coaches to away games – as well as mixing with the self-appointed great and good in boardrooms around the country. And I could count on the invaluable experience of having started and run several food companies, where I had found success using some of the sales-driven approaches I would later introduce at Portman Road. The definitive blueprint of everything we needed to do crystallised in my head during our traditional pre-season Nordic tour. It's a part of the world that I know well, and where I instinctively feel at home – not only have I done dozens of trips up there buying prawns, but my wife is actually Swedish, and we were married in Stockholm.

And so it was, in a land of cray-fish barbeques, Aquavit schnapps drunk under a midnight sun, and skinny-dipping in crystal-clear lakes, that I shaped my plans for how I hoped we could reignite the club.

I had come up with a five-year plan!

## The five-year plan

Having read this far, you could be forgiven for thinking that this is all about me. And, there are certainly plenty of egomaniacs lurking in the business world and, if anything, even more so in football. It's easy to say, but I genuinely hope that I am nothing like that. The simple fact is that my view of leadership was, and always has been, to consult and delegate and involve as many people as possible at all levels. I strongly believe that an essential feature in any business is ensuring that people throughout the organisation feel a clarity of purpose and ownership for final outcomes, so that everyone pulls together as a team.

I had come home from Finland with a plan of what was required, a pretty clear plan. But, more importantly, I knew that I would have to engage with, and draw out, a similar outlook from the people around me, so that it became *our* plan and not just *my* plan imposed on them.

I discussed it with the board. And one of the first things I did was to ask then-manager George Burley and the senior coaching staff to a meeting in the boardroom. Morale was low.

I started by saying that I wanted us to devise a plan together for how we could recover and start the process of getting back to being a Premier League club once more. I asked them if they thought we could realistically be promoted within a year. I remember it vividly, the heads went down and I could hear them thinking, *Who's this joker!*

'Okay then,' I asked, 'what about in two years?'

Again, heads down …

'Alright then,' I ventured, 'what about in five years?'

'Okay,' said Paul Goddard, the youth coach, who was the first to speak, 'I think we could in five years.' George nodded, as did a few others. Progress.

'Okay then,' I continued, 'what would we need to do to make that happen?'

'We'd have to invest in youth, the Ipswich tradition. It's always been the way here with Bobby Robson,' said George. Others agreed.

'What else?' I asked.

'We have to get the supporters back onside,' said someone.

'We need to re-engage with the community,' someone else proffered.

'We've got to become more professional in our commercial management' was mentioned.

And so, the eggs began to hatch. And I added, 'We have got to get our heads up and start believing in ourselves, because if we don't, nobody else will!' We had to rally the club both on and off the pitch, bring it together again and take 100 per cent ownership and responsibility for what we were going to do. It was as fellow director John Kerridge had said to me, we had to 'bring back the loving feeling to Portman Road'.

When I told them I was going to go public with our plan, one or two directors questioned whether it was the right thing to do. But I felt strongly about it, and was sure that it would be much more effective to release a five-year plan to return the club to the Premier League, and make ourselves – and myself in particular – accountable for it.

Of course, the most important stakeholders for any club have to be the fans. And going out so openly with not just a declaration but also a deadline became an increasing burden as the seasons passed by, and with them our chance of getting back to where we knew we belonged.

Nor did it take the sharpest of minds to realise that, having released the five-year plan in 1995, we would really have to be delivering something by 2000. So, as that fateful day at Wembley dawned, I wasn't going to pretend there wasn't immense pressure …

But more of that later. Let's go way back, and start at the beginning.

## Chapter 2
# A Rather Privileged Childhood – Early Beginnings from Another Age

THE JOURNEY that led to my life in football is, I expect, fairly different to most people's. So please stay with me as I take you through what was something of a privileged background, but one that, nevertheless, helps explain my drive and motivation. From my parents' generation onwards, the family money had largely been spent, so what I saw as a young boy was steeped in hard work. My father had to strive for everything, and his outstanding work ethic definitely rubbed off on me.

I was raised in Suffolk from day one, or very nearly, since I actually came into the world at St Mary's Paddington in October 1952. My father later told me how he had made it to London by car in two hours when my mother went into labour. That was some going, as there were no dual carriageways in those days, and no bypasses around Ipswich, Colchester or Chelmsford, and certainly no M25!

My father, Robin Sheepshanks, was a captain in what became the Queen's Dragoon Guards. He retained a strong military presence and a tough exterior, even after retiring prematurely to take over the farm in Suffolk. He had been one of the first to see the Bergen-Belsen concentration camp when it was liberated in April 1945, an experience that profoundly affected him, and no doubt all the other young soldiers, but of which he never spoke. He came to Suffolk in 1952, the year after the sudden death of his own father, who had been a major in the Indian Army and aide-de-camp to the viceroy (Lord

Chelmsford). My grandfather must have impressed his boss, as he would go on to marry the viceroy's daughter, Bridget Thesiger, my grandmother.

It was said that she 'batted both ways'. Whatever the truth, my father was the only son of what turned out to be an unhappy marriage. My grandmother abandoned them both when he was eight, and he was brought up by his father and a governess.

I can't say I remember my paternal grandmother terribly fondly except for the fact that she did teach me how to play bridge. She also smoked 60 Peter Stuyvesant cigarettes a day – and my younger brother, Rick, used to love going to see her on a day out from prep school, as he had taken up smoking at an early age and would always relieve her of a couple of cartons from a stock of thousands under the stairs. Whether she noticed, she never said.

When I took my wife, Mona, to meet my grandmother some years later in a rather smart home for the elderly in Woodstock near Oxford, she was commanded: 'Now stand up and turn around for me dear … Yes, you'll do.' And, after a few seconds' silence, she was asked, 'Have you got any money?' The answer was 'no' and, in my case, Mona was certainly not marrying into any! My grandmother had always been nice to me, but could be pretty shocking by that stage.

On the other side of the family, my mother, Lilias, was brought up in true aristocratic fashion. Her great-grandfather was Sir Andrew Noble, the managing director of Armstrong's, a large arms and ammunition manufacturer based in Newcastle. It would later become Armstrong Vickers, and he clearly made an enormous fortune … that the following three generations then set about spending! There wasn't much left by the time my parents got married in 1951 (in Hexham Abbey), and she inherited very little, apart from some lovely paintings and furniture, including a beautiful desk that had once been Mendelssohn's piano.

Her mother, my grandmother Lady Celia Noble, was always kind, but was nevertheless a terrible snob, and my father – who was immensely practical – never much liked her. He used to say that his mother-in-law had only ever signed cheques all her life, and had no idea what a bank statement was!

Going further back into the family tree, my ancestor John Sheepshanks was a great collector in the 1840s and 50s. He was the archetypal philanthropist, giving 235 oil paintings, watercolours and drawings to found a National Gallery of British Art. The donation was actually made to the Museum of Ornamental Art in South Kensington as he preferred 'the open and airy situation' of the area, as compared to what he saw as the polluted atmosphere of central London. The first of his galleries opened in 1857 in what is, today, the earliest surviving section of the Victoria and Albert Museum. His gift was, in part, an effort to get others to follow suit, and it certainly worked. Queen Victoria agreed to lend the Raphael Cartoons, the greatest cycle of Italian Renaissance pictures in England, and many others followed suit, including Constable's daughter, Isabel. She gave 395 paintings, sketches and drawings, making the V&A's the leading collection of work by one of Suffolk's favourite sons.

I should explain that John Sheepshanks's bequest included several major paintings by Turner, 15 Constables and 40-odd Landseers. When my dear friend and art dealer David Dallas showed me around a Constable exhibition, I asked him what they would be worth today. 'That one I would say 20 million, that one maybe 30 million …' and it went on. It's better to not even think about it! At least they are in the V&A for all to enjoy.

Another extraordinary fact stemming from that era is that my brothers and I are direct descendants, through my mother, of Isambard Kingdom Brunel. The famous engineer had two daughters but no sons, and one of them, Florence, married an Eton housemaster named Arthur James. In the next generation, their daughter (Isambard's granddaughter) married my great-grandfather Sir Saxton Noble, my mother's grandfather.

When I was very young, I remember staying with my grandparents (the Nobles) in Northumberland, where they had a butler, footman, cook, parlour maids, chauffeur and so on. As children, my brother

Rick and I were restricted to the nursery rooms and the garden, and we were really only brought out to see the grown-ups for afternoon tea and maybe – if we were lucky – to play a game. What a glimpse of yesteryear it was. When I was 12 I was finally allowed to sit at the table for dinner, in a scene straight out of *Downton Abbey*. The year before he died, my grandfather insisted I taste the Madeira that he always poured at the end of dinner in small silver goblets.

In the late 1950s and early 60s my father and mother also had a cook and butler, who used to appear from behind a green baize door, but that didn't last. Times were changing and, more importantly, pretty much all the family money had been spent by then. My father stepped into the breach and worked like a Trojan to build up the farm and to pay for schooling for me and my younger brothers: I am the eldest of four boys, the second being Rick, while Andrew and then Christopher were born in the 60s, with 12 years between Chris and me.

We had a very happy childhood. Summer holidays were nearly always spent in Scotland – we would set off every year to visit cousins and friends in Yorkshire, Argyll, Inverness and Kincardineshire.

We used to see our cousins, Charlie and Mary Sheepshanks, and their children, Belinda ('B') Susanna and William. B and I are very close to this day, and she really is the nearest I ever had to a sister.

Her father Charlie was brilliant at all sports, from croquet to tiddlywinks, and earned the nickname 'Pogo' because it was assumed he would automatically win anything, even if bouncing on a pogo stick. Ill health had forced him to retire early from the headship of the renowned Sunningdale Prep School, where Mary must have been the quintessential headmaster's wife, as she could cope with anything that life threw at her, while somehow always smiling and finding the funny side. Although we were actually cousins, the age difference meant we treated them like uncle and aunt. Mary would later become a brilliant novelist and poet, touring the country to give majestic soirée-style talks.

Although my grandfather had moved to Suffolk, the Sheepshanks family originally all came from around Harrogate, and Charlie and

Pogo still lived in the area, at Arthington. We used to have great fun visiting them, as B and Susanna always seemed to have hordes of other girls there, and they loved pranks. The best was, when going up to my room one night, I turned on the light switch, but instead got an extraordinary howling, ghostlike noise from the bed … and hilarious cackles from the darkness behind the curtains. They had hooked up the hoover to the light switch and stuck it in my bed!

**Brian Johnston and an early love of cricket**
And it was at Arthington, in Yorkshire, that my love of cricket was ignited. Among Pogo's greatest friends was Brian 'Johnners' Johnston, the legendary commentator, who often stayed along with his wife Pauline for the Headingley Test matches. Johnners was a naturally funny man, always seeing a joke in every situation. I can hear him even now, in one of British radio's most iconic moments, gasping 'Oh, Aggers, do stop it!' through tears of laughter. Mary Sheepshanks recently reminded me of the time when she asked if anyone had seen the dog bowl. 'No,' Brian had replied, 'but I have seen him bat!'

Brian was also credited with delivering cricket's equivalent of 'the fans think it's all over', with the immortal line: 'Is it the Ashes? Yes! And England have won the Ashes.' The man scoring the winning runs that day at The Oval in 1953, and a great pal of Brian's, was the most famous English sportsman of his day, Denis Compton, a dashing and legendarily good-humoured batsman who raised spirits in a fairly dour post-war era. Amazingly, Denis had taken on the previous Australian side – led by none other than Don Bradman – just weeks after helping Arsenal to the 1948 league title, and he would go on to win the FA Cup as well.

All of this sets me up with an excuse to recount one of my favourite (although possibly rather embellished) sports stories, which involves Denis's 60th birthday dinner, held in great pomp in the Long Room at Lord's. Just as the speeches were about to begin, Denis was summoned to take an urgent phone call from his mother. Returning to the room, he rose to speak when a voice rang out from among the assembled great and good, 'So what did your mother want?' 'Well,' spluttered Denis in slight embarrassment, 'she says I'm only 59!'

One day I was lucky enough to be invited to visit the BBC *Test Match Special* commentary box. What a thrill that was – Brian introduced me to E.W. 'Jim' Swanton and the legendary John Arlott, and I even got to try one of their much-fabled cakes. I had caught the cricket bug!

Around the same time, I pestered my father to take me to Lord's. It was summer 1963 and the West Indies were in town, complete with their fearsome fast bowlers Wes Hall and Charlie Griffith, not to mention Gary Sobers. My father got us tickets for what turned out to be one of the most memorable final sessions in cricket history. England were on the ropes throughout, and we only saved the day after Colin Cowdrey came out to bat with a broken arm and survived the last over to secure a draw. I still have the scorecard from that day!

I was so hooked that from then on I used to try to memorise the county scoreboards from the school copy of the *Daily Telegraph*. My favourite player was England captain Ted Dexter, and because of him I supported Sussex, but I also liked Essex, where my hero was Barry Knight. Much later I developed an affection for Somerset, with Viv Richards, Ian Botham et al.

My parents gave me a crystal radio (which was cheaper than a transistor) and at boarding school I used to listen to cricket commentary from Australia under the bedclothes. But my father wasn't really interested in cricket, and although he did take me to the Scarborough Festival that September, it was many years before I went to another game. Instead, I used to watch Sunday cricket on the BBC and, of course, Test matches when they were on. I vividly remember the 1964 Ashes series, which saw the debut of Geoff Boycott and a memorably high-scoring game at Old Trafford, when Bobby Simpson got 311, before England hit back with Ken Barrington scoring 256 and Ted Dexter 174.

Another great memory from that year was being taken with my brother Rick (I was 12 and he was nine) to see The Beatles at the

Hammersmith Odeon, which is now the Apollo. It was a cacophony of screaming from beginning to end – we saw them, we were there, but we heard nothing apart from the deafening racket produced by thousands of schoolgirls. Nevertheless, I can still say I got to see The Beatles play live.

I had been brought up surrounded by music. My mother had been a very accomplished concert pianist, studying at L'École Normale in Paris under Edwin Fischer (who was said to have once been arrested in Berlin for playing too many encores). When she told him she had got engaged, Fischer retorted, 'Lilias, you cannot, you are married to the piano.' Her father had been chairman of the Northern Symphonia Orchestra in Newcastle, so my mother was well acquainted with all the leading lights of the time, and she was goddaughter to the wonderfully charismatic Sir Malcolm Sargent. Sir Malcolm, who had become famous as the conductor of the Last Night of the Proms, liked to call me his honorary godson, something that pleased me enormously, especially when he took my brother Rick and I to London Zoo (where he was a governor) as he would give me a one-pound note, whereas Rick only got ten shillings.

The composer Sir William Walton was godfather to my third brother, Andrew. My parents used to stay with them in Ischia, an island off the coast of Naples, and it was there that Papa was inspired to become a serious gardener by the fabulous Giardini La Mortella, created by Sue Walton, William's Argentine wife, which is still world-renowned. I remember my father coming back home from Italy one year and putting a bulldozer to a field by the edge of the lawn, which he proceeded to transform into a spectacular ten-acre landscaped garden that was regularly open to the public.

It rubbed off on me, although I am not in his league. I am a bit too impatient – and prone to planting too many things, too close together. My passion is for roses, buddleias and wildflowers. What I did learn from my father is that for maximum effect in a bigger garden you should always plant roses, shrubs or perennials in threes, fives or sevens.

There were lots of other musical figures that passed through our family life, including Benjamin Britten and Peter Pears, who had started the Aldeburgh Festival nearby. My father was one of the locals who served on the committee to raise funds to rebuild the Snape Maltings Concert Hall after it was gutted by fire in the late 60s. Singing was my thing when I was young, and I even had a lesson with Peter, who was possibly the greatest tenor of his day.

Pianist John Ogden was a regular weekend visitor, as was Julian Bream, the classical guitarist. He was always charming company and spoke with a strong London accent. He loved his red wine, and I remember Papa saying, 'Now, Julian, I've got something special for your lunch,' and while he was pouring it Julian turned to him and said, 'Oh, Robin, thank you, I just love a spot of this ol' bojallis' (Beaujolais).

The utterly brilliant writer and philosopher, Laurens Van Der Post and his wife, Ingaret, also became great friends of my parents, regularly coming over to play tennis. It was spellbinding to listen to him speak. He was fluent in various dialects, including the click language of the bushmen of the Kalahari Desert.

My parents also launched the Prince's Trust in Suffolk and so developed a special friendship with Prince Charles (who incidentally is a well-known admirer of Van Der Post). My brothers and I were very touched when we received a message from the King after my mother died in 2023.

An amusing incident I remember from the 1970s involved Joe Levy, the son of my Californian boss, who was staying in Suffolk when the Queen Mother came to the house for a reception connected with Aldeburgh. When we were lined up to be introduced, she asked him where he came from and, after answering 'San Francisco, Your Majesty', he himself asked, 'And where do you come from, Ma'am?' I doubt she had often been asked that. But she handled it very coolly, and replied, 'Scotland' before moving on.

## Chapter 3
# Boarding School

IN JANUARY 1961, aged eight, I was sent away to Northaw Prep School near Salisbury. I hated it! I was so homesick to start with, and we were only allowed to see our parents twice a term: once for a weekend at home and the other when we would go out for Sunday lunch.

I have to confess I was a bit of a goody-goody (partly as I didn't fancy being caned by a trigger-happy headmaster who seemed to enjoy it). I was beaten in my first year for making a puppet with my handkerchief after lights out. And then we were caught having a massive pillow fight before breakfast. Three whacks of a leather slipper, and I resolved never to be beaten, or caught, again!

My younger brother, Rick, who followed me three years later, was a very different case. He was always in trouble and beaten regularly. On one occasion, the geography master, Dusty Miller, had had enough of him and sent him off with a scribbled note that read, 'Headmaster, please beat this boy hard.' In his wrath he had omitted to write a name and, on seeing this, Rick found an unsuspecting new boy in the corridor and said, 'Mr Miller wants you to take this to the headmaster ...'

I settled in over the years. It was a lovely place, having previously been a country home of the Singer (sewing machines) and then Baring (banking) families. We had huge grounds and a tarmac yard, where we learnt to rollerskate. Apart from swimming, which has since become a favourite exercise (I still swim every day), I didn't excel at much, although I did make the first team for all the main sports. That definitely didn't include boxing, and I can still remember a boy called Rickman giving me an incredibly painful bloody nose. Highlights included school picnics in the New Forest and a day out at Alum Bay on the Isle of Wight (with its kaleidoscope of coloured sand). It may all sound idyllic, but wasn't really, and to survive you had to grow a thick skin.

And finally the time arrived for the Common Entrance exam. I passed, and so I was into Eton.

I can't say that I really enjoyed Eton either. Although I have to acknowledge that it did give you a lot of independence, as from day one you had to grow up and start making your own decisions. Every boy had his own room at the age of 13 and, since there was no central heating, you had to ration your own weekly coal allowance. Although, however you played it, there was never quite enough and you knew you would have a couple of cold days in store. When you did your prep/homework was also left entirely up to you. But there were penalties galore for stepping out of line.

When I arrived in September 1965 (aged not quite 13) there were still beatings meted out, not only by masters but also by prefects – who were known as 'The Library'. It was pretty archaic by today's standards, and at the start I lived in slight trepidation. Martin Llewelyn, who was three years older than me, wrote a chapter in a compilation called *Eton Voices*, and said that after 9pm, when we had to be in our rooms, he would lie in bed hearing Library members flicking their canes along the doorframes in the passage. If the noise started nearby, you knew you were safe. But if it was further away, it could spell trouble – and you would be taken to the Library (their private mess room) and beaten with a cane, by one or more of them. That was in 1962/63, but by the time I got there all of that was in sharp decline, and the last beating administered by another boy in my house was in 1967. I managed to avoid it.

Something that sounds equally prehistoric today was fagging. The whole of your first year you had duties to perform (and woe betide anybody who wasn't up to the mark). There were basically four categories of duty:

- *Personal Fag* – each first year was allocated to a Library member and you had to tidy his room, polish his shoes and occasionally run an errand. I had to fag for two captains of house – Nick De Zoete and Charles Mann, who were both good guys. Other fags weren't so lucky!

- *Tea Fag* – you were allocated to a Library member, or even a Debate (vice-prefect), and your job was to make them high tea every weekday evening.

- *After Lunch* – all fags had to wait outside the Library door for whatever errands needed running, which was normally taking messages to arrange matches against another house, challenge someone to squash, rackets, fives, etc.

- *Boy Up!* – any member of the Library could stand in the corridor and yell, 'Boooyyy Uppp!!' – and all the first-year boys (the fags) had to drop whatever they were doing and hare up or down the stairs. Needless to say, whoever turned up last got the job.

**The Sixties – what a time to be young!**
There were abuses of power, of course. However, it sort of worked and taught most of us the importance of discipline. By the time I was in the Library, fagging had been all but phased out and the atmosphere was radically different. My time at Eton, 1965–1970, corresponded with the arrival of the Swinging Sixties, flower power, rock music and drugs. By the end of the decade, standards had dropped and, while still having to wear tail suits, waistcoats and stiff collars, many of us kept our hair decidedly long, which the school strangely tolerated.

Despite my background in classical music, I had by then sadly given up both the piano and clarinet, which in retrospect was a big mistake. I had also been a chorister when younger, but singing rather gave up on me when as a 15-year-old my voice broke in the middle of the school music competition. That was in front of 500 boys, while working through 'Phyllis Has Such Charming Graces'. Anyway, by then I was far more interested in modern music, making the progression from pop (The Beatles, Cliff Richard and The Shadows, Petula Clark, The Everly Brothers, Elvis Presley, Dusty Springfield et al.) to The Doors, Led Zeppelin, Bob Dylan, John Mayall, Fleetwood Mac, Leonard Cohen, Santana … although my all-time favourites would be from subsequent decades: Bonnie Raitt and The Eagles (technically just 'Eagles', of course). I have seen them eight times in concert, including an amazing performance at the O2 in London in the early 2010s when they played a pitch-perfect acoustic set just sitting there on bar stools. The harmonies in 'Waiting in the Weeds' were sublime. We were lucky enough to be near the front, and it was sheer heaven!

I went to my first Eton vs Harrow cricket match at Lord's in 1966. We had to attend in school dress with top hats, while horse-drawn carriages were arranged in a row around the boundary, the last year that ever happened. Champagne flowed and I even remember meeting the legendary comedienne and raconteur Joyce Grenfell. The Eton boys chanted, 'Where's Harrow?' 'On the hill' 'What's it like?' 'Windy.' That all sounds so tame now. Indeed, my son, Tom, said that by the early 2000s the chants had become a lot more risqué.

Playing for the school at Lord's was a dream, of course, but in my case an unrealistic one, as I was never quite good enough. I captained my house in various sports, and played right-back for the school Second XI, but that was about it.

These stories of boarding school life have glossed over one rather crucial element – the education itself. I started off doing pretty well, and after sailing through 11 O levels (like GCSEs, but considerably harder!) I sat down with my father to discuss my future. He was keen that I took subjects that would be valuable in farming (geography, biology and chemistry were chosen), which made sense as all my life he had told me that I would one day succeed him. Indeed, it's fair to say my parents had brought me up to run what they had worked so hard to put together. At the core of that was what my father had himself inherited in 1951, the year before I was born – which consisted of a farmhouse, a few cottages and about 300 acres of land. In the early to mid-50s he set about buying a further thousand acres, in parcels of 200–300 acres each. Land was much more affordable then, but he could only do it with plenty of help from Barclays Bank. So, by the early 60s he had a modern, diversified arable farm growing barley, wheat, rye, oats, sugar beet, potatoes and carrots. He also had 500 'Barley Beef' cattle in a fattening unit, a flock of pedigree Suffolk sheep, and a pig stock of 300 breeding sows, not to mention a fruit-farming enterprise growing blackcurrants, apples, strawberries and raspberries. My goodness, how he worked to build it!

Over the school holidays, I used to accompany my father on Friday afternoons as he took the weekly wage packets around. There were normally 27 to hand out, most of them to full-timers, with the addition of some seasonal workers. It's all different today, of course, with much more mechanisation, and many fewer people employed.

I particularly remember a time in the late 50s when our stockman, Stanley Pinner, who spoke as broad Suffolk as you can find, was asked by my father how he had liked a bus tour to Windsor Castle – his first-ever trip out of the county. 'Well, Cappin,' (they always called him 'captain'!) '… it'ud taik an orful lotta bricks to bild a funny ol plice like 'at!'

So at the time I knew something of the life that awaited me: I was going to inherit and learn to run a working family farm in Suffolk. And I had never considered that I would be anything other than a farmer. I never had any other careers input from Eton, as they – and I – assumed I would specialise in agriculture.

Which meant that what actually transpired came as a real shock. And it was something that would derail me for several years (albeit very entertaining ones), though in retrospect that downward spiral opened the door to the path I eventually took. It would even end up turbocharging a newfound sense of ambition and drive within me to prove my own worth.

What happened was that, the following year, aged 17, I was walking around a field on the farm with my father when he broke the news that I would not actually inherit the farm after all. It was instead to be divided equally. That was entirely fair, of course. There were now four sons, however, so the minute they made that decision, the long-term outcome was always most likely to be that the land would eventually be split up and/or sold off, unless one of us could buy the others out.

It was all entirely reasonable. But the news hit me like a bombshell, and I was left dumbstruck. In today's world (in which, curiously, the issue of tax on inherited farms has taken centre stage in the political debate) it sounds greedy and grasping of me. However, back then it was a hammer blow ... and with my career path curtailed, a slow rot set in. I lost my mojo and became distracted by everyone and everything. I got heavily into rock music, became a fully paid-up member of the anti-apartheid movement, and in the holidays took to haring around on my motorbike (I had passed my tractor and bike tests at 16). I lost my sense of purpose and had no real help finding it, except that my mother sent me on some religious retreats, which I liked, mainly because I got to meet a beautiful girl called Philippa Baillie! When she didn't reply to a love letter once, I remember walking around the garden singing 'The Sun Ain't Gonna Shine Anymore' by The Walker Brothers. Scott Walker was always one of my favourite singers.

I had been planning to go to agricultural college at Wye or Cirencester, but now I had no desire to go to university of any description – apart from the university of life. Nor did I help myself by flunking my A levels. The only thing I wanted to do was travel, and to get away.

So I did ... and went as far away as I could.

## Chapter 4
# Growing Up Down Under

IN SEPTEMBER 1970, and still a month short of my 18th birthday, I jetted off to New Zealand, where my father helped me get a job with the cousins of some family friends. Looking back at it now, it seems like I was so young, but it didn't feel like it then and I relished my chance to strike out on my own. I arrived in Christchurch and set to work for the wonderful Deans family. Tim Deans, their son (a good friend to this day), was my age and he and his father worked a sheep farm called Auchenflower. I loved it there. We worked hard and we played hard. I made some wonderful friends and learnt to shear a sheep, to 'dag' the lambs (clean their mucky bottoms) and to 'lamb' a ewe (even putting one's lubricated hand in to turn or pull a lamb out when stuck). But when Hamish, his father, asked me if I wanted to come and kill a fatted lamb for dinner, I declined. I have enjoyed shooting game all my life, but couldn't bring myself to slit an animal's throat, which is how they do it.

I had a wonderful time in New Zealand. I bought an old 1934 Standard Pennant car with a top speed of 40, but that enabled us to get to Christchurch (which was 30 miles away) in an hour on weekends. After four months in New Zealand, which I loved, it was off to Australia on 30 December 1970 – but not before I had toured the scenic delights of the South Island with Tim in his Mini. One very happy memory was meeting a wonderful girl called Mary-Lou in Akaroa, a beautiful spot that I highly recommend.

I also sold my pink Levi jeans for 45 New Zealand dollars to Johnny Hutton, which was a fortune, despite the fact that they were old and shredded. But the Kiwis were still a year or two behind England, and coloured jeans were a prized novelty.

I headed to Melbourne with Nick Deans (a cousin of the family I had lived and worked with). We became best friends, along with Willie Keddell and John Macdonald. None of us had jobs to go to, which, with hindsight, may have been a mistake! Still, we had a ball. We stayed on Willie's grandmother's floor in her very smart South Yarra house for a week or two. I think her tolerance towards us was partly because it transpired she had been in love with Malcolm Sargent (who was known as something of a womaniser) when he had toured Australia in the 50s. It was almost as if my visit had stirred some latent passion in her.

We partied like anything in Melbourne and were quickly getting through our savings. One evening (after too many ouzo and cokes – please God, never show me another ouzo ... ever!), I met a restaurateur who owned a fashionable place named 'Peanuts' in Melbourne city centre. That was because every table had unshelled peanuts that diners could snack on with their drinks, with the shells all going on to the floor to be swept up each night. It was a fun place, a steak bar with a barbeque hearth in the middle of the room.

'So, tell me, Dave,' asked the owner, 'what's a young Pom like you doing in Australia?'

'Well, I hear you can earn 100 dollars a week in the west, so I am going to head out there and see ...'

'Fair dinkum, Dave. Tell you what, if you can tell me why you're worth that I'll give you a job in my restaurant.'

After hearing some stammering, bullshit answer, he said, 'Or I'll give you a job on the salad bar for three days a week at 35 dollars.'

Apart from eggs, I had never cooked anything in my life, except maybe heating up baked beans when tea-fagging at Eton. So, I took it like a shot!

I bought a clapped-out VW Combi Van for 200 Australian dollars and put a mattress in the back. I met Pam, a very sexy girl and diehard Collingwood Aussie Rules fan. Life was pretty good. We couldn't afford rent, so I shared a condemned house with Nick. It was squatting really, but it was still in the smartest end of South Yarra. We had so much fun. I remember (sort of ...) a pop festival in Sydney where everyone was smashed on magic mushrooms.

**An unusual train ride**
After three months I agreed to meet up with a group of friends in Perth, on the other side of the country. Or, in this case, continent.

Nick and I decided to hitchhike. It was easy enough to Adelaide and up to Port Augusta. But then came the small matter of the Nullarbor Plain, a vast expanse of arid, exposed limestone 1,200 miles across. You could be forgiven for thinking that the name is Aboriginal, but I have recently discovered that 'Nullarbor' actually means 'no trees' in Latin, which is exactly what it's like! There were about five cars a day, all of them full. So, we had a brainwave. We saw a goods train in a siding; it was about a half-mile long with new cars strapped to open trailers. We worked out it was leaving at midnight and were able to creep up in the shadows and find an unlocked Toyota Corolla. After a hasty retreat to stock up on beer and snacks, we made it back to our Toyota – which even had the keys in it so we could listen to the radio. And off we trundled. At about 30mph all the way. For 36 hours. 'Two sleeps and a day,' as Nick would say. We saw the desert, the odd camel and a few roos (as the locals call kangaroos) – it was our own magical mystery train, although without the psychedelic enhancements ...

As we rolled into Coolgardie, the train junction for Kalgoorlie, the old mining town – and still 400 miles short of Perth – we decided to make a run for it, and were duly caught by two railway men. After a few fierce words, they couldn't be bothered to report us, so we made for the nearest bar and a welcome cold beer. Goodness knows how we smelled, but we got a ride to Perth and met up with our Kiwi mates, who were staying with an unsuspecting cousin, where all five of us ended up crashing.

Two weeks later, and with no work around, Tom Kain returned to Christchurch, NZ, where he built a successful property business. He was a real 'player', a great, fun guy, but he is sadly no longer with us.

So, the four of us split into pairs to hitchhike north in search of the mythical 100 dollars a week – or perhaps even more in the north-west. Nick and I went together. We all met up again the next day, 260 miles up the coast, in Geraldton. By now, I was penniless, and effectively a vagrant. So that evening I went into a corner shop and managed to shoplift a watermelon (the only time ever, and something I am still ashamed of). We met up and gorged on our ill-gotten gains before lying down by the highway in our sleeping bags, ready to hitch a ride with an early lorry, or one of their road trains – huge American-style trucks pulling several enormous trailers, in total often 50 metres long or more.

As dawn appeared, I staggered up to find the roadside littered with watermelons growing everywhere. What an idiot I felt. Clearly the shopkeeper had thought I was a stupid Pommy bastard!

I was offered a job in Dampier further up the coast, because I had a tractor licence. But the others weren't, so I turned it down out of solidarity, and we headed north.

In Broome I got a job earning AU$140 a week cleaning down an abattoir, and stayed three weeks during which my 'Pommy bastard' title became official after I beat the town champion at pool. I also met an Aboriginal chief, who took me under his wing and taught me how to throw a boomerang.

We then waited five days for a ride to our next destination in Darwin. There were only three or four cars a day, and we took to clasping our hands in prayer as they passed. Finally somebody stopped, but they only took us 150 miles, to Derby. I then waited another couple of days, before giving up and catching a plane to Kununurra. From there I finally did get a ride to Darwin, where I met up with Nick. Willie and John Mac had meanwhile had enough, and returned to New Zealand.

Darwin was a happening place, with hundreds of young travellers like ourselves, and plenty of long hair around. It's practically at the top of Australia, and in the tropics, meaning the temperature stays in the low-to-mid-30s all the year round, so we slept in communes on the beach. It was there that we met a hippy character, John Otto, and his brother. And what luck – he offered Nick and me a lift to Brisbane. That was to be a three-day trip, and a total of 2,500 miles, through the Northern Territory to Tennant Creek, the mining centre at Mount Isa, before turning towards Cairns and the Queensland coast. Then down through Townsville, and finally Brisbane.

Several things of note happened in Brisbane. We learnt to emboss leather and set ourselves up in another condemned house. We got some tools and went to town twice a week to buy hides from the tannery, from which we made sandals, belts, wrist bands and hair clips. It was a good time for that kind of thing, and we easily sold them to all the local teenagers.

Nick started going out with a girl called Lola, and I met redhead Lesley, the head waitress at an evening hangout bar called Willies. I was very relieved when Nick's grandmother sent him an air ticket to go to London via Malaysia and the subcontinent, as we shared a room in an old deserted house and he kept bringing Lola to bed when he thought I was asleep. He was a great guy, but the one blessing when he left Brisbane was that I no longer had to listen to them at night!

The overland trip through the Far East ultimately cost dear Nick his life as he contracted hepatitis and was never to get over it. That was even after his mother gave him a kidney some 15 years later, when he was married to the sensational, and lovely, Victoria Rhodes. They had three delightful sons, Jesse, Oli and Basti (my godson). Nick, despite his illness, was an incredibly gifted sculptor and the master of understatement. If something terrible had happened, like when he needed the transplant, all he would say is: 'Well, there's a thing, Dave.' I loved that man – and still do – him, Vic and all his family.

Les, the waitress, was gorgeous, sexy and foxy. I fell hook, line and sinker for her. So much so that I stayed on in Brisbane, mostly getting up to no good. It was probably no bad thing when, after six months, my father finally got through to me with an offer of a flight home (by telegram, this being well before the arrival of mobile phones). I knew I had to get out of there. Les and I headed for Melbourne, swearing we would meet again in London, but her parents were probably glad to see the back of me. Her father actually bought me a wig in Southland Shopping Centre, as he warned me that long hair wasn't allowed in Singapore, my stopover point. That my father had also, very generously, booked me a five-day stay at the iconic (and snooty) Raffles Hotel tells all as to how very unprepared he was for the son that would return.

After leaving the old colonels tut-tutting in the bar over their Singapore Slings, I flew home. It was 1 December 1971 when I landed, and some 15 months since I had left our shores. I remember I was wearing my favourite rainbow-coloured shirt and jeans, blissfully unaware of the cold, foggy London that awaited me. My parents walked straight past me at Victoria station. They were actually still reeling (as they later related) from having just seen former prime minister Harold Macmillan check out the full range of *Playboy*, *Penthouse* and *Mayfair* magazines in a newsagent, before buying a paper and moving on. But they were in for an even greater shock when they realised that the long-haired bum with a sharp Australian twang standing on the train platform was actually their oldest son.

Returning home was bizarre and, after giving my mother the most tactless of Christmas presents (Timothy Leary's psychedelic essay *The Politics of Ecstasy*), my father bravely prescribed some tough love and essentially threw me out. 'Go to London and sort yourself out,' he said. 'You are always welcome at home, but much better you get away from here.' And so I went away again, and grew up. But this time for real.

# Chapter 5
# My Informal Apprenticeship and Learning to Work, 1972 to 1978

AFTER ABANDONING an attempt to retake my A levels, I got a job as a motorcycle messenger and started to really find my way around London. It felt almost like being a black cab driver learning 'The Knowledge'. I shared a flat in the New King's Road with an old school friend, John Thurso, who was doing the Savoy Company Hotel Management Course. He was paid £10 per week, which made my £20 per week feel like a fortune.

It wasn't long before we were besieged with Kiwis crashing on our floor, and some of us moved on and rented a flat in South Ealing. I loved haring around London but, after six months of irresponsibility, I was invited to meet the company's head of personnel. It all sounds too corny for words, as when he discovered that the long-haired biker in front of him had, like him, gone to Eton, he adopted a more avuncular tone and asked me, 'David, have you ever thought of a career in business?'

The group I worked for was Ralli Brothers Trading, part of what became Ralli Bowater. They were giants in the commodity world, with companies specialising in coffee, cocoa, jute, sugar, and there was even one that traded container loads of frozen and Cryovac meat, as well as frozen and canned fish. I thought my father would be proud of me if I got a job in meat, but after sitting an exam I was told there were no vacancies there. But there was one in the fish and seafood department. So, seafood it was and, as it turned out, would be for the next 17 years. So not merchant banking or property like many of my contemporaries, or estate management, and not even farming.

Once accepted by Tucker and Cross, the Ralli food subsidiary, I was fortunate to be given an informal apprenticeship with spells in every department, starting with some time on the telex desk. This was 1972, and well before the days of the internet and emails, so it was important to learn how to type up telexes and send them around the world, which was a skill that would serve me well. Then I went on to the shipping desk, where I learnt about certificates of origin, bills of lading and the rest of the documentation needed to ship containers of fish around the globe. Next I moved on to the finance department, which was a great introduction to the world of credit ratings, cash against documents, letters of credit and all the things that generally make the international payment system function.

Finally, and after over six months on the job, I made it to the trading desk. As far as I was concerned, they had kept the best till last. They showed me how to do proper costings to make a profit margin, and then how to buy and sell. It was just my thing. I quickly learnt to love selling, and trading was even better! With a telephone to each ear, I would be saying, 'Just hold on there, let me see if I can do a dollar 30 … no, my seller says it has to be 1.35 or no deal, what do you think? 1.32 – Okay, deal!'

Something that really stuck with me was that it's far easier to maximise profits by buying well, rather than by trying to talk up the price when it comes to selling on, especially in commodity-type situations. I later learnt that is something that applies everywhere, even to buying footballers. The thrill of closing a deal still excites me to this day. That feeling when you hang up the phone and punch the air … Yes! Yes! Yes!

We worked in Bruton Lane, off Berkeley Square in Mayfair, and we were taken over for a short time by Oriel Foods. Their owners had just sold the Fine Fare supermarket group, and were shortly to acquire the Gateway chain, which was a mega deal in 1974. But they clearly didn't fancy our trading world once they had seen it up close, and they soon sold us on to Fisons (coincidentally based in Suffolk, of course).

My immediate boss at Tucker and Cross was Jan Wolf, a brilliant Polish trader, and I met Tim Seward there, a delightful Canadian who would become a lifelong friend. His favourite word was 'horseshit' in a broad North American drawl. We were later joined by Alan Marler and Graham Marler (who, curiously, were not related). It was a phenomenal team. We worked hard and played hard – with plenty of pints and the occasional dry martini. Those were days of toasted cheese and tomato sandwiches for lunch, and countless coffees with a telephone in each hand as we chain-smoked and traded away, with the adrenaline pumping ... I thrived on it.

We were also given the job of selling frozen shrimp produced by Ralli India, as well as 50–100 container loads a year of frozen frog legs! They generally went to the US and French markets, but there was a lingering issue over hygiene arrangements (or lack of them), and salmonella contamination led to countless batches being rejected by the FDA, the all-powerful US Food and Drug Administration. Not that we cared much, because insuring each container for 140 per cent of cost, insurance and freight meant we made a profit either way. That made our directors happy, and kept our bonuses flowing!

It transpired that the frogs were actually harvested in Northern India, and sent down in wicker baskets with ice (that melted in a split second) to Cochin in Kerala in the hot and steamy south. And then frozen when they were already smelly.

I sadly never went to India at that time to see for myself, but I was sent on my first business trips abroad: the first was to a sardine factory in Zagreb, the capital of Croatia, which was then part of Yugoslavia, and then on to Vienna.

I loved the travel, and have always enjoyed meeting people, regardless of where they are from. My skill for communication and relationship-building clearly didn't go undetected, as I was summoned to see the MD, Egon de Laskay, and asked if I would like to work in Dubai. What an opportunity!

### 1974: Dubai and Ajman, the UAE

Flying out, I was sent to meet one of our big frozen shrimp suppliers, Jamal, in Pakistan. Being taken out on the town in Karachi and only being allowed to drink coke was quite an eye-opener.

After a couple of days there, I can still remember arriving in Dubai and hearing the hostess announcing, 'We're coming in to land and the temperature is 46 degrees.' When I got out of the plane, I realised what that meant. It was centigrade. My suit stuck to me like glue, and my hands were instantly wet. I had never been so hot, not even in Australia.

Dubai is so very, very different now, of course. At that time it had only just gained independence from Britain, as one of the seven emirates that make up the UAE. In fact, the small shrimp factory we owned – employing 30 or so Pakistanis and Indians – was actually based not in Dubai but Ajman, which at only 100 square miles is the smallest of the emirates.

One of the first things I had to do was to sort out a situation involving the previous manager, who had got himself into some difficulties.

On top of this there were major doubts as to how plentiful the local fishing grounds were. So my brief, in March 1974, was to run the factory for six months and assess the general viability of the whole project. I would also have to manage the political side of things, with the top man in Ajman, Sheikh Humaid bin Rashid Al Nuaimi. He was filling in for his ageing father, and was the effective ruler, so I spent many a morning sitting in his court drinking Arabic coffee, waiting my turn to be spoken to. However, there was no escaping the fact that Fisons was a leading global company in those days, and Ajman didn't have any oil. So it was important for them to hang on to us.

I started out in the old Bustan Hotel in Dubai, getting up each morning to drive 30 miles through the Sharjah Desert, past Dubai Airport (which was huge even then), the RAF base and then into the creek area of Ajman. In those days, I could do the journey in 30–40 minutes, as it was mostly a desert road. Now it's one gigantic urban sprawl, and utterly unrecognisable.

Evenings at the Bustan were given an extra allure by a brilliant Italian band (led by a guy called Marcello) that featured a gorgeous and honey-voiced English singer, who we will call 'Fay'. Her performance of Roberta Flack's 'Killing Me Softly' and 'Jesse' (my favourite) could melt every man in the room. So, after a meal of sheep eyes in aspic, she was a very welcome distraction.

We used to go swimming at Jumeirah Beach, without a hotel or even a house in sight, which is not quite the case these days. One thing inevitably led to another, and I invited Fay to come along on my week's leave in Beirut, where my other direct report, the legend that was Stuart Matthieson, lived with his family.

Stuart, a wonderfully charismatic man who sadly died many years ago, was one of only a handful of British officers who went with the Pakistani side at the partition of British India in 1947. He spoke fluent Urdu and Pashtu, the language of the Pathans, a fiercely proud people in the north of the country. I had a Pathan driver in Ajman, and when Stuart came to visit, I discovered that he was revered as a hero back in Peshawar. When staying with him and his family in Lebanon, I remember drinking bottles of wonderful Chateau Musar and then lying on the floor listening to *Parsifal*, an album by the Italian band, Pooh, which was a favourite of his wife, Agnese.

Fay and I had an absolute ball in Beirut. What an amazing city it was. A gateway between East and West, it was Muslim, Druze and Christian, and also Arab – but with a distinct French influence. We partied day and night, and visited the legendary Casino du Liban, where dancing girls put on shows to match the Folies Bergère in Paris. As well as the beautiful parks and beaches, and magnificent cedar trees, the city was also full of elegant, high-cheeked women, all of whom seemed to be called Leila!

Tragically, civil war broke out not long afterwards and many of the best bits of Beirut – including the waterfront Phoenicia Hotel where we had stayed – were destroyed.

Back in Dubai, I had moved to a flat at the end of the airport runway and remember seeing Concorde take off while I was shaving one morning. That was as part of a world tour it did before entering service with British Airways and Air France.

As time went on, I was increasingly alarmed by rumours that there weren't actually any shrimp in local waters and that they were being smuggled in, as part of a local racket, from Bandar Abbas, an island off the south coast of Iran.

So, I hired an Arab dhow with a Bedouin crew and set off to search the local waters with powerful spotlights, which attract prawns at night. For a week I lived like a Bedouin, with cockroaches on deck at night, eating with our hands and abluting in a net hanging over the side of the boat.

The nearest we got to finding any shellfish was me turning lobster red! One day we had beached on a deserted island to take a swim, and a military helicopter landed to check us out. They were looking for boatloads of illegal immigrants from India, but relaxed when they saw a red-raw, sunburnt Englishman.

The findings, or lack of them, meant going back to Beirut to discuss with Stuart how we could extricate ourselves from the area. When the time came for me to return from Lebanon, for some reason there were no flights back to Dubai. So I was driven to Damascus Airport through numerous checkpoints across the infamous Golan Heights, which had seen a pitched battle between the Syrians and Israelis just a few months earlier.

More delicate meetings with Sheikh Humaid followed. He was generally accompanied by his brilliant Palestinian chief minister, Adnan Dajani, who used to invite me to join his family in breaking the fast after sunset during Ramadan. That was an honour, and a very special experience – sitting on cushions and savouring some really delicious Arabian sweet dishes. Ramadan made life, especially work, even slower than usual. In fact, 'bukra' (tomorrow) and 'inshallah' (if Allah permits it) were words you heard all too frequently at the best of times. It was frustratingly hard and slow to get anything done. And then there were temperatures of over 100 degrees Fahrenheit every day in the summer. Still, at least my Toyota Corolla had good air conditioning ... plus it moved a bit faster than the one that had taken me across the Australian outback a few years earlier.

Negotiating and organising our withdrawal was a challenge, but an enjoyable one, and my bosses appeared to think I had done a good job. So it was time to pack up and leave after an extraordinary six months. Back in London, Intermas (as the trading company was now called) found itself in trouble with so many frog leg rejections, and there were some very upset customers at the major frozen seafood importers right across the US. To make matters worse, Jan Wolf had left for the Netherlands to work for Henk de Bruijne, a wily giant of the European market, while my pal Tim Seward had joined one of our customers, Albert D. Levy, in San Francisco.

I was charged with the responsibility of negotiating non-delivery damages for the frog legs, and set off on a whirlwind peace mission with customers in New York, Boston, Chicago and Miami.

Throughout this time I was avidly following match reports, going to Portman Road and even away games when I could. It's hard for people these days to grasp what it was like back then, with no website or anything like that to keep you up to date, so every weekend I would try to get a copy of the *Green'Un*, a weekend football paper produced by the *Ipswich Evening Star*, with the last print version coming out in 2008.

### Scandinavia calling – in more ways than one!

In March 1975, I got a letter from Al Levy, swiftly followed by a call from Tim Seward. 'Sheepshanks,' asked Tim, 'do you fancy setting up a Northern Europe office in London to sell Del Monte's frozen salmon production?' I jumped at it, resigning from Intermas, and was quickly in action accompanying my new boss, Al Levy, together with Dick Rhodes from Del Monte, on a tour of European cities: Amsterdam, Hamburg, Copenhagen, Oslo, Stockholm and Helsinki were our destinations. We stayed in only the best hotels – I particularly liked the Vier Jahreszeiten (Four Seasons) in Hamburg, the D'Angleterre in Copenhagen and the Grand Hotel in Stockholm. As luck would have it, that last one would later become especially memorable.

In Stockholm we met up with Nils Ullbin and Kaj Jägmo, the partners who dominated the seafood industry in Sweden (the brand name Ullmo exists to this day). We were wined and dined in Operakällaren, the world-famous restaurant, and taken on to a cabaret at Berns nightclub, featuring the big star of the day, Lars Berghagen. One thing that stuck in my mind from that trip was the picture of a beautiful blonde on Nils Ullbin's desk ...

In those days, there were no salmon farms, so if you were lucky enough to eat Scottish or Irish smoked salmon, it was caught wild, and therefore was rare and expensive. So the vast majority of smoked salmon consumed in Europe was imported frozen from Alaska and the west coast of Canada – the so-called Pacific North West. Del Monte was the second-largest supplier in the world, and my job, along with Hubert Jonglez who handled the substantial French market, was to sell it all.

That meant getting to know all the big smokehouses in Britain and Northern Europe. When I wasn't travelling to meet them and sorting out the quality issues that sometimes arose, I worked out of a one-room office at 194 Old Brompton Road, with three telephones, a telex machine and two brilliant secretaries – Anne Griffith-Jones and Xenia Howard-Johnston. We were later joined by a debonair Frenchman, Philippe Barbe.

They were busy 12-hour days and intensely fun. I would spend practically the whole time selling – typically ten to 15 a week of the 20ft containers, which weighed 17,500lb, or about eight tons, each. The fish was generally worth between $1.50 and $3.00 per pound, so the batch would be $30,000 to $50,000 dollars a pop then, and the equivalent of over five times that amount now. In addition to the Del Monte output, Tim Seward was a master trader and he would find production from other suppliers in Alaska and Canada and offer it to me to sell. So, we grew an even bigger trading business, buying and selling containers of not just salmon, but also Alaskan prawns.

After a year, in spring 1976, Al Levy was so pleased with our progress that he invited Hubert, who was based in Paris, and me to San Francisco. Al was an avuncular figure and, although not very tall, he had immense charisma and stature. In his earlier life he had run the canned tuna giant Ralston Purina and developed the 'Chicken of the Sea' brand. His own firm, Interocean Seafoods, was an altogether smaller concern, but it had global reach, selling to the huge Japanese market as well as Europe and domestically in the US.

I would send daily sales updates by telex to San Francisco and receive shipping schedules back from Barbara in our office there. Every Friday we would get to speak on the phone to iron out any issues. Barbara had a Californian drawl to rival any heroine in the Harold Robbins novels that were then in vogue. I couldn't wait to meet her ... and convinced myself that she might be one for me.

And so it was that we got to San Francisco. Arriving in Al Levy's swish Pacific Heights home for the drinks reception, I saw two girls sitting on a small sofa, right in front of me. One was blonde and tantalisingly gorgeous, and the other a bit of a plain Jane. 'You must be Barbara,' I offered my hand to the blonde. 'No, I'm Barbara,' said the other, 'this is Mona from Sweden, Mona Ullbin.' My heart jumped. So this was Nils Ullbin's daughter, the one whose picture I had seen a full year earlier. Mona was in San Francisco taking a few months out from her law degree in Stockholm and doing work experience with Al Levy.

After drinks, we were all taken to a private dining room at the top of the Bank of America building, where they had filmed the disaster movie *The Towering Inferno*, with Steve McQueen.

Al was so proud of his new cosmopolitan company – he even made us all sing our national anthems after dinner. Cringe! Mona, as the only Swede, and I, as the only Englishman, had to do it alone. Still, embarrassment is supposed to hasten attraction.

Tim Seward organised some really fun dinners in Mill Valley (on the other side of Sausalito over the Golden Gate Bridge) and after a couple of days Mona and I had our first kiss on the top of the Coit Tower, which is a memorial to the firemen who died in the 1906 earthquake and subsequent fires. To say Mona and I became keen on each other was an understatement! We spent a week together before it was time for me to go back to London via various stopovers to meet more customers. I went to Vancouver and Chicago, and had got as far as Detroit by the following Friday, from where I was due to go to Boston and home. Instead I bought myself a four-hour flight back to San Francisco for the weekend. I was now hooked. We were hooked!

There were no emails in those days, so we wrote to each other nearly every day and occasionally spoke on the phone. After three months I persuaded Mona to leave San Fran and come to live with me in London, in my room in a large bachelor house at 53 Shelgate Road, Clapham. I had great housemates, who remain close friends to this day – Peter Gossage, Ted Turner, Mark Hedderwick and Peter 'Spike' Marling-Roberts and his girlfriend Gerry. It was lots of fun, but not at all what Mona was expecting. She got a job with the cosmetic company Avon, and pretty quickly moved out to share a flat with Mark's girlfriend. I really couldn't blame her.

Eventually she disappeared back to Sweden. But I couldn't leave it at that, and we got together for a weekend in Copenhagen. It was then that Mona announced she was leaving to do a degree at a top merchandising and fashion school in Los Angeles, where she got a house at the poor end (!) of Beverly Hills. My heart sank at the news, but my father had drilled the *perseverando* family motto into us. So I did just that. I managed to persuade her to spend Christmas with my family in Suffolk, which was a good sign. And when I next flew out to California, it was to propose.

We got engaged on 23 March 1978. The idea was to get married that summer in Sweden so, to make that work, Mona, who is extremely bright, crammed her two-year course into one.

(Tractor Boys will be aware that there was another big day between the engagement and the wedding on 26 August 1978 ... but we will get to that later!)

Our wedding was held in a beautiful 18th-century red wooden church called Seglora Kyrka (kyrka means 'church') on the island of

Skansen, in Stockholm. We mixed a bit of English into the service, but mainly followed the local tradition, including a dress code of white tie and tails, and long dresses.

My legs shook throughout, and I have never been more nervous in all my life, which was not helped by the bride being nearly an hour late, as she was sorting out a problem with the bus bringing the guests from the hotel. There were 120 of them in total, with 40 coming in from the UK, US, France, Iceland and elsewhere.

Then came an English-style stand-up reception at Saltsjöbaden, half an hour away, which was followed by a Swedish banquet, complete with songs and speeches. Mona's girlfriends – led by her best friend Ulla Hemlin – performed an embarrassing song they had composed called 'Ravy Davy', and Christopher, then aged 13, made a charming speech (while my other younger brother, Andrew, had played the trumpet in the ceremony itself).

We then danced the night away, before Mona and I headed for the Grand Hotel, which, of course, is also where I had stayed my first time in Stockholm. I think we had a four-hour wedding night before leaving to Arlanda Airport, en route to an epic honeymoon in Trinidad.

We transited through London en route to our honeymoon in the Caribbean, only to find a huge queue at the immigration desk. So I asked Mona to join me at the UK passport counter. When we showed her Swedish passport I explained to the officer that we were newly married, and after a couple of questions he said, 'I hope you have a very happy life,' and, adding a permanent entry stamp, 'Welcome to the United Kingdom, Mrs Sheepshanks!' Who said immigration was difficult …?

We had a wonderful time in Trinidad, Barbados, St Lucia and Tobago – where I got horribly sunburnt. Meanwhile, Mona had to be rescued from sea urchins and was carried out of the water by a very large man called Samson.

# Chapter 6
# Early Businesses – from Prawn Star to Mayo Man

MONA HAD come back from Los Angeles the month before the wedding, and we went over to Iceland together. It was part business, part fun, and it was at the beginning of a period when I used to go there five or six times a year, with over 60 visits in all.

We bought prawns and scallops by the container load – prawns for the UK (and ultimately our own factory) and scallops for the US market.

It wasn't all work, and I got invited along for some wonderful salmon fishing and memorable Icelandic safaris. We made plenty of friends there, especially Agust and Rakel Sigurdsson, who had the most modern scallop factory in the country, which was nestled among the beautiful scenery at Stykkishólmur.

We met Agust and Rakel when they had a parcel of some 200 tons of scallops ('queenies' and 'roe off', as they are known in the trade) that needed selling. It was a distressed lot, in the sense that their normal American counterparts, Coldwater, couldn't sell them because the scallops still had the tendon (that attaches the roe), and that was held to be a defect.

With the guidance of Ottar Yngvason and Ingi Konradsson from the Iceland Export Centre, I flew out and then had to drive over a hundred miles on dirt roads to Stykkishólmur, inspect the scallops in their cold store and then get back to my hotel, where I defrosted a five-pound block in the shower, dissected them and tasted them raw.

All the time giving a blow-by-blow description to my friend Tim Seward, who was on the other end of the line in San Francisco. Tim sold them to Ben Kozloff, a great walrus of a man, who was admired as one of the great fish traders of his time. So we got Agust and Rakel out of a jam, they got their money and we became the closest of friends.

**Starting Starfish**
The Interocean seafoods business was expanding fast, but in late 1979 I made the momentous decision to leave and go it alone.

So Mona and I set up our own business, Starfish Ltd, in our flat in Ifield Road in West London, taking Mike Lewis, one of our salesmen, with us. There was invaluable support at the start from Agust and Rakel, who had appointed us to manage their scallop sales to the US. Other than that we hustled, buying and selling pallets (and containers when we could) of frozen salmon, prawns, scallops, scampi and even cod and haddock.

After a year we decided to sell the flat in London and move back to Suffolk. Mike left, and in 1982 we were doing well enough to set up a retail packing plant in Martlesham. In those days, the prawn factories in Iceland and Norway didn't have the equipment to meet UK retailer requirements. But we did, so we built a production line and imported and packed to precise specifications for Marks and Spencer in their own St Michael brand, and in our Starfish brand for Tesco, Safeway, Bejam and many others. We quickly became the main competitors to the market leaders, Young's Seafood. What a high-octane, fast-paced life it was, but the effort paid off and we built up a brand and became increasingly successful.

I travelled to Iceland about 60 times over that decade, and also to Norway several times a year, where the Sky Bar in Tromsø in the north of the country became a regular haunt. I was often accompanied by Villy Johnasen, the sales director, and his boss Bodil from Helge Richardssen – the largest cold-water prawn factory in the world at the time.

I saw the Northern Lights on numerous occasions and made plenty of memorable small plane flights across the frozen landscapes. On one of them in Iceland I asked the pilot why the lights on the wing were flashing brighter than usual, and he told me not to worry, as it was just the lightning bouncing off the airframe.

It was all going well and I threw a 30th birthday party, with 30 of us squeezing around a makeshift table at the Old Rectory in Hasketon, where we lived at the time. When it was time to prepare the langoustines for dinner, I was already extremely merry, and I set about wedging the pincers into the tails so they looked like they were dancing, a trick I had learnt. They all looked highly decorative, but as we served them, one of the guests, our Norwegian friend Bodil, suggested they were 'very fleshy'. To everyone's amusement, and my intense embarrassment, I had completely forgotten to cook them. Too many drinks!

The discomfiture didn't stop there, however. An hour later, my brother Rick let on that he had organised a strippergram, something that would be very much frowned upon these days. Anyway, in came this pretty girl, and as she opened her coat to reveal lacy underwear, there was a shriek of recognition from two of the guests, who had been at school with her. She was horrified but soon saw the funny side of it, covered up and joined us for a drink. It transpired that she was earning some extra money while at university.

## Opening a factory

My 30s and early 40s were taken up with huge amounts of travelling, as – in addition to my new football life – I was charging around buying and selling prawns. Young's were our main competitors and they were very good – but they were expensive, so there was room for another brand to come in and undersell them for the same (or, dare I say, better ...) quality.

So that is exactly what we did. I was the head salesman and campaigner, while my brother Rick had come back home to run the factory. He had effectively been given the boot from Zimbabwe, after working as a security guard for some of the foes of former revolutionary guerrilla Robert Mugabe, who was busy seizing power in the newly created country. Rick knew next to nothing about the seafood business, but soon proved his worth and kept the production and operational side of things ticking over nicely while I handled sales and finance.

We soon grew, and were able to hire Chris Sheen to run finance, Gavin Cornall and Simon Muse in sales, before Tony Newman and Tim Mack (pinched from Young's) joined us to head up that department. Sandra Firman was a brilliant PA to me, Colleen ran the reception, and in no time we had taken on more than 50 people and were turning over £15 million a year. Among the stalwarts at the factory were Greg O'Donovan (aka 'GOD', who I regret to say is no longer with us), Steve Curran and Richard Woodcock. I will never forget them all turning out to empty our cold store by hand into refrigerated shipping containers the day after the hurricane in October 1987, when we lost power in the factory. Disasters can certainly have a positive effect on camaraderie.

The game that people worked in the prawn world was to sell ice for the price of prawns, or breadcrumbs and batter for the price of scampi or fish. Some of our competitors tried to do just that, and even some of our suppliers too, but we were seen as the good guys. So we regularly sent inspectors to Iceland and Norway to check we were getting our money's worth, because you could be sure our most discerning customers would be doing so too. The upside of this was that it meant many a happy Scandinavian trip with buyers, including Robin Tapper, John Wood and Ben Hood from Marks and Spencer. My, how those guys could drink!

So we won M&S's confidence – and that of Tesco, Safeway and Trust House Forte. They knew we weren't out to cheat them, and were a serious outfit. They backed us, and the business grew.

There was just one drawback. Despite its great commercial success, Starfish was intrinsically a risky business. We took all the risks – quality, shipping, the ice glaze and exchange rates (there being no euro back in those days).

The whole thing worked if we could generate high volumes with no complications, as we were only able to add on a small amount to cover packaging for the retail market. The margins wouldn't have been much even in a completely stable environment, but – especially with currency fluctuations – they were all over the place. So one year we would come out £300,000 on top and the next year lose more than that. A yo-yo existence like that wasn't viable in the long run – indeed, nowadays, all the factories over in Iceland and Norway supply UK supermarkets directly and the product is now mostly sold chilled/defrosted, so ice is no longer an issue. In our day they simply didn't have that ability, so we fulfilled a need.

I didn't have enough money to fund the up-and-down financial results, so as good as we were, we were vulnerable to takeover. And when Alistair Salvesen (who had a top scampi company, which was part of the Salvesen business empire) came along, aided by his top man John Catherall, I eventually agreed to sell him a majority stake, which meant that the firm would now be much better funded. I was to stay as managing director, and we carried on successfully, but my enthusiasm waned. I had sold 'my baby', and while Alistair – who sadly died recently – was a good man and a philanthropist, he wasn't the easiest to work for. We became friends, and meeting him was a good thing, as it gave me the time to acquire perspective and to understand that I would have to look beyond fish to do something really profitable in the food industry.

By 1989 my brother Rick had resigned. He didn't have any shares, and in any case didn't get on with Alistair. In May of that year I followed suit and agreed a more complicated exit, which ended my 17-year journey in the world of fish – it had been tremendous fun and, although there was also plenty of heartache, it had been full of friendship.

Above all, I had also learnt a lot. One of the main lessons from my time in prawns was that there is no point taking a manufacturing risk unless you actually make the product yourself to control your margin. Which is exactly what I set about doing.

## Suffolk Foods

A good friend in Ulster, Trevor Kells, had been one of our trading partners in Starfish. He had also got fed up with the lack of profit in the seafood sector, so one day rang me and asked, 'David, how do you feel about making mayonnaise?'

At the time I was still extricating myself from Starfish, so I suggested the idea to Rick and we agreed to give it a go. He bought a black Volkswagen van and went over to Belfast to learn how to make it at Trevor's new firm, Rich Sauces. Rick started going over every week to pick up a couple of pallets of mayo, which we would then sell. And that was the genesis of Suffolk Foods, which we incorporated later that year.

Just as people had asked why we needed a new brand of prawns, now they were saying that there wouldn't be any demand for a new mayonnaise when they already had Hellmann's, Kraft and Heinz. My answer was that most of the stuff tasted like upmarket salad cream, and that although Hellmann's was excellent, it was expensive, and we thought we could do better. And we did!

I just love a crusade! The new product gave me the energy, the fervour even, to get out there again and tell everybody how good it was.

We gave Trevor a small share in the business in exchange for his recipe, which was absolutely delicious. We won all sorts of blind tastings run by magazines and, more to the point, the end-customers loved it. I had decided we should stay away from the retail trade (so bottles of mayonnaise on shop shelves), other than to supply the supermarkets in bulk for their sandwiches, which is an enormous market. We won all the Tesco business and many others besides.

Luckily I still had some money left as Suffolk Foods was starting out, and we expediently sold our house in Hasketon at the end of the year, which funded both our new home near Eyke and also the capital that we needed to start up a new mayonnaise factory in Rendlesham.

This time around Rick and I were partners, although the work was divided much like it had been: Rick would make it, pack it and deliver it, and I would sell it and run the financial side of things. And, crucially, we agreed that – unlike before – the focus had to be not on turnover, but on profit. Cash was king! Although we still couldn't afford to pay ourselves in the first year, we did turn £100k profit, and that doubled the next year and the year after that. So by the late 90s we were making seven-figure profits and earning well.

All of which meant that Suffolk Foods was already motoring by the time I was appointed chairman of Ipswich Town in August 1995. I carried on in both roles, combining away matches with customer visits all over the country. I recall, for example, once going to Sheffield United for an evening game, after dropping in for marketing calls on Pauleys in Stamford, and then Binghams in Sheffield itself. When I drove myself around, I would often give friends high-speed lifts home. I was always in a hurry in those days!

That all worked well. But I am still not quite sure how we kept all the balls in the air when I went to take on the Football League and the various FA committees and management board responsibilities. Rick was absolutely heroic and assumed a lot of the leadership role, and we brought back Tim Mack to lead mayo sales, meaning both Suffolk Foods and the county's standard-bearing football team would enter the new millennium at the top of their game.

# PART TWO

# Chapter 7
# Bobby Robson – Glory Days

BOBBY ROBSON joined Ipswich in January 1969, and after four fairly challenging seasons in the old First Division eventually shaped a team that would challenge the best in the country, and indeed in Europe.

After alleged fisticuffs with veterans Billy Baxter and Tommy Carroll, Robson had to win over and shape his own team, dressing-room spirit and work ethic. And just when Robson was under the most pressure and the target of chants from some of the fans, chairman Johnny Cobbold called him in and handed him a new contract!

Demonstrating faith in your key people (if you are sure about them) is such an admirable and powerful quality in a leader.

In 1973, we won the Texaco Cup – beating Norwich 2-1 both home and away! Amazingly, it was Bobby's first trophy either as manager or player, and everything grew from there.

We jumped up from 13th to fourth place in the league, the first of nine seasons in the space of a decade when we would qualify for Europe. The only season when we were outside the top six was the poor showing in 1977/78, which, of course, came with the unbeatable sweetener of winning the FA Cup.

So here for the record are those years, ones in which a town of little more than 100,000 people sat on merit at the top table with the biggest clubs and cities in the land, and indeed in Europe:

1972/73    4th
1973/74    4th

| | |
|---|---|
| 1974/75 | 3rd |
| 1975/76 | 6th |
| 1976/77 | 3rd |
| 1977/78 | 18th |
| 1978/79 | 6th |
| 1979/80 | 3rd |
| 1980/81 | 2nd |
| 1981/82 | 2nd |

Any leader or coach will tell you that sustaining success is one of the biggest challenges in a job. You are talking about managing human beings, who can easily have their heads turned by success and the money and attention it brings, so there is always a risk the team will lose the hunger to make the sacrifices necessary to stay in peak condition. There is also a fine balancing act to be played in terms of recognising when the big-name players have passed their prime. So it's essential to manage the squad to maximise their value to the club, knowing when to trade them on and find somebody younger who is as good or better, if possible for less outlay.

Bobby was unquestionably a master of doing just that, and practically every one of the 14 players he brought in from other clubs over his 13-year tenure at Portman Road seems to have been the right move at the right time. Some clubs seem to burn through 14 new players practically every season these days!

From an early juncture, Robson built his teams around the youthful, versatile and multi-skilled Mick Mills, who he soon installed as captain.

Three important early signings came in 1971: Rod Belfitt, Bryan Hamilton and Allan Hunter, and the latter pair would form the basis of the first of what were effectively two different teams, both of them very successful.

Allan was a rock-solid centre-half, while fellow Ulsterman Hamilton was a shrewd signing from Linfield. He would replace one of my favourite players of that time, Jimmy Robertson, who was coming to the end of his career, and Bryan proved to be a potent goalscorer from his wide midfield role.

Rod Belfitt replaced Frank Clarke, who, like Robertson, had been a great signing a few years earlier, but Robson saw the need for fresh blood, and Belfitt was itching to prove himself, having largely been an understudy to Allan Clarke in the great Leeds team of the day. But, in another example of how alert Robson was to opportunities in the transfer market, the very next season – and not quite 12 months after making his debut – Belfitt was moved on again, to Everton, in exchange for David Johnson. A real fan favourite, I remember David as a true fashionista, and he even had his own men's clothes boutique, Jonty's, in the town.

With Robson bringing in so few players, and constrained by a tight budget, success inevitably also came – and had to come – from our own youth ranks. Robson's avuncular presence was a key factor with the youngsters, but a lot of credit for developing the system should also go to 'Wor' Jackie Milburn. Sadly, that is the most that can be said of the legendary Newcastle striker's disappointing stint as Ipswich manager.

## Real Madrid, Lazio and unzipping a fly!

So, in 1972/73, Robson brought in Kevin Beattie (replacing Derek 'Chopper' Jefferson), and the following season would see debuts given to George Burley and Brian Talbot. By then we had Colin 'Ace' Viljoen (signed from South Africa back in 1966), Peter Morris, Trevor Whymark and local boy Colin Harper all as regulars. David Best and Laurie Sivell were vying for the gloves in goal, while Mick Lambert and Clive Woods competed for the No.11 shirt. Meanwhile, Hamilton and Whymark (who had a leap like a gazelle) bagged 11 goals apiece.

Hamilton increased his tally to 19, and Whymark to 17, while Johnson got 15 in the 1973/74 season, which saw us finish fourth again. Mills, Hamilton and Beattie were ever-present ... and Norwich were relegated in bottom place – alongside the mighty Manchester

United! One of the highlights of the season was a 7-0 thrashing of Southampton, but the really big treat was seeing us knock Real Madrid out of the UEFA Cup, our first-ever fixture in the competition. An own goal early in the second half gave us a narrow win in the first leg, and Hunter and Beattie were immense in keeping it goalless in front of a daunting 80,000 crowd in the Bernabéu.

Then it was Lazio, who we beat 4-0 at home, Trevor Whymark grabbing all four. How Lazio kept all their players on the pitch only the ref will know as they completely lost their discipline, with David Johnson getting a nasty stud mark on his manhood. The story goes that the club chairman, Johnny Cobbold, asked him how he was, and to his horror Johnson unzipped his fly and showed him on the boardroom table! In the return leg, we went through, despite losing 4-2 on the night after the Lazio fans had pelted the team bus. Then we beat FC Twente 1-0, with Whymark again on target, before trading early goals in the away leg to seal a place in the quarter-finals. Next, and once more having to play the first leg at home, a late Kevin Beattie strike was enough to see off Lokomotive Leipzig at Portman Road. But we went down by the same score in the return leg in East Germany and lost the shoot-out 4-3 after Allan Hunter missed his spot kick, our sixth and the first in sudden death.

**An epic cup tie**
In 1974/75 we went one better in the league, to finish third, with only Derby and Liverpool ahead of us. We won the FA Youth Cup for the second time in three years, and had future stars such as Eric Gates and Johnny Wark coming through.

Lowestoft boy Laurie Sivell was now first choice between the sticks, Burley and Mills were at full-back, Hunter and Beattie centre-halves, Talbot and Viljoen in the centre of midfield, with Hamilton and Lambert wide, and Johnson and Whymark the strikers. What a team!

My highlight of that season was our FA Cup run. Having knocked out Wolves and Liverpool, we found ourselves 2-0 down to Villa, but clawed our way back and ended up 3-2 winners. That earned us a quarter-final tie against Leeds, which we drew 0-0 with our all-time record gate of 38,010 – which included me! Although we led much of the replay at Elland Road through a David Johnson goal, the mercurial Duncan McKenzie equalised for them in the 90th minute, leaving us to somehow hold on through extra time in front of a partisan crowd of over 50,000.

This was before the days of penalty shoot-outs in the FA Cup, of course, so those were just the openers in what, over 30 years later, the *East Anglian Daily Times* would remember as 'a remarkable war of attrition'. Filbert Street, Leicester was chosen as the neutral venue for the second replay, which ended goalless. Just two days later the teams met yet again on the same ground, and with the same referee – Jack Taylor, who had been in charge at the World Cup Final the previous year. Years later, I had the privilege of working with Jack when he was a live TV ambassador for the Football League. What a gentleman!

Beattie was out injured, so Robson brought in 17-year-old Johnny Wark at centre-half for his debut – and it's worth recalling that the likes of Billy Bremner, Allan Clarke and Peter Lorimer were then on their way to the European Cup Final, and had developed something of a nasty reputation.

This time round Whymark and Hamilton scored for us, and Clarke and Johnny Giles for them, before Clive Woods curled in an absolute beauty to win it, after over 400 minutes of football.

And then came the travesty. FA Cup semi-finals weren't held at Wembley back then, so we set off to Villa Park to face West Ham. Despite an injury crisis, we hung on for 0-0 and a replay at Stamford Bridge. And we again kept the same referee, Clive Thomas, something that would never be allowed these days. We eventually went down 2-1, but only after he had denied us a goal that the linesman had given, and ruled another from Bryan Hamilton out for offside. It felt very unfair, and a case of bias towards a bigger and more fashionable club.

Amazingly, Clive Thomas disallowed another seemingly quite legal Hamilton goal, which would have been the winner, for his new club, Everton, in their own semi-final two years later against Liverpool.

We only lasted one round in Europe that season, with FC Twente – featuring a certain Frans Thijssen – getting their revenge on us through the away-goals rule, after two draws.

It's a reflection of quite how much we had improved, and how high our expectations now were that sixth place in the 1975/76 league season came as a bit of a disappointment. Meanwhile, the UEFA draw seemed destined to deny us any sunny southern destinations, as we faced Feyenoord (ending as 4-1 aggregate winners) before squandering a 3-0 lead from the first leg to crash out 4-0 at FC Bruges.

We bounced back to third domestically in 1976/77, behind Liverpool and Manchester City, and were boosted by securing Paul Mariner from Plymouth Argyle for a club record £220,000, with David Johnson going to Liverpool. This was a masterstroke from Robson, his best signing of all, I would say, and it was done in the face of competition from West Ham and West Brom. Trevor Whymark was on target in two memorable victories that season – getting four as we thumped West Brom 7-0, and a hat-trick in the 5-0 win over Norwich.

## 1977/78 – the FA Cup and containing Cruyff

Whymark suffered a bad knee injury the following season, as did Kevin Beattie, leading to a poor league showing and a final finish just three points from relegation. Nevertheless, what an absolutely epic year it was! The FA Cup run of 1978 is indelibly printed on my brain.

It all started when a Paul Mariner double saw us through a potentially tricky third-round tie at Cardiff City, and we followed that up with a 4-1 home win over Hartlepool (Mariner, Brian Talbot and a brace from Colin Viljoen – his last goals for the club). In the fifth round we managed a 2-2 draw in icy conditions at Bristol Rovers, thanks to two goals from Robin Turner, his first at senior level, one of them very late on.

The replay at Portman Road saw normal service resumed and we beat Bobby Campbell's side 3-0. Clive Woods was in flying form, and the third came when he cut inside to leave his marker flailing, before firing an unstoppable rocket past Martin Thomas. I met Martin many years later, when he was training keepers in the FA set-up at St George's Park.

In European football, the third round of the UEFA Cup saw us up against mighty Barcelona, who featured Dutch duo Johan Cruyff and Johan Neeskens. What a thrill it was to be there that night to see the legend that was Cruyff. He was extraordinarily gifted, but our very own home-grown Roger Osborne pretty much marked him out of the game. The 3-0 win – with goals from Gates, Whymark and Talbot – left the 33,633 fans who had packed into Portman Road utterly delirious.

The second leg in a soaking Camp Nou didn't go so well. We hit the bar twice and Paul Mariner had a goal disallowed. Barcelona drew level just three minutes from the end, which meant extra time and then penalties, which we lost 3-1, with Mick Mills converting our only successful spot kick.

Johan Cruyff became one of the most admired innovators in the game, further developing the concept of total football while coaching Ajax and then Barcelona, where he was a formative influence on none other than Pep Guardiola. He wanted every player to be able to practise and play in each others' positions so they could learn the art of real teamwork and understand how everybody on the pitch needs to receive or give a pass to suit their respective strengths. It's an approach that has now been widely adopted in a range of sports, and even in the business world.

Back to the FA Cup, where we were drawn away at Millwall in the sixth round. I just had to go, and took along my brother Rick as my minder. Rick – it should be said – is not really a football fan. Anyway, off we went to the notoriously inhospitable Den, and somehow ended up standing among the home supporters in a packed crowd. The game was pure magic from my point of view, but we didn't dare celebrate. George Burley opened the scoring with a terrific strike, which was followed up by goals from Wark, Talbot and a Mariner hat-trick.

We didn't know it at the time, but it was the biggest quarter-final away victory in over 50 years. Ipswich were sublime that day, and having to restrain ourselves from cheering six times was frustrating in the extreme. The game was marred, somewhat predictably, by local yobs attacking our supporters – and even their fellow Millwall fans! – and the game was stopped for 18 minutes while order was restored. Fortunately, Rick and I were on the other side of the ground among the tamer supporters, who by the end resorted to some amusing South London gallows humour. I remember they had a player called Walker who copped most of their ire.

So, on to the semi-final against West Brom, which was held at Highbury and proved to be another epic! Brian Talbot opened the scoring with a brave diving header that left him and opposing skipper John Wile holding their heads and in need of bandaging. It was a real blood-and-thunder tie. Our captain, Mick Mills, scored a second after a mistake from Cyrille Regis at a corner, before Allan Hunter gave away a penalty. Things were on edge at 2-1, before John Wark stole in unmarked with a great header just below where I was standing at the Clock End. And that sealed the deal, booking our place at what would be the club's first-ever Wembley final.

It all seems so strange to say now, especially after the great times I would later have on supporters' buses when I became a director, but I went to the semi-final alone. Back then I would get tickets and go to games all over the country on my own, often fitting client visits in around them.

And I never went to Wembley for the final; I can't think why really. Perhaps I just couldn't get a ticket. But I did invite 'Uncle Bilham' from the farm (one of the group that had taken me to my first-ever game in 1966) over to watch it with me on television.

As to the final, many people reading this now will have been there that day, and practically everybody else will know exactly what happened. But it's easy to forget that not only were Arsenal strong favourites to take the trophy (we had done really poorly in the league and Trevor Whymark was missing, replaced by the valiant

David Geddis) but we could easily have beaten them by a hatful. Paul Mariner hit the bar in the first half, and poor Johnny Wark smacked the post from distance in almost exactly the same place twice after the break. It was beginning to look as though fate was against us when Roger Osborne capitalised on a defensive slip in the 77th minute. It must have seemed like something out of a fairy tale to Roger, who was born in Otley and is part of a large Suffolk family. Indeed, shortly afterwards he had to be substituted after collapsing from the excitement and an excessive goal celebration.

### Robson's masterstroke – and European triumph

It's a mark of Bobby Robson's strategic shrewdness that he started dismantling and reshaping the team almost as soon as the FA Cup was sitting in the Portman Road trophy cabinet. He showed himself to be an early adopter of 'if it ain't broke, fix it', a reversal of the old cliché that many businesses and sports leaders apply these days in the pursuit of success in an ever-changing world.

The rebuilding meant jettisoning half the side. So tireless midfielder Brian Talbot and goalscoring winger Bryan Hamilton were replaced. So too were penalty expert Colin Viljoen, prolific striker Trevor Whymark, tricky left-winger Clive Woods, and Mick Lambert – all eased out as they approached the end of their careers. And not long afterwards, FA Cup hero Roger Osborne would go out on loan to Detroit and then eventually to Colchester, where he played over 200 games.

The remaining core, and the backbone of the success yet to come, was formed by Paul Cooper in goal, Mick Mills and George Burley at full-back (with the injured George replaced by Steve McCall in early 1981), along with Johnny Wark and Paul Mariner, plus Kevin Beattie on the occasions when he was fit.

In place of local boy Talbot (who went to Arsenal for £450,000), Robson brought in the amazing Arnold Mühren, who was joined in midfield the following season by Dutch compatriot Frans Thijssen. Otherwise it was entirely home-grown talent that stepped up to fill the gaps left by the departures. So Russell Osman and Terry Butcher came in at centre-back, Alan Brazil replaced Whymark, while Eric Gates – rather than playing winger – sat 'in the hole' behind Mariner and Brazil. 'Gatesy' was an impish terror to defences. A short man who nevertheless had the strength to shield and pass the ball, he also possessed a ferocious shot, scoring regularly.

And the results would quickly show that Robson knew exactly what he was doing. He had pulled off a managerial masterstroke.

Over 40 years on, a game from that time that really sticks in my mind, and undoubtedly that of everybody else who saw it, is the 6-0 drubbing of Manchester United in March 1980. They were a team full of famous names but, if anything, the result flattered them, as we missed two penalties, three if you include one that was retaken. The team sheet shows why that was – spot-kick supremo Johnny Wark was absent, on compassionate leave back in Scotland.

Although we won the UEFA Cup and were FA Cup semi-finalists in 1981, in many ways it was a season of might have beens. We didn't lose until our 15th league game (to bottom-placed Brighton), and were top of the league from January to the end of March, winning six games on the trot. After a stutter, on 14 April we beat title rivals Aston Villa away, but the wheels fell off four days later when we went down at home to Arsenal, and we inexplicably lost three out of our last four matches.

April also saw us lose an FA Cup semi-final against Manchester City. I drove up to Villa Park together with Mona, and we had tickets in the Holte End. But she had eaten something that disagreed with her the night before, so when we arrived she didn't feel able to go to the match. Being a diehard fan – and not the gentleman I should have been – I parked up in a slightly dodgy area, she locked herself in and I paid two boys to protect her and the car. And off I went to the game!

We should really have won, with the only goal coming from a free kick given very debatably against Terry Butcher in extra time – the first occasion it had ever been played, as they had always gone straight to a replay back then.

In Europe, a brace from Mariner and an absolute rocket from Mühren helped us to an impressive 4-1 quarter-final win after going behind at Saint-Étienne, the pre-eminent French side of their day, who boasted Michel Platini and Dutch star Johnny Rep in their ranks. I unfortunately missed that famous victory over *les Verts*, which was seen as one of the finest club performances of the era. But I was there when we followed up with a 3-1 result in the return leg, and we went on to secure 1-0 wins in both legs over FC Cologne in the semi-final.

So although things at home had flagged slightly, we were on a European roll, which continued with a 3-0 win in the first part of the two-legged final against AZ '67. Two weeks later, Mona (sporting blue and white ribbons in her hair) joined me on the ferry to the Hook of Holland along with thousands of Ipswich fans. It's hard to explain how exhilarating it was to be among all of the crowd from Suffolk who made the trip over on that memorable, and memorably hot, day. We were under the sun in an open section of the old Olympic Stadium in Amsterdam, which AZ had preferred to their own, much smaller ground in Alkmaar.

It was an ecstatic afternoon, albeit a fair bit tenser than we would have liked. Frans Thijssen scored soon after the start, but AZ equalised immediately and then took the lead through the great Johnny Metgod. Johnny Wark pulled us back level with another potentially vital away goal, and we had our first-leg cushion thank goodness, because from then on we were really under the cosh, conceding two more. But we eventually got over the finish line, winning 5-4 on aggregate. And wow! At last, after years in Europe, we had won a trophy.

A fact I still find incredible is that we remain unbeaten at home in continental competition. We have never lost a match! Not one of the 31 games at Portman Road since 1962, starting out when we beat Floriana of Malta 10-0, and then AC Milan 2-1, until 2002 when we last played (in my time as chairman) and beat Slovan Liberec of the Czech Republic, 1-0.

Our UEFA Cup triumph was confirmation of the dominance of English football at the time, as Brian Clough's Nottingham Forest had won the European Cup in 1979 and 1980, and in 1981 Liverpool regained the trophy they had won in 1977 and 1978, by beating Real Madrid 1-0 in Paris.

To conclude, here's a favourite story from our European campaigns of that era. We were playing away in Norway, and after the match some of the players glimpsed one of the club officials (who shall remain nameless!) disappearing upstairs with a beautiful blonde. When they left the hotel bar later they couldn't help hearing 'ooooh, that's luuuvvely' from outside his door. Getting on the team bus to head home the next morning, the individual was greeted by a loud chorus of 'ooooh, that's luuuuuuvvely!!' from the players at the back.

# Chapter 8
# The Players that Made It Happen

**Mick Mills**
Mick joined as a 16-year-old from Portsmouth, who had closed down their youth scheme. A gentle and soft-spoken man, Mick was tough as nails as a player and was a role model as our captain for over ten glorious years. Extremely versatile, 'Bomber' also had a huge engine, and would often pop up to score important goals. Capped 42 times for England, he was made captain for the 1982 World Cup in Spain. The same year and, after playing a club record 741 games over 17 seasons, he left for Southampton, where he would play another 103. He went on to manage Stoke City for several years, and then Birmingham City with Trevor Francis, though he never quite hit the heights that he had done as a player. I should add that the girls always seemed to take a shine to Mick as he had tree-trunk thighs!

**Kevin Beattie**
The late (how terribly sad it is to have to write that) Kevin Beattie came from Carlisle. He was discovered by John Carruthers, a northern scout, and put on a train south in his mid-teens. As a supporter, it was genuinely thrilling to have Kevin on your side. He was a real Trojan, a leviathan, a giant of a man, yet at the same time incredibly humble, modest and gentle off the pitch, and – in the nicest possible way – almost a bit hopeless … but loveably so!

Beattie seemed to have every possible attribute. Apart from one. He had terrible problems with his knees, which severely restricted his playing time. My favourite memory of Kevin was from a bitterly cold UEFA Cup tie against Bohemians of Prague (who featured Antonín Panenka). Beattie came on as a late substitute wearing a short-sleeved shirt as if to prove that nothing fazed him, and slammed a free kick from 30 yards out that nearly wedged in the top corner of the goal. I had never seen a ball hit so hard, nor do I think I have since!

**Paul Mariner**
Along with Kevin, Paul Mariner (or 'PM') was probably my favourite player, out of the many to choose from. He made his debut on my 24th birthday in 1976, in a 1-0 win over Manchester United. From Chorley in Lancashire, Paul was an amusing character, with a distinctive northern accent and nasal twang, and he had a personality on the pitch that the fans loved. He developed a special understanding with Johnny Wark – the two of them just seemed to feed off each other. I have so many memories of watching Paul, who was a quite brilliant centre-forward, but two hat-tricks stand out. One was in March 1978 in the FA Cup quarter-final at Millwall, and the other two years later when we demolished Man Utd 6-0. Paul is also no longer with us, but I was lucky enough to get to know him after his playing days were over, and I spent a memorable evening with Paul in Tokyo drinking, and singing, in numerous karaoke bars during the 2002 World Cup.

**Johnny Wark**
With George Burley and Alan Brazil, Johnny made up a triumvirate of Scots, all of whom had come up through our youth scheme. You knew where Johnny was from as soon as he opened his mouth, and it's said that his accent was so strong that he had to be dubbed in the classic footie film *Escape to Victory*. He was homesick at first, and was one of a number of young players who looked up to Bobby Robson as a father figure. 'If it hadn't been for the boss, I would have been straight back to Glasgow,' he said. Johnny was a midfielder, but he could basically do everything – jump, tackle and score goals. The 14 he bagged in our

UEFA Cup-winning campaign was a tournament record, and all the more remarkable given the position he played, helping him win the PFA Player of the Year award that season. Johnny had three spells with us, and even beat the prolific Ian Rush to finish as top scorer in one of the seasons he spent at Liverpool. He is a gentle man in every respect, except on the pitch, of course, and became a great friend, singing Elton John's 'Your Song' at my 40th birthday (a karaoke party with the theme 'Black and White, Short and Tight').

**Terry Butcher**
Terry is from Lowestoft, where his father was a prison officer. A commanding presence, he succeeded Mick Mills as captain in 1982, and would later wear the armband for England too. Terry indirectly played a part in me becoming a director at Portman Road: in 1986 we lost a vital relegation game controversially at West Ham, after which Terry kicked the dressing-room door down, such was his passion for the club. He then left for Rangers, which led me to write a letter of complaint to the chairman. Not about the door, but about the deafening silence from the club about selling him! Terry playing on in a vital World Cup qualifying match, head bandaged up and absolutely covered in blood, is one of the most iconic images in English football. He was a true warrior on the pitch, but is also caring, considerate and modest off it, and is blessed with a wonderful sense of humour. And, like me, he is a Suffolk man through and through, who adores our club.

**Russell Osman**
Russell was an extremely talented all-round sportsman, and played rugby for England Schools before opting for football. He played alongside Johnny Wark in the side that won the 1975 FA Youth Cup and, upon becoming established in the first team in 1980, developed a formidable centre-back partnership for both club and country with his great friend Terry Butcher. Russell was an extremely personable guy, while his fluent, easy style made him a favourite player for many to watch. Alan Brazil tells a story about the time he was about to buy

an expensive car to celebrate signing a new contract, only to find that Russell had put down the same amount as a deposit on a house. So Alan changed his mind, and bought a place to live and a secondhand Triumph instead.

## Allan Hunter

Allan was a tough, uncompromising centre-half who joined us from Blackburn Rovers in 1971. Although beset by injuries in the later years, Allan played 355 games for us and won a club record 47 international caps while at Portman Road, with many of his total of 53 appearances for Northern Ireland coming as captain – he was a true leader, though, in truth, we had them all over the pitch. Allan was modest and incredibly funny, as he is to this day, continuing to live in Ipswich as so many of our ex-players choose to do. He was also a smoker, and there were plenty of stories of how he and Kevin Beattie would sneak in a quick puff behind the groundsman's hut in the middle of training.

## George Burley

George came down to us from Cumnock in Ayrshire as a 16-year-old, and played in the FA Youth Cup victory in 1973, before making his first-team debut against George Best at Manchester United. Although we lost 2-0, our George is said to have marked their George out of the game! Burley was a model pro, always first out and last in at training. He was strictly brought up, and his manners and standards were impeccable. In 1981, George badly injured the cruciate ligament in his knee and became one of the early patients of legendary Cambridge surgeon Dr Dandy. There will be much more about George the manager, later.

## Arnold Mühren

With English football now awash with foreign talent, it's hard to imagine how few foreigners there were before the late 70s. But it was an absolute revelation when Spurs signed World Cup winners Ossie

Ardiles and Ricardo Villa from Argentina, and not long afterwards Bobby Robson brought Arnold Mühren over from the Netherlands to replace Brian Talbot (but for a third of the fee). Arnold quickly showed himself to have the sweetest left foot in the country, and his pairing with fellow Dutchman Frans Thijssen gave us the most skilful midfield around. Arnold also became very adept at putting Alan Brazil into the one-on-one situations with the goalkeeper that Alan excelled at. Both would eventually move on to Manchester United, but while Arnold did well, as a pair they didn't flourish there like they had with us. Arnold ended up back home, and at the age of 37 would crown his career by winning the 1988 European Championship Final with the Netherlands.

**Frans Thijssen**
The other half of the Dutch midfield duo, Frans joined us for £200,000 from FC Twente in 1979 and, together with Arnold, helped drive changes that the tactically astute Bobby Robson was eager to embrace. 'The English style was to kick it forward as much as possible,' Thijssen would later comment. 'Bobby changed the style, he told the defenders to play it to the Dutch guys ... that suited the team very well.' As well as adding a touch of 'total football', the pair were also instrumental in developing new approaches off the pitch, especially in increasing the intensity of pre-match warm-ups. Thijssen's absence because of a hamstring injury was undoubtedly a major factor in the collapse that cost us the title at the end of the 1980/81 season, but he was nevertheless named the Football Writers' Association Footballer of the Year (to go with Johnny Wark's own accolade). Frans went to Nottingham Forest in 1983, and ultimately left for Vancouver, apparently on the recommendation of Bobby Robson, who had worked there before coming to Ipswich.

**Paul Cooper**
The son of a publican, Paul had started out as a striker before putting the gloves on. He joined us from Birmingham City in 1974 when

they brought Gary Sprake in from Leeds. After edging out the excellent Laurie Sivell as first choice, Paul quickly established himself as one of the top keepers in the country. Although under six foot and considered short for the position, he was a magnificent shot stopper, a superb penalty saver and was remarkably quick getting off his line. Had he not found himself playing at the same time as both Peter Shilton and Ray Clemence, Paul would surely have had a glittering England career. He served Town brilliantly, being incredibly loyal even after Bobby Robson left in 1982, and making a total of 575 appearances over 14 seasons.

## Eric Gates

The son of a miner from the north-east, Eric was part of the team that won the FA Youth Cup for us in 1973. Gates packed a punch much greater than his 5ft 6in stature would suggest, proving adept at holding the ball up and also scoring plenty himself. He got both of Town's goals in the legendary 2-1 win over Barcelona in 1979, and would be our top scorer in his last two seasons, before finally leaving for Sunderland in 1985. Eric's mischievous temperament earned him headlines in his last-ever professional appearance, or rather non-appearance, for Carlisle. He reportedly walked off down the tunnel and got straight into the bath when told to get off the bench and warm up in the dying minutes of a game.

A few years earlier, Gatesy (as he is known at ITFC) and his great pal Alan Brazil apparently had a snowball fight during the UEFA game at Widzew Łódź in 1980 (we had won the first leg 5-0, so it wasn't quite as bad as it sounds). And like Brazil, Eric did well in his second career in the media, on local radio in County Durham. He now lives and works on a farm in the area. Famously scared of flying, Gates hasn't been on a plane since he stopped playing in 1991.

## Alan Brazil

A true Glaswegian, Alan spent time at the Celtic academy under Jock Stein, and shortly after joining us was sent on loan to US side Detroit

Express. He quickly established himself on his return, with his finest hour coming in February 1982, when he grabbed all our goals in the 5-2 win over a Southampton side featuring Kevin Keegan. That was part of his 22-goal tally that season, placing him second only to Keegan in the top flight. He was one of the best finishers I ever saw one-on-one with the keeper. A few months later, Alan turned out for Scotland in the World Cup, though television commentators were spared the problem of him taking to the pitch in the game against Brazil.

Alan didn't get on with Bobby Ferguson, who he claims to have had a fight with, and left in 1983. But his career would stutter to a halt before he turned 30 because of a persistent back injury. He briefly ran the Black Adder pub in Ipswich, before turning his hand to broadcasting, where his good-humoured straight talking has made him a great success. Talksport allegedly gave Alan his marching orders after he overindulged, even by his standards, and missed his programme slot the day after the Cheltenham Gold Cup one year, only to bring him back a fortnight later. Alan's love of racing is well known, something that he says began with visits to Newmarket while at Ipswich.

**Steve McCall**
Like Kevin Beattie, Steve came down from Carlisle to join the youth set-up. A superb passer of the ball, Steve was both Mr Dependable and Mr Versatile, being able to fit in at left-back, or centre- or left-midfield, and became a regular in 1981, after George Burley's injury. Steve held the club record for the most consecutive games played, until overtaken by Matt Holland. A brilliant guy, Steve went on to play for Sheffield Wednesday in 1987, and then Plymouth and Torquay. We brought him back to be European scout, and then chief scout in George's time as manager, and then as a coach under Joe Royle. Having also worked for Carlisle United, he is now back in Suffolk, and attends all of our home games.

## Chapter 9
# Life Without Robson … and a Lunch Invitation

IN 1982, after another tremendous season as runners-up in the league, but having lost to Alex Ferguson's Aberdeen in the UEFA Cup, Bobby Robson was lured away by the FA to manage England. That was despite the Town board trying their hardest to keep him with the offer of a ten-year contract. It was the second time in as many decades we were to lose our manager that way, and both times it was a hammer blow to the club, which in Robson's aftermath was already likely to struggle by the drain on finances from building the Pioneer Stand.

Big players started to be sold for seemingly low sums. Mick Mills, who had started out with us back in 1966, was the first to leave, joining Southampton. Then Arnold Mühren went to Manchester United, and Alan Brazil followed him there, via a brief stay at Spurs. George Burley and Eric Gates both went to Sunderland, and Paul Mariner left for Arsenal. I remember being very upset when Paul played his last match, against Coventry, as he clearly didn't want to get injured and never had a worse game (the bright point that day was seeing 16-year-old Jason Dozzell score on his debut). Russell Osman went to Leicester. It was a constant stream.

So as a devoted fan it all became rather soul-destroying. We had become used to a special kind of excitement before and during nearly every game. I suppose you could say we had been spoilt, watching our side compete with – and often beat – the best in the country, and seeing the best players week in, week out. The departures were hard to fathom. Of course, as happens everywhere, new players and new favourites emerge, but it just wasn't quite the same.

Coming in to fill the gaps under new manager Bobby Ferguson were Ian Atkins, the captain and a tough Brummie centre-half, while John Deehan would later join us from Norwich to play alongside prolific striker Kevin 'Jockey' Wilson. Also featuring was Romeo Zondervan, a Dutch Surinamese midfield general who had cost just £70,000 a couple of years earlier from West Brom and who proved to be both skilful and wholly committed on the pitch. Except at Christmas that was, as he always seemed to be injured over the festive season. I really liked Romeo, and we became friends, although I will always regret selling him my old Mercedes 450 SLC. I sometimes dream that I still own it, I loved it so much.

There was an amusing story about Romeo when we were playing at Manchester United shortly after he joined us. Bobby Ferguson went into the dressing room just before kick-off to give his final team chat and was supposedly in full flow about keeping Remi Moses tightly marked when he suddenly saw he was in the wrong dressing room! He had glimpsed what he thought was Romeo and followed him in – whereas in fact it was Moses himself. Tractor Boy legend at the time had it that Ferguson was in the process of telling them, 'Now listen up, I want you to nobble Moses …' or words to that effect, when he realised his mistake.

I remember being glued to the radio listening to our penultimate game in the 1985/86 season at West Ham. Kevin Wilson got the opener for us, but then they equalised and got a dubious penalty in the 86th minute, leading to Terry Butcher's encounter with the dressing-room door. We could have stayed up had we beaten Sheffield Wednesday away a few days later, but we went down 1-0 and were duly relegated.

The result meant Butcher left for Glasgow Rangers, which was such a sad end to that era. I couldn't contain myself – my sense of desperation was extreme! I was really affected by what I saw as poor leadership, the total silence from the club, the lack of any kind of PR, the absence of any explanation as to why players were leaving and a complete lack of anything for fans to look forward to. As supporters all we saw were the transfers and an utterly frustrating, stiff upper lip and seemingly cavalier approach from the board. So I wrote to the chairman, Patrick Cobbold, to complain, but also to ask if there was anything I could do to help as a younger businessman. I didn't get a reply. Not immediately anyway ...

I later learnt that they may have appeared cavalier, but it was actually nothing of the sort. All the directors loved their football, and the club. They may have lacked modern-day business skills, but what they didn't lack – and were big enough to recognise – was the realisation that they really did need those skills. So they had recently brought in John Kerridge (head of Fisons) and local businessman John Kerr as much-needed directorial talent. And I was to be next.

## Passing the Cobbold test

Completely out of the blue in early February 1987, and months after my letter of complaint, I got a call from Patrick Cobbold and an invitation to lunch before the game that Saturday. I was left speechless and didn't even dare to hope it would be some kind of interview.

There were no other guests, just the board members. In the (old) First Division it was tradition to invite the visiting directors to lunch before a game. However, the Town board weren't so sure they liked all their opposite numbers in the Second Division, so they decided to only invite selectively! That day we were hosting Portsmouth, and their lot clearly hadn't passed the test.

Lunch consisted of several large gin and tonics, followed by cold meats and salads, then cheese and biscuits and lashings of wine, washed down with port and brandy. I relaxed and remember telling them all manner of stories that afterwards I wasn't so sure I should have. I was still lost in a bit of an alcoholic blur during the game afterwards, which is perhaps just as well, as we lost.

However, in terms of my candidacy, if that is what it was, all seemed well, and the directors couldn't have been more welcoming. As I later worked out, anyone who knew how the Cobbold family did things wouldn't be surprised that the day had essentially consisted of assessing:

- how much I loved and knew about the club;
- whether I could hold my drink (and plenty of it); and
- whether I had a sense of humour, especially when it came to telling funny stories.

I think there may have been a couple more criteria, perhaps something about having a sensible business brain. And I believe the fact that I am a Suffolk man through and through, and proud of it, counted for a lot. But there was not a single question about how much I might be able to invest. 'Oh no, that's not the way we do things here!' was what they told me later when I asked. And in those days it wasn't.

When I got home that night my head was spinning, in more ways than one!

When there was no immediate contact from Patrick, I had no idea what to make of it. Nobody had actually said anything about an interview, so was it, after all, simply a lunch invitation?

A few days later and one of the most portentous weeks of my life was to unfold. On Monday, 16 February our gorgeous daughter Sophie was born. We didn't realise how completely unprepared for parenthood we were when we brought her back home, but Sophie was a joy from day one.

Two days later, Patrick called and asked me to join him for coffee. My heart was racing as I went in. 'David, so good to see you last week,' he said. 'The thing is you are the unanimous choice of the directors to join the board, might you possibly consider?' I have no idea what I said, although it was of course an emphatic 'yes'. However, I will never forget Patrick's words once the formalities were completed, and that only later would I see as prophetic: 'Very good of you to take it on!'

Those words have stayed with me forever, and I have often mused over what exactly he meant. I realise now that he probably sensed then that he might have picked a future chairman of the club. We will never know.

What happened that day would permeate every aspect of the rest of my life. The seed that had been sown back in April 1966, and that had been nurtured ever since, had exploded into bloom!

My debut as director came against Birmingham City on 21 February, and we won 3-0 with goals from Deehan, Cole and Cranson.

**Away games**

The following Saturday was my first-ever away trip, to Sunderland. David Rose our much-respected club secretary used to take his car to the games and give a lift to the first three directors that asked. Any others had to drive themselves, and there were often at least five of us.

When the distance was too great, we would go up the afternoon before on the team bus, which is what we did on this occasion, and it was an enormous thrill. We were one of the few clubs outside the top flight to have our own coach, which was painted blue and white, needless to say.

The manager and his staff, board members and any media accompanying us would sit in the front compartment, but there was also a galley area and WC downstairs, leaving the players the larger rear section. It was actually very plush for the day, and we had a video machine so the manager could go through the game on the way back home. It was tradition that the away side was handed a video of the match before they left.

The non-playing subs and squad members had the job of heating up the pre-made meals and serving us all lunch or supper. Otherwise we kept ourselves entertained playing card games, usually Hearts. Occasionally one or two of the older players would come and join in with us.

I absolutely loved it. Being part of this remarkable brotherhood was a sheer delight. I had to pinch myself that I was now part of the extraordinary Ipswich Town family ... and on the inside!

We stayed in the team hotels, but they were never smart ones. That time in Sunderland I remember we were at the Seaburn, on the beachfront close to the old Roker Park ground. For some reason there was a group of nuns staying there too, and I recall telling a couple of risqué jokes slightly too loudly and seeing them tittering on the other side of the room.

We would have a drink before and after dinner with the manager and the Ipswich press people, who were all good and trusted friends in those days – Dave Allard from the *Evening Star* and Bryan Knights were regulars. There was great camaraderie, with plenty of outlandish football stories, as well as speculation as to what the next day would hold. What fun we had!

The day of the match itself would generally involve lunch with the opposition board, but that wasn't always the case, for the reasons I mentioned earlier. It's all quite different now, but in those days football clubs were still run by boards of non-professional, non-executive directors, which is what I then was. There was generally great fellowship between us behind the scenes, even if we did want to wallop each other on the pitch. And, sometimes, it became a genuine friendship. All of which was in stark contrast to the money-driven and increasingly detached world of the people sitting at the top of the game today.

Over the years we had become close with several clubs. The ones that come to mind are Coventry and Blackburn (who both featured some very entertaining characters), Leicester, West Ham, West Brom, Brighton, Barnsley and Sheffield Wednesday – where a top-notch lunch was always served by an elegant butler. Surprisingly perhaps, we got on particularly well with the Norwich City board, even in the days of the late Roger Munby, and then with Delia Smith and Michael Wynn-Jones, with whom we enjoyed many a happy curry.

When it comes to liking the board, but not necessarily the club, I have to confess that for some reason Bolton were never my favourite side. But we were very friendly with their directors, and they always entertained us royally. Their chairman Phil Gartside served with me for many years on the FA Board, and I supported Brett Warburton, a director of Warburton's Bakery, when he became an FA councillor.

Being a division below them, I didn't experience it immediately, but the strongest bond of all was always with Arsenal. It went back to the 1930s, and owed a lot to the Hill-Wood and Cobbold families, and specifically the Arsenal chairman of the day, Sir Samuel Hill-Wood. He was a member of the same London club, White's, as Ivan Cobbold, the father of Johnny and Patrick – all three of whom would become ITFC chairmen over the years.

The story goes that Ivan had been planning to go to Kempton, but the racing that day was called off. So Samuel invited him along to Highbury, and he enjoyed the game so much that he was inspired to invest in Ipswich Town – then an amateur set-up that had just been promoted to the newly formed Eastern Counties Football League. Ivan took over the club, turning it professional in 1936, joining the Southern League, which we duly won in 1937, before finishing third in 1938.

That second year we applied to join the Football League and were immediately accepted (at the expense of Gillingham) into the Third Division South. At one stage Ivan Cobbold apparently asked Samuel Hill-Wood who he should get in to run the team. That led to him approaching Manchester United's manager of the day, Scott Duncan, who he somehow persuaded to drop down into the third tier. Ivan then sent the Manchester United chairman two cases of port by way of apology. I think it's safe to say none of that would happen nowadays.

### The Cobbold legend

The eccentric Johnny Cobbold loved to have a bit of fun at the expense of those he found too much like hard work. In the decade before I arrived, he and the ITFC board had found their Manchester United counterparts all too grand, as were Liverpool. Many years later a Liverpool director told me of one such occasion in the 1970s at the Copdock Hotel in Ipswich (which is now the Best Western).

During a stony silence at lunch, the eccentric Johnny reached under his chair, took out a packet of frozen sausages from a shopping bag and put them on his head! After a couple of minutes, their dry-as-dust chairman John Smith asked, 'Forgive me, is there a reason why you have those sausages on your head?' 'Oh,' said Johnny, 'I quite forgot, I was defrosting my supper!'

There were plenty of similar stories about Johnny. In fact, the entire Cobbold family were the stuff of legend locally. Sadly, I now find myself as one of the few people left that really knew Johnny, and particularly Patrick, so I rather feel it's my duty to recount some of the things they got up to.

Like the time that, after his customary liquid lunch, Johnny was sitting next to Bobby Robson at Filbert Street, the old Leicester City ground. They, of course, play in blue and white at home, as do we. Town were two down, and seeing Bobby muttering as half-time approached, Johnny touched him on the arm and pleaded, 'Don't be too harsh on them, Bobby, we are after all winning 2-0.'

Or when greeting a pompous alderman, the chairman of Bolton Wanderers, Johnny said, 'Come in, welcome, would you like a glass of Chablis?' 'Neh, sir, alcohol is the curse of modern man, never a drop has passed my lips' was the reply. 'Oh well, in that case would you like a cigarette?' 'Neh, sir, smoking is a cursed habit, an addiction for weak men.' 'Well, I am sorry,' said Johnny, 'in that case we have fuck all in common!'

Before a league match in Blackpool, the directors were walking on the promenade and Johnny saw someone with a sign saying 'monkey for sale'. He paid the man £5 and duly took the monkey along to the Blackpool boardroom, introducing it as the latest director.

When we won the FA Youth Cup in 1973, the club held a party for all the players and their families. At the end of the dinner, Johnny stood up and said, 'Well done and congratulations, boys, but most of all, well done to the parents. Why don't you go home and have a bloody good fuck and we will win it again in 17 years' time.'

On another occasion, as chairman of the South East Counties Youth League, Johnny stood up to make his speech at their annual dinner and promptly passed out. He was then carried out to a standing ovation.

Johnny had two donkeys, which he called Alka and Seltzer. Somebody gave him a third one, which he christened 'Burp'.

During a live television interview in the 70s, Johnny was asked by Gerry Harrison, the Anglia TV commentator (who died very recently), 'What do you do as chairman of Ipswich Town, Mr Cobbold?' To which Johnny replied, 'Fuck all …'

Ken Friar, a long-serving Arsenal executive, says that on his first visit to Portman Road in the late 60s/early 70s he walked into the boardroom to see six bottles of champagne, six bottles of white wine, three bottles of gin, three bottles of whisky – and six sausage rolls. And that was the catering for the day. By the end of the afternoon there were five sausage rolls left and Johnny Cobbold held an inquest to find out who had eaten the other one.

His brother Patrick's favourite grace before a meal was apparently: 'For what we are about to receive, the chef should be shot.' The squad went out for dinner in Puerto Banus after a pre-season friendly in Spain, with Bobby Robson saying how much he was looking forward to having lobster thermidor. So Patrick quietly asked the chef to remove all the lobster meat and replace it with bread. To the amusement of all assembled, Bobby nevertheless tucked in and exclaimed how delicious it was.

It ran in the family. When asked how all the 400 windows in Glemham Hall were cleaned, Patrick's nephew, Philip Hope-Cobbold, replied, 'I do the ground floor, and when it rains God does the rest.'

Johnny and Patrick's mother was Lady Blanche Cobbold, the daughter of the Duke of Devonshire, who had grown up at Chatsworth. She was a fearsome *femme formidable*, who briefly chaired the ITFC board. It's said that, at the 1978 FA Cup Final, she was asked if she would like to meet Prime Minister James Callaghan, and she replied that she would rather have a gin and tonic. Patrick Cobbold's close friend, Andrew Napier, was leading the band of the

Coldstream Guards on the pitch that day, and as a joke they played the tune 'The Old Grey Mare Ain't What She Used to Be'.

Lady Blanche died the night of the hurricane in October 1987, after which Patrick remarked, 'At least she went out with a bang.'

Some of what the Cobbolds did was rather silly schoolboy stuff, and what they said was often littered with four-letter words. But it was always full of good humour. Most visiting directors had never met anyone like them before and, despite the occasional insults, the majority took them very much to their hearts.

But, as you may have gathered, it was important to click with the Cobbolds. And among those that didn't were Chelsea (they never could get on with the Ken Bates, and it was reciprocal), Aston Villa and Crystal Palace (they were suspicious of Doug Ellis and Ron Noades respectively). I made a point of trying to build good relations with them all in the ensuing years. In the case of Ken Bates, probably not good enough, as it would turn out.

By contrast, we had a great rapport with the Barnsley (John Dennis and Barry Taylor et al.) and Leicester boards, as well as with the people at Stoke City, where they seemed to have a very similar mix to our own ITFC board. An eclectic blend of local businessmen who had a great capacity for fun (usually involving copious amounts of alcohol) while sharing a deep-seated passion for their club.

### A warm reception ... and a goodbye

I had to drive to one of my first games in the Potteries, as I was too late – and junior – to get a place in David Rose's car. It was early March, and somewhere near Birmingham it started to snow ... and snow ... and snow! And soon it was a blizzard. As I turned on to the A50 into Stoke, I saw what I was sure was the Ipswich team coach coming back the other way. The game had been postponed. Our instructions had been to meet in the city at the Potters Club. As a new boy I felt that I had to go anyway, so I fought through the weather to get there.

In I went, out of the cold, to the very warmest of welcomes. Peter Coates was fairly new as chairman, and also owned a local radio station, and as I was a director of Orwell FM we had an immediate bond, which I am pleased to say remains to this day. There was also a food link, since he headed up Lindley Catering, one of two firms that dominated the stadium catering world. They had the contract for Trent Bridge, and Peter would often issue an invitation to watch the Test match (complete with plenty of Pimm's!) to me and others from ITFC.

I will never forget Peter happening to tell me one day that he wasn't quite sure what to do with a chain of betting shops he owned. Years later I asked him what he had done with them. 'Oh,' he said, 'I've handed them over to my children to run – they seem to think they might be able to make something of them.' As it turned out, that 'something' was turning the chain into bet365, one of the most inspirational stories of business transformation that I know. Despite his mega wealth today, Peter remains modest, amusing and delightful. A true gentleman of football.

The end of my first season as a director, 1986/87, we managed to get into the newly introduced play-offs. The rules then in place meant that, by finishing fifth, we had to play the third-from-bottom team of the First Division, which was Charlton Athletic. The first leg ended goalless, but was certainly not without incident, including a Paul Cooper penalty save.

Things quickly went downhill in the return leg, which was played at Selhurst Park, Charlton's own Valley ground being closed at that time. Jim Melrose, their Scottish forward, grabbed two early goals, and our top marksman (Kevin 'Jockey' Wilson, who had hit 25 that season) went off injured at half-time. Although we came back into it after the break, Steve McCall's late strike proved no more than a consolation.

Steve and Paul Cooper were by that stage the only survivors from our heroic UEFA Cup side of six years earlier. Bobby Ferguson, who had been a brilliant first-team coach to Bobby Robson in the glory years, had been forced to sell his stars. In retrospect, the steady decline (ninth, 12th, 17th and finally 20th in the old 22-team First Division) was understandable, inevitable even. He really was being asked to manage under severe financial constraints.

So I had very mixed feelings and really felt for Bobby when the board opted not to renew his contract, which had expired. Tradition said this was the Ipswich Town way – it was much better than sacking. As the new boy, I went along with the decision, which had largely been taken in advance. Letting someone go is never easy, as I was to find out on more than one occasion.

Chapter 10

# John Duncan Arrives: Adventures Behind the Iron Curtain

SUMMER 1987 saw us interviewing a new manager to replace Bobby Ferguson. We talked to Ian Bowyer (a Nottingham Forest veteran), Charlie Woods (the first-team coach) and Keith Peacock (then managing Gillingham, but who was return to his old club, Charlton, as Alan Curbishley's number two). Peacock made it through to the final two, before losing out to John Duncan. The former Spurs striker had been successful at Chesterfield and was felt to have done well at getting the best out of players on a low budget, much as he had done at Hartlepool and Scunthorpe.

Upon his arrival, John made the decision to let goalkeeper (and expert penalty stopper) Paul Cooper go to Leicester, Steve McCall to Sheffield Wednesday and, sadly, to sell striker Kevin 'Jockey' Wilson to Chelsea for £300,000. It doesn't sound much today, but back then ... However, in came strikers David Lowe from Wigan, Neil Woods from Rangers and left-back Graham Harbey from Derby. We also recruited goalie Ron Fearon, and Andy Bernal, a combative Australian midfielder. And we shouldn't forget one very special signing: Simon Milton, from local side Bury Town. I remember standing next to Simon, who was looking as nervous as I think he ever got as we both waited for the pre-season team photographs on the main pitch. It was a symbolic moment as the directors got to sit with the players and coaches in the main photo. And it was a debut outing for both of us.

## Sergei Baltacha, a historic signing

I got to know John Duncan very well over the next few years as I threw myself into being a director. It's fair to say that, although John never failed as our manager, he never really succeeded either. The first two years we had almost identical seasons, finishing eighth both times. A case of so near and yet so far. In the second season we bought central defender, and future captain David Linighan, from Shrewsbury, as well as cultured midfielder Ian Redford from Dundee United. However, the really eye-catching move came just before Christmas 1988, when we signed Dynamo Kiev star Sergei Baltacha on loan, which later became permanent. This was the first-ever transfer business done by any English club with the Soviet Union, which at the time was rapidly changing under Mikhail Gorbachev. It was definitely seen as a landmark deal, and with all the talk of glasnost (openness) and perestroika (restructuring), the whole business became the subject of intense public interest.

Club chairman Patrick Cobbold didn't want to make the trip, so picked me to go with John to complete the formalities (or what we assumed would be formalities). Although I didn't have much experience in the football world, he knew I had travelled extensively on business and knew how to negotiate abroad. Nothing quite prepared me for what unfolded on the trip, however.

We flew out on Aeroflot and arrived in Moscow, to be collected by some faceless state representative. It felt like a scene out of an old James Bond film, with all the men in black suits, hats and dark glasses! We were taken to a crummy place outside the city that had been a hotel for the 1980 Olympics, with pokey rooms and cockroaches crawling all over the bathrooms. It was pretty dire. Almost as soon as we arrived we had to field calls from the British press, both local and national.

Next day we decided to be adventurous and try out the Moscow Metro. John's father had been there once, so he had encouraged us to visit the stations, some of which are resplendent with huge marble halls. Somehow we found our way to the city centre and arrived at the forbidding doors of the official state-owned agency, Sovintersport. The fact that we were even admitted was a surprise, given what came next.

We were shown into a dark office with only one shuttered window. Twenty minutes had elapsed before the door finally opened, and in came three very officious-looking characters, then two friendlier-looking men, and lastly Sergei Baltacha himself, who was almost frogmarched into the room.

All the preliminary details had been completed by telex and telegram, there of course being no email back then.

'Well, Mr Sheepshanks and Mr Duncan, how can we help you today?' we were asked.

'Good morning,' I said. 'We are here to discuss the details of the proposed loan transfer of Sergei Baltacha to Ipswich Town.'

'What transfer? We have not agreed to anything.'

'That is strange,' I replied. 'I have a copy of the telex in which you signify your agreement, which is the reason we have travelled here to meet you and the player.'

'We have not seen this before. We do not agree to anything.'

'Gentlemen, can I ask if you will please read this copy, perhaps we can move forward?'

And so it went on for about half an hour, with their intransigence still prevailing until a man called Mikhail Oshenkov interrupted and said, 'Gentlemen, I think we should go to lunch and, in true Russian and British diplomatic fashion, I think we can solve this problem.' At which point we were escorted out into the minus-20-degree cold for the short walk to their chosen restaurant.

We had left the state officials behind and were accompanied only by Mikhail, who we had now learnt was the general manager of Dynamo Kiev, and the president of the Soviet FA (who I think was Boris Torponin, but seeing as we couldn't converse much I could never really get his name properly). With Sergei himself, that made us a party of five. So we entered the dining room of the Hotel Rossiya, not far from Red Square, which had been the largest hotel in the world but has subsequently been demolished. It was an absolutely enormous room that could easily have seated a thousand people. But there was only one table in the middle, set for five, while the rest of the space was entirely empty. It was utterly bizarre.

We were ushered to the table. I think it was 11am, certainly no later, and over the next five hours we were treated to about 25 toasts! We were saying *nasdrovia* every ten minutes or so and knocking something back as we toasted everything from the health of the Russian Football Federation, to the English FA, Sergei Baltacha, Dynamo Kiev, Ipswich Town, each of the individuals present, and the weather. We made our way through three half-litre bottles of vodka and two bottles of brandy, and that was only four of us, because throughout Sergei would raise his glass to his lips but never drank a thing.

What was it that I said about being able to hold your drink being a requirement of becoming an ITFC director? The adrenaline was actually pumping so strongly that I never felt remotely tipsy; that is, until we went outside into the cold five hours later.

The deal wasn't entirely closed, but Mikhail seemed much happier, and relationships were being built. 'Right,' he said, 'we meet at midnight, and I will collect you for a special event.'

Midnight? John and I looked at each other and immediately wondered how we could get out of it. On getting back to our hotel we were hit by an avalanche of calls from pressmen and broadcasters back home, which we somehow handled between us. Mona said we were even on the *Nine O'Clock News*! At about 11pm we were both completely knackered, so John suggested we should give our apologies to Mikhail and meet him in the morning. I rang him and explained. 'David,' he told me in no uncertain terms, 'I would take grave exception to you not attending this evening at midnight.' I pleaded with him and explained how tired we were. 'I understand,' he said. 'However, if you do not come tonight, the deal will be in jeopardy.'

So we met him downstairs, our minds racing as to what was intended and being slightly wary that he might have been laying on some dubious late-night entertainment, or possibly a honey trap! We were duly driven to a suburb full of high-rise and rather forbidding-looking apartments, and took the lift up to a flat on the tenth floor, where we were warmly greeted by Moscow's top sportswriter. His wife had prepared a feast for us and we ate and drank and regaled each other with football stories galore until four in the morning. What became very clear was that they were really excited to meet fellow football people from the West, and that they were still very much stuck behind the Iron Curtain. Starved of contact, they had to make do with scraps of old newspaper and magazines. It was a real eye-opener. And they couldn't have been kinder or more delightful.

Next day we (somehow) returned to the office, and the mood was utterly different. That was very largely thanks to Mikhail Oshenkov, and the alcohol-fuelled diplomacy that had smoothed the way.

I found out later that Mikhail had actually hit the news in Britain because of a spat two years earlier involving Rangers' boss Graeme Souness, who had narrowed the pitch at Ibrox by a full eight yards overnight, even after Dynamo had trained on it. That led to an official complaint, and Oshenkov condemning the ruse (which had stymied their star winger, and helped the Scots take the tie) as 'un-British'. Souness has some form in the spat department, of course, but that incident came after the Rangers party had found themselves obliged to use an official Soviet plane to fly out for the first leg, before being detained and subjected to questioning at Kiev airport. All of which I could fully believe, after our own experience.

The next day we secured an appointment with the British Ambassador, who helped us understand the process to secure visas for Sergei, his wife Olga, son Sergei junior and daughter Elena.

That was all in early December, and a month later we were duly able to welcome the family at Heathrow, amid immense media excitement. We also hired the top football interpreter, George Scanlon, from Liverpool, as Sergei only spoke two words of English: 'no problem!'

I will never forget Sergei's face lighting up when we told him that we had organised a sponsored car for him. Or how it practically hit the floor when he realised that it wasn't the Jaguar or Range Rover he was probably imagining ... but a Lada!

We arranged a house for them locally, next door to a great friend of ours – the late Bob Shelley – one of several people associated with the club who took them under his wing. Mike Noye, our commercial manager, and I would take it in turns to host the family to Sunday lunch. And it was actually on our court at home that their young daughter Elena first hit a tennis ball. She went on to turn pro and become British number one! It was desperately sad when the family lost Elena to cancer aged just 30, soon after marrying her devoted husband Nino Severino. A tennis academy was set up in Ipswich in her name that still operates to this day.

Sergei made his debut for Town on 21 January at home to Stoke, who were managed by Mick Mills, and brought the house down on 46 minutes when he opened the scoring from a cross by Chris Kiwomya. We went on to win 5-1, and everybody felt on cloud nine. However, it never got any better than that.

After having had the courage to sign him, John Duncan insisted on playing Sergei in midfield or at full-back. He had suddenly got cold feet when he realised that Sergei wasn't a dominant, British-style centre-half, but rather a sweeper-style central defender. He was one of the best in the world in that position, and played 45 times for his country. But he would only turn out 28 times for us in what felt like a lost opportunity for all concerned. After a year, Sergei left to become a stalwart at St Johnstone in the Scottish Premier League, where he was much valued and happy, playing 90 times for them before moving on to management at Inverness Caledonian. He remains a close friend, and I used to go to stay with him and his family in Perth.

### A Ukrainian interlude

Largely because of having Sergei in the team, and with the Cold War rapidly thawing, the summer of 1989 saw us not in Scandinavia, but on an unprecedented trip to the Soviet Union. It was very much a first in English football. Upon arrival in Moscow we were taken by bus to the railway station, where a carriage had been set aside for our overnight journey to Kiev. It had old-fashioned compartments with double bunks on each side, the lower of which also worked as seats. I shared a cabin with Patrick Cobbold, manager John Duncan and David Rose. Also along for what was a hugely interesting, not to say groundbreaking, ride was our good friend Dave Allard from the *Ipswich Evening Star*, and also Tony Jones together with a crew from Anglia TV. Fortunately, someone in our cabin had brought a bottle of whisky as, apart from a delightful hostess offering tea and coffee, bar service was not forthcoming.

It felt utterly bizarre. We were well and truly behind the Iron Curtain. The Berlin Wall, to everybody's immense surprise and relief, would fall only a few months later, but it certainly hadn't yet. It felt almost unreal. I remember the countryside was largely flat and very green as it was the height of summer. We were also hit by an immediate sense of poverty, with very few cars, and people in villages tending smallholdings, largely by hand or with horses.

Finally we got to Kiev, which had plenty of exquisite palaces and churches that were in complete contrast to the rather dour and gloomy tenement blocks that made up most of the city. There were also interminable tram and trolley bus wires everywhere, and very little traffic. We saw hardly any shops, and no restaurants or bars anywhere. When I did find one, it was an austere room of tables set out with all the décor of a 1960s classroom.

We were staying at the Hotel Kiev, which I think was as good as it got. I was very lucky and had a top-floor room with a balcony and view over the park to the glorious golden domes of St Michael's monastery in the distance. Not far away was the equally sumptuous Mariinsky Palace, a truly captivating building that is now the official presidential residence.

Practically every maid in the hotel looked like Rosa Klebb, the villain in *From Russia with Love* who had poisonous blades in her toe caps. Perhaps most alarming was our discovery that the first floor was completely out of bounds. It didn't take us long to work out it was the

KGB listening area, and that all of our movements and conversations were being observed. This really was an adventure!

After spending a couple of days exploring, we set off to the airport for the internal flight south to Krivoy Rog. The plane was a Russian version of a propeller-powered DC3 Dakota, and when the captain got on he looked more like Biggles or the Red Baron. It was certainly not an experience for the fainthearted. I will never forget Mich d'Avray and Jason Dozzell taking turns sitting in the co-pilot's seat, and praying they weren't going to be called on to help fly the plane.

After a rickety flight of about an hour we landed at a deserted airfield and split into two groups. There was one bus for the team, who were to proceed to the match, and the other for the rest of us to be taken for refreshments.

We were given a splendid guide and interpreter who apparently was one of the few people in the city who could speak English. We also discovered two astounding details about the place: firstly, that we were the first Western visitors to Krivoy Rog since the Russian Revolution in 1917; and secondly, that the iron ore and smelting facility that it was built around meant that it was 29 kilometres long at one point, giving it an entry in the *Guinness Book of Records*. That was what we were told, at least.

We moved on to the match, where, after meeting the local dignitaries, there was great excitement and a capacity crowd of about 10,000. I seemed to remember winning, but the records suggest it ended two-all. Perhaps it was all blotted out by what happened next. After the match we were all driven off, including the players, to a feast night with lashings of local wine and far too many vodka toasts.

Feeling rather more than merry, we were taken back to the airfield, and the bus pulled up next to the plane ready to board. I was bursting for the loo, as were a few others, so I retreated into the shadows and suddenly found myself falling six feet or more into a trench. As I was lying in inebriated agony, bumped and bruised, all I could hear was Patrick Cobbold appealing in his very upper-crust accent, 'Help, someone, David's fallen into a hole.' I was hauled out, with nothing more serious than scratches and a sprained wrist. But what I then realised was that a few feet away there were huge security spikes, and that, for some reason – and to my lifelong relief – there were none in the tiny section of the trench that I had fallen into. Phew!

I was helped on to the plane, where Patrick and David thought it all called for a medicinal drink. Another one! And so we flew back to Kiev.

Our next game was against Dynamo Kiev Under-21s (a 1-0 win), but before that we were invited round by Sergei Baltacha and his wife, Olga. We crowded in and enjoyed drinks and local snacks. What became clear to us all as we spent time with Sergei was that he was revered in the country and he was cheered wherever we went. He also very kindly drove me out to the Dynamo Kiev training ground.

It's worth recalling that Dynamo had provided over half the Soviet Union squad that had beaten England on the way to the final of the European Championship the previous year. Their facilities were enormous, as befitting the club's stature, but it all felt dowdy and old-fashioned. It was pre-season so very few of their stars were around; however, I did meet the great Oleksiy Mykhaylychenko, who was working on an exercise bike and greeted his former team-mate warmly.

It was interesting to see how the players all had their own bedrooms in the centre, as they often stayed together before matches. They were managed by the legendary Valeriy Lobanovskyi, a giant in the game over there who was very much in the Shankly/Ferguson mould.

After a couple of days we were off again (in an altogether safer-looking plane), this time to Chernovtsy in the south-west of the country, very close to the Romanian border.

It was the same sort of thing as in Krivoy Rog; however, this time it was an afternoon kick-off and there was considerably more ceremony involved. The Soviet officials assembled and their rather snooty boss, who we shall call Comrade Bolokoff, introduced himself with a very formal air: 'Good morning, gentlemen, welcome to Chernovtsy,' he announced, looking down his nose. 'I am the president of the Communist Party for this area,' he said, self-importantly. 'Very good to meet you, Comrade Bolokoff,' said Patrick Cobbold with a glint in his eye. 'I am the chairman of Ipswich Town Football Club and my uncle was Prime Minister Harold Macmillan.' That rather put our host in his place, and Bolokoff was much more interested in speaking to us from that moment on. For the record, we notched up another draw, 1-1.

On our final evening back in Kiev, Sergei invited some of his other former team-mates to the hotel for a drink, and we met Igor Belanov, Anatoliy Demyanenko, Gennadiy Litovchenko and Vladimir Bezsonov. These were world-class players, with that extra bit of mystique as they were hidden behind the Iron Curtain most of the time. I felt very privileged to meet them. Somewhere around there must have been a young Andrei Kanchelskis, who was soon to become a star for Manchester United, but I don't remember meeting him then.

I will always hold a deep affection for Kiev, its courageous people and its amazingly beautiful palaces and churches. Ukraine became independent only two years later, and we now call the city 'Kyiv' in their national language. It was like a different planet back then, and probably would have remained a bit like that from our perspective. Instead, most of us will have seen footage of Kyiv on an almost daily basis, and could probably even place it on a map. For the very saddest of reasons.

Mona and I attended the Ukrainian carol service in Bury St Edmund's Cathedral at the end of 2024, and it was packed and very moving. We have the Ukrainian flag on one of our cars, and my brother Rick wears the blue-and-yellow badge every day. What the Ukrainian people are living through is horrific. And we salute their courage.

## Chapter 11
# New Arrivals: the John Lyall Era

THE 1989 campaign started with good news for me and my family, as our son, Tom, was born on 29 September. A huge baby at 11.5lb! Literally two months later we moved from Hasketon to Eyke, where we still live. We substantially rebuilt a bit of a wreck of a house that had been turned into two flats, on the farm. I set about the garden, while Mona worked her interior design magic – she was so good at it that she had two shops, called Sister Moon, in Ipswich and Woodbridge.

As it turned out, the 1989/90 season was to be John Duncan's last. We had a strong team that simply didn't live up to their potential, and the fans started to get on John's back for using overly defensive tactics. We finished ninth, with David Lowe (13) leading the scoring, followed by Simon Milton (12) and Johnny Wark (10), while Jason Dozzell got nine. The decision to sign Brian Gayle from Sheffield United mid-season created a formidable centre-half pairing with David Linighan, and Neil Thompson had settled in at left-back, complete with his thunderbolt shooting. Never could you meet a nicer bloke! We won three out of the last four games, ending the season with a 3-1 victory away at Brian Talbot's West Brom. But it was too little, too late for John Duncan, and Patrick met him soon afterwards to deliver the bad news.

Then six days later, working in quite un-Ipswich-like fashion, we made a masterful appointment. John Lyall, no less, was unveiled – to the media's great surprise. Lyall had been sacked the year before after

15 years in charge at West Ham. But he was revered as a disciple of former England manager Ron Greenwood, and was very much committed to the passing game. John was also full of fascinating stories about East End gangland feuds, and the fearsome Kray twins in particular.

Along with the changeover in my business life from Starfish to Suffolk Foods, I was throwing myself into being an active director, making more away trips on supporters' coaches, and watching every reserve game at Portman Road, as well as Saturday morning youth matches on the way to first-team fixtures. I had some great journeys to the north with the late Irene Davey, John Catton, Kevin Everritt, Nicola Martin, Colin and Edie Haddock, Sue Thrower and many other diehard Town followers. It helped me learn what was really important to the fans, and to build bridges with them, something that helped me when I became chairman a few years later.

I have always genuinely enjoyed communicating with people, whoever they are. The fans have generally accepted me very well, which is to their credit, as I probably spoke a bit posh, and that comes with all kinds of connotations of superiority that I have never in the least identified with. But they soon worked out that I was a diehard Super Blue.

I also remember being deputed by Patrick Cobbold to try to build a rapport with Roger Lynton, who had become a vocal opponent of the club board. Roger and I soon got on well. Things like that are so often just a matter of proper dialogue and keeping the lines of communication open. And to be frank, you could see where Roger was coming from, as the Ipswich board, while brilliant in so many ways, were not great at PR – which is exactly what I had been complaining about before joining them.

I always thought that spending time with fans, even disgruntled ones, was an essential part of the whole business of running a club. I enjoy their company and, when it comes down to it, share all of their concerns, and am essentially one of them. The only difference was that I had been granted some power to do something about those concerns.

There were certainly some other things I had to do as director that were far more onerous than talking with like-minded people.

And then there were other tasks that were pure, unadulterated pleasure.

In the summer of 1991, for example, I was invited to Cornwall, to attend centenary celebrations, by the delightful people at St Austell FC, where we had played a friendly. I was there to speak as a warm-up act to one of the absolute legends of the game. The guest of honour that night was none other than Sir Stanley Matthews. And I was placed next to him at dinner. Wow! Winner of the very first Ballon d'Or, he had played across four whole decades, winning his last cap at 42 and retiring in the top flight aged 50. And that as a winger! Despite all that, he was remarkably modest and humble, and a great man – in such contrast to some of today's self-appointed superstars.

## When everything suddenly clicked

John Lyall was an inspired choice, a strong character, revered by players and staff alike. He was also extremely bitter about his departure from West Ham, so really had a point to prove. We brought in the genial Mick McGiven from Chelsea for him, but kept the rest of John Duncan's staff – Charlie Woods, Bryan Klug and Peter Trevivian.

Needless to say, Lyall's arrival had got the fans very excited. But they would have to wait a little bit longer. It was entertaining stuff at times, but we had to write off 1990/91 as something of a 'getting to know you' season. John had managed West Ham in the second flight before, but obviously didn't know our squad. We finished a disappointing 15th.

What came next was a completely different story. We didn't have much money, as usual, but we targeted goal poacher Paul 'Sarge' Goddard (he had been a sergeant in the Boys' Brigade), as John knew we could have him from Millwall – which was an unhappy place for ex-West Ham players. Another former Hammer, giant goalkeeper Phil Parkes, had arrived the previous season, on a free transfer.

John had also signed Steve Whitton, a tall centre-forward from Sheffield Wednesday, and showed his capacity for out-of-the-box thinking by putting him on the right wing. To some people's surprise, it worked – Steve could jump and had pace, which meant he could nearly always beat the full-back in the air and then cut in and either shoot or cross to Chris Kiwomya, Jason Dozzell or Sarge Goddard.

After that first year, the pieces that John Lyall had been assembling suddenly slipped into place, and although not much was expected of us – less than 9,000 people turned out to see our first home game of the 1991/92 season against Port Vale – we ended up winning the division by four points. The 12 draws and ten defeats that campaign, including a painful one at home to Cambridge United, show that it wasn't all plain sailing at the start. But the Christmas turkey seemed to hit the mark (as it did quite a few times in that era), and our 2-0 win over Charlton on Boxing Day was the first of nine, a run interrupted only by losing at promotion rivals Middlesbrough. We beat Derby at the end of March to steady a minor wobble, and that was the first of a further five consecutive victories – all tight games – in just 15 days, curiously four of them at home.

John Kerr – whom I very much liked and respected – was by then club chairman, having taken over after Patrick Cobbold's retirement at the start of the season. With promotion now very much a likelihood, John and his wife Jill had taken along a case of champagne to Bristol City, a match we ended up losing. So it stayed in their car boot.

And it was only after the 1-1 draw that secured the title at Oxford United in the penultimate game of the season (with their goal coming from Jim Magilton) that the boot was finally opened!

On previous visits to Oxford we had been hosted by one of the many colourful characters in the football world, their larger-than-life (and quite simply large) former owner, Robert Maxwell. Always controversial, Maxwell was posthumously disgraced when he was discovered, after a very mysterious death, to have left the *Daily Mirror* pension fund in some disarray. And, on one occasion I recall, alongside him was his daughter Ghislaine, whose own infamy now rivals her father's.

We also reached the FA Cup fifth round that season, holding Liverpool to a goalless draw before taking them to extra time at

Anfield. Jason Dozzell gave real hope to the many thousand Town fans who had made the long trip north when he put us 2-1 up, only for Jan Mølby to score a free kick from right on the edge of the box – whereas the original foul had been at least five yards further back. And in the end we went down 3-2.

Anyway, promotion meant we were to become founder members of the Premier League, something that I will forever be proud of.

Given the titanic presence it now has, not just in Britain but all around the world, it's easy to forget the scepticism that surrounded the unveiling of the Premier League experiment. Some dismissed the new top flight as simply a ploy, the First Division under a new name, and just a way to draw more attention. It was more like marketing genius, in my opinion.

I was an early convert. And before it all kicked off, I accompanied John Kerr and David Rose to a high-octane presentation of the BSkyB vision for revolutionising how football was televised. This was back in 1992, of course, and I recall marvelling at the fantastic images of satellites beaming transmissions down from space. And I was starstruck in more ways than one. Even being in the same room as the likes of David Dein from Arsenal and Rick Parry, the league's new CEO, was quite a head-turner for somebody still under 40. The whole experience was a real education for me. Little did I know that within a few years I would be rubbing shoulders with them on pretty much a daily basis, and becoming friends.

The excitement of promotion carried on through the following months, as we held some phenomenal concerts at Portman Road. With the help of local promoter Barry Dye we had got the ball rolling the previous year with none other than Tina Turner, who descended down a giant stairway from what is now the Sir Alf Ramsey Stand (then known as the 'Churchmans'). She certainly woke us all up in sleepy 'ol Suffolk that night, and held every man in the audience by the testicles for two riveting hours.

We followed that up in the summer of 1992 with Bryan Adams. And did we rock! In addition to the main stage in front of Churchmans,

Bryan also belted out some of his numbers from a smaller one in the middle of the pitch. If Tina was the raunchiest, Bryan was the best live performer I had ever seen.

And then there was Dire Straits. I have a great memory, actually from a couple of years later when Mark Knopfler, who was a big buddy of our close friend Andre de Moller, came to stay with his new girlfriend, the lovely Kitty Aldridge, and his two children. One evening Mark saw our daughter Sophie's tiny beginner's guitar, tuned it up and treated us to a rendition of 'Sultans of Swing'.

### Founder members of the Premier League

It all kicked off on 15 August 1992 at Portman Road, with our new all-seated capacity of 22,500, against Aston Villa. For me the day was actually most memorable for my first meeting with their legendary chairman, package holiday tycoon Doug Ellis – the man Jimmy Greaves had nicknamed 'Deadly Doug'.

What everybody else remembers will probably be a strong debut by the only newcomer to the squad, midfield dynamo Geraint Williams, who fired up the whole side. Maestro that he was, John Lyall had fashioned a very competitive team with just a single acquisition. Things were looking good for us when local boy Gavin Johnson smashed home a 30-yard rocket, only for them to capitalise on some defensive errors and equalise through our former star, Dalian Atkinson – who would later die in tragic circumstances.

Gavin Johnson scored again, the only goal of the next game, away at Wimbledon. That was followed by five more draws – but since the opponents included Manchester United, Liverpool and Spurs, things could have been worse, especially since we had attracted crowds of over 20,000 for the latter two games.

Needless to say, we came back to (artificial) earth with a bump at Oldham. Yes, at Oldham – with that terrible plastic pitch of theirs. They were a top team back then, under the masterful Joe Royle, and always seemed to knock four past us. This time it was 4-2, with Ian Marshall getting one for them. In truth, they had learnt how to master the bounce and could gauge the run of the ball better than the opposition. So it was no surprise when synthetic surfaces were eventually banned. The quality available has improved immeasurably since then, of course, and they are now used at senior level in various countries, including Scotland.

Some highlights of the season were a 2-0 win over Tottenham (with Frank Yallop cracking one home from 30 yards), which was swiftly followed by beating Manchester United 2-1, with Frank again on target. He hadn't scored for four years at that stage, and then got a brace in just four days against two of the biggest sides in the land! A double from John Wark also helped us beat reigning champions Leeds United, complete with Eric Cantona, 4-2 in a really memorable game.

There was also the small matter of a home match against Norwich in April, when Jason Dozzell scored with two lethal finishes, with Micky Stockwell adding the other. This was Norwich's best-ever league season, but beating us in that fixture would have meant them finishing second rather than third! That satisfaction was one of the few bright parts of the second half of the campaign, and having been as high as fourth in January, we ended up a disappointing 16th out of 22.

Still, we didn't care, we were Premier League, and John Lyall and Mick McGiven had worked a miracle on slender resources.

I will never forget the final game of the season at a packed Portman Road, against Nottingham Forest. We won 2-1 thanks to Simon Milton and a Steve Whitton penalty, but what really made it memorable was that it was Brian Clough's final match. He left the pitch to resounding cheers from the entire crowd.

Although he was a shadow of his former self by then, and looked an ill man, Clough had been a colossus, and fully deserved the universal respect he got that day. Winning titles on limited resources with Derby County and Nottingham Forest, not to mention two European Cups, was in many ways his own two-fingered salute to the establishment, and what he saw as the entitlement of the big boys in the game. No wonder the Ipswich crowd applauded him.

We will probably never see Clough's like again. Although those feasting at the top table did get another taste of what happens when the peasants revolt when Leicester City slayed giants all season long a few decades later. Moments like that give us all hope.

Of course, I had been able to see many of those larger clubs at firsthand when we visited them during that first Premier League season, which, all in all, was one to savour. We even made the quarter-finals of both domestic knockout competitions, eventually losing to Arsenal and Sheffield Wednesday (in the FA and League Cup respectively).

**A dreadful day at home**
Although things didn't look too bad on the pitch, 1993 was a pretty awful year for us at home. Mona had a bad fall from her horse in Tunstall Forest where she used to hack. I was in a meeting when I got the call, although at first it sounded as though everything would be fine. She was wearing a riding hat, but it looked as if she had been concussed, and a doctor said she just needed some rest.

After enduring a series of truly dreadful headaches, she went to a specialist, who failed to diagnose the real problem. The excruciating pain continued, and so six weeks later she saw a new doctor in Ipswich, who immediately sent Mona for an MRI scan, and then told us she had to be operated on that very day. She had a three-quarter-inch blood clot between her brain and the top of her skull. It was a slow bleed, but was now creating potentially lethal pressure on her brain.

Stunned and frankly terrified, we drove straight to London, and the renowned neurosurgeon Professor P. K. Thomas. The pre-eminent man in his field and a founder of the Association of British Neurologists, he calmly explained that Mona had a serious subdural hematoma and required immediate burr hole surgery. That meant drilling four holes of about two inches in diameter in her skull to drain the fluid. All of this sounded utterly horrifying, and that was before he told us that, because it involved the brain, he wouldn't be able to administer any pre-med anaesthetic.

After sitting together crying, we hugged as bravely as we could, and I left. I paced endlessly around the streets, stopping only to call in for updates. Finally, at 10pm, and a full five hours later, I was allowed in, to find Mona covered in tubes. She was awake, and could squeeze my hand.

The operation had been successful. The brilliant Professor Thomas had saved Mona's life.

It was 18 June 1993.

# Chapter 12
# Discontent – and an Unexpected Elevation

AMONG THE events held over the summer, one we always looked forward to was the club golf day. In those days, most of the players would come along (whether golfers or not), as well as the coaching staff, supporters and the board (actually, just me as its sole representative). Jason Dozzell swore he had never swung a club in his life, but still managed to shoot a very respectable score. I remember watching him at one hole and wishing it was all so easy.

When the squad started training again in July 1993, physio Dave Bingham organised some aqua aerobics for the injured players at Fore Street Baths in Ipswich. I started going along for the 8am sessions, and was soon hooked, learning all kinds of exercises that I still do to this day. There were normally between six and ten of us, and we swam lengths in the various strokes, as well as doing leg kicks and float routines. An exhausting 45 minutes was capped with a fiercely competitive game of water rugby polo. Just like in a playground kickaround, we would take turns at picking sides, and I always wanted to end up with Richard 'Bam Bam' Naylor, who even as a young academy player had been one of the strongest guys at the club. Goalie Craig Forrest was probably the best at it, blessed as he was with the physique of an Olympic swimmer.

'Duck the Director' quickly became a side game, but I had always felt at home in the water, and could hold my own – it was probably the only sport where I could have competed with the guys.

It was incredibly good fun, and sometimes even the fit players came along. It wasn't his fault, but I still have a scar from one of our longest-serving players, Micky 'Stumpa' Stockwell, to remember it by. And remember it we do, at the various player reunions and anniversaries, which for many years were organised by our legendary manager's secretary, Pat Godbold. Meeting my heroes of yesteryear is still a thrill to me, and many have become genuine friends who have shared the experience of being part of this remarkable football club.

The excitement for the new season was building to a crescendo. However, it was then that John Lyall sprang a big surprise on us. He wanted Mick McGiven to take over as manager so that he could 'move upstairs'. That would leave John, who was only 52 at the time, as a kind of supremo overseeing, but not directly running, the team. None of us on the board were happy with the sound of that, but he was a major figure in the game. Looking back, we should have been stronger in resisting his demands. But despite our misgivings, Lyall won the day.

Despite all that, things started well with three consecutive wins – and debutant Ian Marshall, signed from Oldham, scoring in all of them. But things came unstuck from there on, and we didn't win a single one of our last 11 games. A heroic goal-line clearance from Micky Stockwell right at the death on the very last day gave us a 0-0 draw at Blackburn Rovers, a team spearheaded by 33-goal Alan Shearer. Even so, it required a late Chelsea goal to beat Sheffield United and relegate them instead of us. Phew!

It had been a terrible season. Mick McGiven (a delightful and highly knowledgeable man) had returned to an ultra-defensive approach, as John Lyall had largely left him to it. Our reputation, built upon decades of attractive open football, was left in tatters. The papers were saying that we made George Graham's dour Arsenal side look like Brazil, and after the Blackburn game *The Guardian* reckoned it would have been 'good riddance' if we had been relegated. Meanwhile, the *Daily Star* said, 'Ipswich Town were the most bland and negative waste of space in the Premiership!' I even recall someone writing that Shearer and his mates had betrayed the nation by not beating us. Hurtful stuff indeed for all Town fans.

With the natives distinctly restless, in July 1994 we asked John Kerr to call a board meeting that the now-retired Patrick Cobbold generously offered to host at Glemham Hall. There were strong feelings around the table that day, led by John Kerridge and myself, that John Lyall could not be allowed to stay in the background any longer. Either he was to be the manager or he should go. To my mind, the problems had all been caused by Lyall. Good a man as he was, Mick McGiven had struggled to the point where change was needed. I would even go so far as to say that we felt let down; however, ultimately it was us, as the board, that had allowed it to happen. In my view, it's a classic mistake in business to allow strong CEOs to appoint their own successor through sentiment.

In the end, Lyall agreed to stay on as manager. There was a reshuffle beneath him, with Charlie Woods made assistant manager. McGiven, who really didn't deserve the criticism, was made a face-saving 'Head of Football Development', while Paul Goddard became first-team coach and Town legend John Wark became player-coach – an appointment that John himself only heard about later. It all felt like a bit of window dressing by Lyall.

We began the 1994/95 season with some optimism, especially after buying Steve Sedgley for a club record £1m from Spurs, Claus Thomsen from Aarhus in Denmark, Adrián Paz from Uruguay and a young Mauricio Taricco from Argentina. That feeling didn't last long. Despite a memorable 3-2 win over Manchester United in September, things went badly downhill. The return fixture at Old Trafford in March was a disastrous 9-0 drubbing, a woeful performance that I was unfortunate enough to witness, and was part of a run of eight straight defeats. We ended the season bottom, a full 21 points from safety ... which was effectively 22 because we had a catastrophic goal difference of minus 57.

Needless to say, we couldn't keep faith with John Lyall throughout all this. With the fans in open revolt, at the beginning of December we asked him to resign. Paul Goddard took over as caretaker as we looked for a permanent replacement. The media went into their customary overdrive and had decided that Mick Mills would be the next man in the hot seat. But as it turned out, it was not Mick but another veteran club servant, George Burley, who got the nod. The shortlist comprised George and the distinguished former Everton boss Howard Kendall, but in the end we felt that there may have been a question mark about Howard's suitability for the job. By contrast, George was the future, he was steeped in Ipswich and the good standards learnt under Bobby Robson, and was hungry for the job.

**Two painful losses**

At around the same time, we lost the great Patrick Cobbold, who had nobly suffered the indignity of seeing his nephew Ivan Paul become a leading light in the fan protest. It all seems rather tame compared with today's relentless social media harassment, but the radio phone-ins and letter-writing to local newspapers all took a toll. I had known Ivan (also long since deceased) since school, we were even in the same house for a bit, and I think many people had expected him – rather than me – to become a director back in 1987. For a time Ivan had followed his other passion (and that of his family) and opened a wine business in France, but nobody could dispute the sincerity of his love for the club, even if we on the board felt it was misdirected.

The same week as Patrick, we heard the equally shocking news of the death of my best man and great friend from school, Jamie Elphinstone. He was a generous, larger-than-life character with an infectious giggle, and we had shared countless happy times together. I spent some very memorable weekends with him at the house he had rented in Bibury, when he was at Cirencester Agricultural College (where in another life I might have been as well), one of which I spent decorating his staircase while singing 'Rhinestone Cowboy' at full pelt. At about 9pm one evening, and after a liquid dinner, we decided it would be a good idea to pay a visit to the very large mansion Jamie had just inherited from his uncle in Perthshire. But neither of us was in a state to drive to Scotland, so he called up the local police station to ask if there was somebody off duty who could help us (and, of course, be paid). The officer who answered was, unsurprisingly, intrigued by the request, and said he would get back to us.

Half an hour later, seven or eight officers turned up at the doorstep. They clearly weren't taking any chances. They piled in and we offered them all a drink! It didn't take long for them to work out that we weren't a threat, and most of them left, leaving a couple behind who said they needed to make a call. They duly found a colleague who said he might be interested, but he wanted to know what sort of car it would be. The answer was a BMW 5 Series!

So, not long afterwards, a delightful officer named Robin arrived and off we went. We chatted away and dozed off, arriving at seven in the morning. There was clearly a policeman's code, as he had evidently not paid too much attention to the speed limit. Drumkilbo was a very splendid house, complete with staff, housemaids and all. There was even a gong for dinner. Robin couldn't believe the swish dining room and the full English breakfast served to him by the butler, Geordie, who would later amaze Mona upon our first visit by asking if she would like her bag unpacked.

Robin was then given a generous fee (I can't remember what exactly), a ticket home and taken to Perth station. The best part of the story is that the two became friends, and for many years he used to take a week's leave to drive Jamie to pheasant shooting parties at various friends' houses around southern England.

So losing Jamie was a terrible blow for all of his many friends, and of course his family. I was to have been one of his pallbearers, along with his eldest son (and my godson) Alexander. I was dreading it. But Stansted Airport – and indeed everywhere in the south – was blocked by fog. Fortunately, I was able to give a eulogy for him at a memorial service in Surrey a few weeks later.

George Burley made his managerial debut in the 2-0 home loss against Arsenal on 28 December. There was a brief glimmer of hope in January when a solitary Adam Tanner strike gave us our first win at

Anfield, but the woeful run of results continued, and the discontent eventually came to a head at a highly charged extraordinary general meeting (EGM) held at the Novotel. It had all become very personal, with Ivan spearheading a push to unseat the entire board. They would have needed 75 per cent at the EGM for that, but in the end only got around 15 per cent, so it was very a comfortable win for the board. Comfortable or not, John Kerr – who had ridden the storm in a very dignified fashion – was deeply hurt by the whole business, and at the end of the season announced he was going to step down.

There was a general assumption that John Kerridge would take over. I certainly thought he would. He was, after all, the big-hitting head of what was then a very big-hitting FTSE 100 company, Fisons. But over the summer he told me he thought I should take up the reins, and rather to my surprise I won unanimous support from the rest of the board as well. John Kerr offered to step down entirely, but I asked him to stay on. We also reiterated our backing for George Burley, who was still young and had been appointed for the future. He was clearly not to blame for the decline, or the relegation. And thank goodness for that! It would turn out to be a very good decision.

# PART THREE

## Chapter 13
# 1995/96: Setting Out as Chairman

I STARTED out as chairman with a pent-up frustration from having seen things go so badly wrong in the preceding couple of years and a burning energy to try to put it right.

I knew what needed to happen at the club. It needed to be professionalised. And it needed a new sense of oomph! I knew that it was a great place to be, with people who were well meaning and customer-centric. But we needed drive, and a much more business-like modus operandi. With the advent of the Premier League, the game was professionalising, and there was no escaping the painful truth that, at an organisational level, we were being overtaken.

I sharpened my thinking on the five-year plan on our now customary, pre-season Scandinavia tour, where we would play four or five matches against smaller clubs. Both Finland and Sweden play through the summer, so they were mid-season and the games proved competitive. Johan Bjork, from Umeå in northern Sweden, used to organise the trips for us, and I always took a week or so off to go along too. As did fellow director Harold Smith and, when possible, John Kerr.

It was serious football, but also great fun and an important bonding time for manager, coaches and players. During the 90s, we must have visited just about every football-playing town and city across the north of Sweden and the whole of Finland. The hospitality was amazing. There were nearly 24 hours of daylight, we had great barbeques, often beside lakes, followed by skinny-dipping in ice-cold, crystal-clear water.

I remember the first time I got in the shower with some of the players, I found myself wondering what they did to be so well endowed (even after the arctic plunges). Some of the lads were enormous!

As fate would have it, during the second game of the 1995 trip – all four matches of which were in Finland – Micky Stockwell got injured and Mauricio Taricco, then a reserve player, came on at full-back and did really well.

Getting home, after a press conference to announce my appointment, my first league game as chairman was away at Birmingham, and we lost 3-1. However, with the flying Dutch winger, Gus Uhlenbeek, now in the team, we beat Crystal Palace 1-0 and, after a goalless draw with West Brom, we then whipped Stoke and Sunderland 4-1 and 3-0. That put supporters' minds at rest that we were not going to 'do a Swindon', as they had been relegated again after dropping out of the Premier League the year before us. There was so much pessimism after our previous two seasons, and our average home crowd had dropped to around 12,500, while the gate against Luton in October was down to 9,123. So there was much to be done to win the sceptics back.

And there were certainly plenty of sceptics around. Ipswich as a town can be a bit glass half empty in mentality, and feeds off the football club for its mood.

I didn't have a particularly high profile, and – to the disappointment of many – it pretty quickly became clear that I certainly wasn't a knight on a white horse leading a baggage train full of treasure.

I was always very open about the fact that all I had to offer was bundles of passion and energy for the common cause. Which was combined with a business brain and experience from my own companies that gave me a good grasp of how to professionalise an organisation and build momentum. I had found that it all starts with the lessons from Stephen Covey's brilliant *The 7 Habits of Highly Effective People*. The first three chapters have titles that would become my mantra: 'Be Proactive', 'Begin with the End *(i.e. your goal)* in Mind' and 'First Things First'.

In some ways the disastrous preceding months actually made it easier to bring about change, as there was simply no disguising the fact that things couldn't go on as they were. To me it was clear that we needed to introduce a much more customer-focused and sales-driven approach to everything done at Portman Road. So, once George and others had laid their own ideas on the table – and bought into mine – we set about doing just that.

To give it structure, in very simple terms, this was my five-year plan:

*In the short term*:
- To confirm 100 per cent commitment and responsibility from everyone, on and off the pitch, and to ensure that everybody at the club is fighting the same corner.
- To aim high – not just to survive but to thrive and become winners once again.
- To bring back the atmosphere, excitement and friendly feel that makes Portman Road such a special place for Ipswich players and supporters by investing in community engagement.

*Medium-term objectives*:
- Recapturing Ipswich's position in the Premier League at the earliest opportunity – hopefully this season – and progressing so that, by the year 2000, the club once more has a team capable of mounting a sustained challenge for honours, both at home and in Europe.
- Develop and improve the youth system to offer a superior level of care, education and training to young players and to attract and recruit the very best players to Portman Road. It is no coincidence that winning the FA Youth Cup in 1973 and 1975 led to nearly a decade of unprecedented success.
- To build a commercial department that generates revenue at an altogether more advanced level, to aid and sustain the club's efforts in the years ahead.

One of the first things I introduced to all the staff at Portman Road was what is known as the 'Fish Philosophy', which was very much a 90s thing, and was inspired by the can-do culture of the Seattle fish market. It focused on four core practices: Be There, Choose Your Attitude, Make Their Day, and Play. We used it as a fun device, to rally everyone behind it, and to get people to choose to be positive. One of my favourite quotes is from Dale Carnegie, the author of *How to Win Friends and Influence People*, who said, 'People rarely succeed unless they have had fun in what they are doing.' That is so true.

We also started work on getting our BS 9002 ('Say what you do, Do what you say'), making Ipswich one of the first clubs in the land to achieve this certification, as well as Investors in People accreditation. A lot of what we did came down to starting with the end in mind, and asking, 'What does success look like?' It goes without saying that in broad terms success would be getting promotion, but we were breaking it down to try to ensure everybody in the entire organisation had the right mindset and were being all they could be. 'One Team, One Dream' was our mantra, and one that we kept repeating in the years that followed. It takes a little bit of time for changes like that to trickle through to results on the pitch, of course, but I would like to think there was a perceptible change of mood.

Something else I did was to take George Burley to London to meet former UK Athletics supremo Frank Dick. My brother, Rick, had seen him speak to the Institute of Directors and told me Frank had left the whole room with hairs standing up on the back of their necks! Rick thought he might be exactly what was needed at Ipswich. So I cold-called Frank and asked for a meeting.

George was sceptical but, as a fellow Scot, he came. After that, Frank visited us regularly at ITFC, and even ran some training for the players until one of them pulled a muscle, so that stopped as the coaches were suspicious of anyone from outside the game. However, his motivational questions and techniques were inspirational and we soon got Frank engaged with Bryan Klug at the academy, where he was a tremendous catalyst to new thinking. Most of all, from my point of view, he challenged and galvanised me, and I learnt an enormous amount from him. I cannot praise Frank highly enough. His book, *Winning*, became a bible. He was my coach!

### A Burley masterstroke – Mogga arrives

Something that really stood out in George Burley's extensive managerial armoury was his exceptional judgement and uncanny ability to spot just the skills he wanted in a player. That autumn, he came up with a masterstroke by signing Tony Mowbray, a former Middlesbrough legend who was then at Celtic. Tony wanted to move on as he had suffered the tragic loss of his wife and was keen to start a new chapter. It was a real coup to land such a leader, as the years to come would prove. It would also turn out to be a much happier time for Tony, as in Ipswich he found love again and married the lovely Amber.

The results ebbed and flowed, and for a good time it looked almost certain we would make the play-offs. We were also in the Anglo-Italian Cup and played games away at Foggia and Brescia – who featured Andrea Pirlo playing just the second game of what would become a fabled career. We eventually lost in the semi-final to Port Vale, but the trips to Italy were a fun distraction from the routine of the domestic calendar, and our first little taste of what Europe was like in a new era.

Another feature of the season was the emergence of young goalkeeper Richard Wright. He replaced Craig Forrest in January and put in a stellar performance in an FA Cup replay, away at the reigning Premier League champions, Blackburn Rovers, who featured a striker by the name of Alan Shearer. Alan's face was an absolute picture as he trudged off after our 1-0 win!

Sadly, after an unbeaten run of 12 games, our form dipped at the end and we missed the play-offs on the last day when Millwall played 11 men behind the ball, thinking a draw would save them from relegation. We fought hard to break the deadlock, and Johnny Wark (by then 38) went down injured in the cause. James Scowcroft, who had come through the youth system to make his debut that season, hit the post near the end. But no, we just couldn't quite get over the line. It was heartbreaking to finish seventh, and seeing Millwall being relegated was little cheer.

By making it to the fifth round of the FA Cup and an honourable defeat by Aston Villa, after beating Blackburn and Walsall, we had at least begun to serve notice that Ipswich Town were no longer the basket case that the nation had dismissed the season before. The 79 goals we bagged that season, 45 at home and 34 away, were the most scored by any side in all four divisions. But we also let 69 in, so the neutrals must have found us exciting to watch! Ian Marshall got 19, as did his M&M strike partner Alex Mathie, while Paul Mason hit 13 and Simon Milton (voted Player of the Season) scored nine, with other contributions all across the team. Essentially we were developing a new togetherness and a growing sense of *esprit de corps*.

One of the best moments that year came at home to Norwich with over 20,000 in the ground in a feverish state. It was 1-1, and near the end Robert Ullathorne's back pass took a bobble, leaving their goalie, Bryan Gunn, kicking at air as the ball rolled across the line. We were delighted, of course, and the crowd erupted, but poor Bryan (a real gentleman) probably wanted the ground to open and swallow him up. You really had to feel for him. I have had the privilege of getting to know him since, and his son Angus later became the Norwich keeper.

That incident was in part caused by the state of the Portman Road pitch, which in previous years had been immaculate – they even used to play a cricket match on it in the pre-season. I talked to our secretary, David Rose, and he agreed with me that, hard as it was, we needed to replace Winston 'Wiggy' Chapman. After some research, we found Alan Ferguson, who was unsettled in Scotland with Rangers at Ibrox Park, and had a fine pedigree from his time working on the golf course at St Andrews. He proved expensive, as in addition to ripping up and relaying all the turf – which it has to be said was necessary – he wanted to acquire every piece of equipment you can imagine. However, he did restore the pitch to its former glory, going on to win countless groundsman of the year awards. We were lucky to have him, despite the challenges in managing him and his budget. He always wanted just one more bit of kit!

# Chapter 14
# 1996/97: So Near, Yet So Far

SO, ROLL on my second season in the hot seat, which began with what might have been the most pivotal of signings, but was actually to prove the source of plenty of heartache and distraction.

In May, before the previous season had even ended, we became excited by an unexpected opportunity to sign Norwich playmaker Ian Crook. Ian was set to become a free agent from 30 June, the termination date on all player contracts, so he came down to Portman Road to discuss terms and do a medical before then, as he planned to go on holiday at the end of the month. All went well, he signed for us, we took the obligatory photograph of him in his new Ipswich shirt, and locked it all in a drawer for 1 July. Wow! What a coup! Ian was a proper midfield general, and was to be a key part of George's plans for the following season.

At least, so we thought.

In the meantime, former Norwich manager Mike Walker, having left Everton, had returned to Carrow Road, and immediately expressed his disappointment that Crook had been allowed to leave. He apparently made contact with the player in Greece and persuaded him to change his mind. So the next thing we knew, Crook was calling us to say that he couldn't join us after all. You couldn't make it up.

It all sat very uneasily with me and the rest of the board, and our legal advice was that he was breaching contract. However, the Football League ruling was that, because it had been signed ahead of the 30 June expiry date, Norwich and Crook were within their rights to change their mind. Whatever the ins and outs, it certainly soured relations with the Canaries for a while. To say we were furious was an understatement. And when the Football League only fined Crook £250, that just added insult to injury. To be fair, he did apologise but it stuck in the craw for a good while. The only thing that cheered me was wondering what our fans would have to say about it when we next played Norwich.

Unfortunately, it wouldn't be the last time on my watch that we found ourselves in dispute with a club from our neck of the woods.

Instead, we signed Danny Sonner (a stylish midfielder who had been playing lower league football in Germany) and another flying Dutch winger in Bobby Petta – he came on a free transfer from Feyenoord. With James Scowcroft and Richard Naylor coming through, as well as Richard 'Bam Bam' Naylor, we made the decision to sell Ian Marshall for what I seem to recall was around £900,000.

The fans all knew we had to balance the books somehow but, even so, selling Marshall didn't go down well at all. And when Alex Mathie dislocated his shoulder, it left us short up front. That injury, which put Alex out for the whole season, came after he had scored twice in a 4-1 cup win over Palace. Losing him added to an indifferent run of league results in October, so we were true to form in delivering the fans plenty of reasons to grumble in the lead-up to November's annual general meeting (AGM) – for some reason it just always seemed to go wrong for us at that time of year!

When you sell one key striker, the other one is badly injured and you only have unproven youth leading the attack, it's no surprise that things don't always go as the supporters would like. Happily, we won the game immediately prior to the AGM, 3-2 over Swindon. Unhappily, however, the crowd was only 7,086 and, although that figure was partly caused by a massive storm that had hit the town earlier, it meant the average gate had slipped below the 10,000 mark, and was a clear sign of the enormity of the task ahead of us. Bringing back the loving feeling to Portman Road was certainly proving a challenge.

The AGM was a major event in those days and would typically be attended by about 200 to 300 shareholder-supporters, with the board of directors, chairman and manager all present on the stage in front of them. After my opening speech, they were encouraged to ask the manager and myself questions. We were always well prepared and forthright in our answers, and I would try to pre-empt their grumbles, but there were inevitably a few people who would go out of their way to try to embarrass us. Still, in the end, it was usually good-natured, and I continued the policy started by Patrick Cobbold of giving the assembled 'the only dividend they would ever get', in the form of a drink!

Around then we signed Jason Cundy, the former Chelsea and Tottenham defender, and he proved a great addition, a thoroughly spirited guy with a winning mentality, whose approach rubbed off on those around him. Jason's wife, Lizzie, a former Bond girl, also helped brighten the outlook around what was a slightly dreary Portman Road at the time.

Jason was a real, no-nonsense centre-half, but after only a dozen games he was diagnosed with testicular cancer. He recovered, thank goodness, and returned the following season, but even in his first few games he had become a catalyst for better things. At this point, we reluctantly decided to accept Everton's £900k offer for the Dane Claus Thomsen to help fill the coffers.

Being chairman immediately introduces you to the national scene, which meant attending quarterly meetings (usually in the Midlands) of all 72 Football League clubs. Club secretaries would also turn up, so David Rose always accompanied me. Some of it was fairly tedious administrative stuff, but there were plenty of very interesting sessions too, mostly focusing on commercial and TV rights. David Dent was Football League secretary then, and he would prepare an agenda of current issues and regulation changes – all things that would take centre stage in a distinct chapter in my life that began around then, of which more later.

Meanwhile, back at the ranch, things were hotting up on the pitch. We didn't lose a single league match in 1997 until 15 March, going down at home to Bolton (who were all too often our nemesis back then) – a run that had peaked in a 5-0 thumping of West Bromwich Albion. It's a great testament to George Burley and his staff that we had managed to turn the season around. With no real established strike force, and relying on loan players such as Bobby Howe and the Swede Niklas Gudmundsson, we had climbed all the way from near bottom in November to sixth after beating Stoke away on 3 March (1-0, with a Mauricio Taricco goal, on the full league debut of our very own academy player, Kieron Dyer).

We also saw the emergence of a reserve striker, Neil Gregory, who hit a hat-trick against Sheffield United. So, after a brief stutter, successive 4-0 wins over Oldham and Swindon in early April meant we were suddenly looking good for the play-offs, and we sealed the deal with three more wins on the trot, to finally finish fourth. That included beating Norwich 2-0 in the Old Farm Derby, with goals from Taricco and Mason, in front of another highly charged full house of 22,397, our all-seater capacity in those days.

The goals had been spread around the team, with Paul Mason getting 15 from wide midfield, and Alex Mathie nine in only 16 games, while James Scowcroft with 11, Micky Stockwell (nine) and Steve Sedgley (eight) all chipped in.

**Everybody's favourite player**
Geraint (George) Williams, Micky Stockwell, Paul Mason, James Scowcroft and Richard Wright all played 40 or more games (out of 46), as did Mauricio Taricco, who was voted Player of the Year. What a competitor he was! He brought such energy to every game, and he was infectious to team-mates and supporters alike, not to mention managers and directors – we all loved him.

After losing away to Norwich, I saw him sulking by the team bus. I put my arm around him and said, 'Come on, Mauricio, it's done now, we have to focus on next week.'

'No, Mr Chairman,' he said, 'I just want to kill somebody!' Not that he really meant it, of course, but nevertheless the leader in me knew we should try to cool it down. That said, it was difficult not to be drawn to the kind of passion that every fan really wants to see.

In the play-off semi we would have to face Sheffield United over two legs for a chance to get to Wembley. We had plenty of ding-dong battles with the Blades over the years, but we were nevertheless optimistic, having done the double over them during the regular season.

The tension was sky-high for all of those play-offs (and, of course, there were far too many of them), and I will never forget a moment. But even by those standards our first match at Bramall Lane was a supercharged affair. However, we gave ourselves a really good chance after the tireless Micky Stockwell secured a 1-1 draw in front of 5,000 of our travelling support in a raucous upper tier.

We went behind in the second leg, before Scowcroft drew us level, and Portman Road was rocking when Gudmundsson put us in front. But then, in the 77th minute, heartache ... they equalised. And in the last minute it got even more agonising when Steve Sedgley's free kick rebounded off the post. It went to extra time and, although Paul Mason went close, we found ourselves being dumped out on the away-goals rule.

It was really painful to take. For two seasons now it had been a matter of so close, but yet so far. And it felt so unfair - as the team that finished below us, which meant they were away in the second leg, then had the whole 30 minutes of extra time for away goals to count. I was determined to lobby for change.

And yet again it was a case of the media demanding, 'So now we are out, come on Mr Chairman can you level with the fans and say you are going to have to sell once more to balance the books ... so is that the end of the promotion challenge?' No, I would say, far from it, we are all hurting. We have to take stock, learn from it, make plans and go again. And mark my words, go again we will!

I learnt quickly that the leader's mood always sets the tone. Confidence breeds confidence and, equally, any flicker of doubt will be picked up on.

## Chapter 15
# A Day in the Year 1997

I STILL have stacks of diaries and notes from board and management meetings, as well as a heap of other material that I have worked through to produce an idea of a typical day in a typical season. No season is actually typical, of course, but I ended up choosing the 1997/98 campaign, to give an idea of the kind of issues we were then facing ...

- Redecorating the stadium bars
- Deciding whether or not to open a club shop in Bury St Edmunds
- Promoting Mother's Day as a 'Ladies' Day' at the club, to encourage more female supporters
- Taking on a full-time electrician for the stadium (Charlie Cocker)
- Painting the Churchman Stand
- Agreeing policing costs, with the Suffolk force asking for a ten per cent increase over the coming three years
- Installing new public address speakers in the Pioneer Stand
- Deciding on the new third strip
- Making a decision on replacing the players' coach for away travel (we made comparisons, and found that Leicester City paid £25k a year rental for theirs, and Bolton Wanderers £30k)

- Setting up special deals to bring more young families and kids to games, and implementing customer care training for family-friendly stewarding
- Getting flu jabs for all the staff
- Asking Fisons and Cranes about renting their sports grounds for academy training, and ultimately buying them to expand the training ground
- Coaching the ticket office manager to benchmark the pricing with other clubs
- Working out how the new executive boxes would be priced
- Reviewing the entry criteria for player lounge passes
- Discussing the changes needed to our alcohol licence
- Arranging player visits to local companies, hospital wards and community events (we always encouraged injured or squad players not involved in that day's match to interact with fans)
- Organising supporter roadshows with George, myself and a couple of players
- Getting the ladies' loos replumbed ...

And the list went on. So it was all go! As it was for anyone running a football club back then, when – even as the boss – I sometimes had to roll up my sleeves and get my hands dirty. It is so different nowadays, as clubs today are unrecognisable, and vastly more sophisticated operations. Every part of an organisation has to function and click into place with the other pieces in the jigsaw to maximise the chances of delivering a good end product – in our case, results and promotion. But at least everybody at Portman Road felt they were on the same team, and we certainly all shared the same dream.

Some weeks a whole series of issues would come together at once; for example, in late August 1997, I see we had to have a big debrief after the Coca-Cola Cup match against Charlton Athletic. We won 3-1 (Mark Stein and James Scowcroft on the scoresheet, adding to an own goal from them), so it was not so much about what had occurred on the pitch, but more about what had – or hadn't – happened off it.

To start with, the ticket office had been missing four regulars and had a real 'mare' of an evening, so we decided more people should be trained. Then there were a whole host of problems with the catering people (Lindley, the company owned by Stoke chairman Peter Coates). Only half their booths were open, and they ran out of drinks in the visitors' area – which is revenue we would never get back. Meanwhile, Letheby & Christopher (to whom we had let the Centre Spot Restaurant) had complaints about their food.

It all called for a 'let's pull our socks up' discussion ...

## A key signing – Paul Clouting joins as commercial director

A lot of these were commercial issues, and at the time we were looking for a new commercial director. David Kimbell at executive search firm Spencer Stuart (who is extremely modest, despite being easily the best-connected man I have ever met) set us up with a shortlist, and I was immediately convinced by Paul Clouting. I wrote in my diary at the time that he had the 'right personality – we can teach any added skills required'. That is a belief I hold dear to this day. Recruit for attitude and train for skill.

We had excellent people in Mike Noye and Richard Powell running corporate sales and lottery respectively. However, we needed to add new commercial skills to realise our growth plans. So getting Paul on board was a massive boost, as it freed me up to concentrate on other issues, some of which I had been too busy to address. He got straight down to work by looking at a proposal to develop executive boxes in the Pioneer (soon to be 'Britannia') Stand alongside BDP (the Building Design Partnership, who had designed Wimbledon's new No.1 Court). And Paul would go on to spearhead our push to generate more revenue across the board, particularly matchday income, and to expand corporate hospitality – both of which had been somewhat lacking until then.

Even so, in many ways I was continuing to do the job of a CEO as well as chairman.

## Finances

As always, one of our chief concerns at this time was money. Or the lack of it. My notes are peppered with references to meetings to try to raise finance, and I spent an inordinate amount of time with the bank. We seemed to be permanently, and perilously, close to our overdraft limit. It had been 'ever thus' in my time at the club, and was a situation I inherited, as had John Kerr before me, from the Cobbold era. Quite simply, Ipswich Town was, and had always been, undercapitalised.

One of the issues we were exploring at the time was acquiring the freehold of Portman Road from Ipswich Borough Council, which would have strengthened our balance sheet. But they were never very keen on the idea, since they felt there was a danger we might then sell it. They did, however, seem interested in the possibility of developing the area opposite the stadium, possibly with a hotel. We were also excited by the idea of buying our own training ground at Bent Lane on the other side of town. Land (unlike players) can be bought with a mortgage, if at this point you are wondering how we could possibly have afforded it.

Something else that cropped up at that stage was how to most effectively, and tax efficiently, secure the 32,000 so-called 'Chairman's Shares'. These had previously been held by the Cobbolds, and were then passed on to the chairman of the day for voting purposes, to be used non-beneficially; that is, not to own. At one stage the family's Tolly Cobbold brewing business had sold them (with other assets) to property developers Brent Walker, but the club had negotiated to buy them back, and since that time they had been available to the chairman, if required, at AGMs.

At that time we began hosting lunches at Portman Road as a way of bringing in income and increasing our connection with the local business community. The guest speakers included Frank Dick, legendary Arctic veteran Ranulph Fiennes, and Francois Pienaar, who was fresh from winning the Rugby World Cup (and would later be played by Matt Damon, who is actually six inches shorter than him, in *Invictus*). I will never forget Pienaar's strong Afrikaans drawl when asked how he thought Ipswich would get on the following day:

'Losing is not an option,' he replied, in a tone of iron determination that emboldened everyone listening.

## One-to-one meetings

I have always very much believed in the importance of having regular, scheduled one-to-one meetings with department heads and their direct reports. This is not so much about telling people what to do, more a matter of keeping quiet and letting them talk about how things work, and – more importantly – how *they* think things should work. So at that time I would typically have what we called 1:1 appraisals with all department heads: Mike Brooks (retail), Richard Powell (lottery), Dave Williams (head physio), Mike Noye (commercial, programme), Mark Andrews (finance), Bill Leggate (ticket office), Geoff Sheppard (security), David Brooks (community), Sarah Scarlett (commercial sales), Colin Suggett (academy).

And then came head groundsman, Alan Ferguson, who was always so energetic, so informative and so infectiously passionate about his job that he drew you right in and made turf care sound like a thriller. But I had to prepare myself to resist, as he always wanted just one more bit of equipment. I recall him pleading his case for a £6k multicore machine in February 1998. But we had the budget for it, so he won the day that time!

I would later start doing 1:1 sessions with my fellow directors as well, which freed them up from the constraints of trying to say what they thought sounded like the right thing around the boardroom table (something I had been guilty of in the early days). I have got better at the whole 1:1 thing over the years, especially with the coaching I now do, having learnt to focus on asking open, deep-dive questions, often with a follow-up. Experience has taught me that you don't always get the full picture the first time around and that taking time to probe helps people to open up and yields the best results! In simple terms, by taking an interest in others and how they see things, you become a better boss, or leader.

## The academy

It probably doesn't need to be said, but without having much cash to splash in the transfer market, youth development has always been our lifeblood. It was a critical investment in our future, and not even in the especially long term, which was why it was one of the core planks of our five-year plan. We tried to set our sights for the academy plan high, and studied the model developed at Auxerre, a town of only 35,000 where the legendary Guy Roux had recently won the league and the French cup, twice.

So when the FA released the criteria needed to be accredited as a top academy, we were keen to ensure the funds were found to make the changes. These included pitches for exclusive academy use, a 60 x 40-yard indoor playing area, full-time academy manager and physio, dedicated youth scouts, a minibus, changing rooms, canteen, lounge, offices, a dedicated study area and classroom – plus a head of education! At that stage we even had a discussion over the possibility of opening a satellite ITFC academy in the Leeds/Wakefield area.

Related to all that was the more strictly revenue-generating/ brand-building activity we developed around things such as running summer courses, putting on Saturday soccer clubs and skills centres, hosting birthday parties and the introduction of a Junior Blues membership scheme.

**The Colchester dispute**
Something that had rumbled on throughout the opening part of my tenure was an unfortunate dispute with Colchester United over the recruitment of George Burley. It all happened in my predecessor John Kerr's day; however, since summer 1995 it had become my issue to deal with. I was clear in recognising that technically we were in the wrong to have spoken to George while he was under contract. Nevertheless, Peter Heard, their chairman, seemed to almost enjoy portraying us as Goliath bullying David and almost to enjoy stringing it out!

It had all become an aggravation, and the board took further advice on the issue from Roland Sharpe of Prettys Solicitors. I was keen to come to a resolution, as it was a silly distraction, but we agreed that it was best not to appear too anxious. We had always been ready to settle for something in excess of £100k if that was what they wanted. But negotiating with Peter was a nightmare.

The following month we began exchanging witness statements ahead of the arbitration hearing. I have to say, we had real concerns about their efforts to influence the proceedings.

The case was eventually heard in June 1997, just off Fleet Street in London, well over two years after George's appointment. It was actually my first time in a courtroom; however, apparently it would be much like normal proceedings, but with fewer people. The judge (in this case, the arbitrator) and his staff were in the middle, with club secretary David Rose and me on one side, and the Colchester people on the other. In the end they were awarded 150k. So more than we had offered, but it really wasn't worth the bad blood that I thought Peter Heard had engendered between us.

We reported on the settlement at the ITFC board meeting of 23 June 1997, and agreed to put a dignified public face on it. Even if, inside, we, and I in particular, didn't feel that way.

## Pat Godbold

The end of the 1996/97 season had seen the (first) retirement of our inimitable treasurer, Pat Godbold, as manager's secretary, after starting way back under Alf Ramsey. On 16 October 1997, we held a special testimonial dinner for Pat, with guest speakers including the extremely amusing Bob 'the Cat' Bevan, her all-time icon Bobby Robson (who she called 'Mr R') and several of 'her boys' – Bobby's star players. The inimitable John Motson presented a 'This is Your Life' session, and I would later arrange for the FA to make a special presentation to her, which was very richly deserved.

But there was no holding Pat back, and until very recently – and in her late 80s – she had been back at work part-time, as club archivist. That meant seven decades of service to the Town! She had a player's contract on the wall from her early years for Len Fletcher, who was a regular first-teamer. In 1957 he was earning £9 a week during the season, and £7 a week over the summer break. No comment needed ...

## Chapter 16
# 1997/98: the Same Old Questions

AS THE dust settled on another so-near-yet-so-far campaign, our attention turned to somebody whose time with us had begun back in the glory days – John Wark. He had only played twice that season, making his 678th and final appearance for us back on 30 November 1996, at the age of 39. Despite only playing as striker towards the end of his career, with 179 goals in all competitions he is still Town's joint second-highest scorer, alongside Ted Phillips and behind Ray Crawford (with 227). He was also brilliant at holding the ball up and shielding it for the other forwards to run on to.

As the summer began, Johnny asked to see me in private. He obviously got on well with George Burley (who had been keen to keep him on board in one capacity or another) but he said conversation was drying up when other people came into the room. Johnny was feeling unsure about things and unsettled as to his role, and when he asked to be involved in scouting it seemed he might be encroaching on the domain of chief scout Charlie Woods. There were specific instances; one that stuck in my mind was Johnny said he had driven all the way to Torquay, on the south coast, to watch somebody who wasn't even playing.

He wanted to do specialist positional coaching and generally support the first team. The situation was complicated by the fact that, as well as being an utter legend, Johnny was also a personal friend both of mine and his former team-mate, George. In the end he had to accept that there wasn't really a role for him, which felt harsh considering his service.

Meanwhile, we sold Steve Sedgley for £500k to Wolves and secured Mark Venus in part exchange. Mark turned out to be a really fabulous acquisition. Blessed with a sweet left foot for a defender, he could pass the ball as well as hammer it at free kicks. And he was a great guy too!

We also sold Canadian goalie Craig Forrest to West Ham. That was a shame, as he was a gentle giant of a man and another super guy, but Richard Wright had established himself as No.1 and Craig wanted a new challenge.

A bigger deal at the time was selling home-grown defender Tony Vaughan to Man City for £1.35m. It was a tribunal decision, as Tony was under 24, and City had only wanted to pay half a million. Just beforehand, I had a call from Francis Lee, their chairman, to say that the deal was off because of Vaughan's unrealistic wage demands. He said he would only be prepared to go ahead if Tony lowered his expectations and showed a desire to play for Man City. I responded by saying it was entirely up to City, and that I had been disappointed to read about the deal and their enthusiasm to sign him in the paper. That kind of gamesmanship was pretty normal in the transfer market.

During July we were immersed in negotiations with Bournemouth, and their chairman Trevor Watkins, over Matt Holland – who George had shrewdly identified as an option for the future. We knew they needed the money, so we were offering 66 per cent down, 33 per cent in six months and further amounts depending on appearances and whether (when!) we were promoted. On 14 July, Trevor called to say they had rejected our £535,000 offer, and wanted £800,000 as they had lots of interest from other clubs – Liverpool was the name he came up with, I seem to recall. It was more of the usual stuff. We shadowboxed around one another, with me offering different terms and makeweight squad players that I know they liked, but who shall remain nameless.

George was also interested at that time in the Watford striker Kevin Phillips – but wanted to check on his fitness. We met with Kevin at Portman Road in George's office, and really liked him. The big problem was that money was very tight and the priority signing, Matt Holland, still wasn't concluded. The Phillips deal obviously didn't go through and Sunderland nipped in to poach him from us. I got blamed by the media for us not signing Kevin; however, we couldn't do what we couldn't do! We got reminders of what we had missed out on nearly every year, including even a full decade later, when Kevin got a hat-trick for WBA as they drubbed us 5-1 at Portman Road.

Around then Fulham's Bill Muddyman asked us to put a price on our centre-half, Chris Swailes. Chris had been in our youth system, before leaving for Peterborough and ending up at Doncaster. George Burley had brought him back to Portman Road for £300,000 in early 1995. He had made 27 appearances the previous season, and, with hindsight, maybe we should have let him go when we had the chance. As it happened, he only played six more games the next season before we sold him to Bury for £200,000. A big-hearted Geordie and a good man, Chris carried on, quite remarkably, until 2016, when at the age of 46 he became the oldest-ever scorer in a Wembley final (for Morpeth Town, as they beat Hereford United 4-1). In the interview afterwards he looked practically unchanged from the player I remember in the 90s.

In late July we headed off to Sweden on the pre-season tour and a few days later Trevor Watkins rang to say that he was upset about newspaper articles naming the players who might be included in the Matt Holland deal. The whole issue was further complicated by Bournemouth having to pay 30 per cent of any fee on to West Ham. But a few days later, eureka! We agreed a deal of £750k with 50 per cent down, and the rest spread over the year.

### Matt Holland, captain fantastic

Matt turned out to be a tireless warrior on the pitch, a real role model, and ultimately a brilliant captain. We did some great transfer business in my day: Marcus Stewart is right up there, but Matt has to be my personal favourite, and most important-ever signing. I was delighted to see him appointed as a director on Mark Ashton's club board.

Needless to say, the amounts involved back then seem almost insultingly small these days. The wages were also correspondingly less – in the mid to late 90s established first-team players were mainly on £1.5k to £2k a week, plus £400–£500 appearance money, as an incentive to make the team. The world of football, spearheaded by the Premier League and global television rights, seems to have detached itself from any semblance of reality in the intervening years. Even some Championship players are earning as much as £2m a year and more nowadays, and positively stratospheric numbers in the tier above.

It took a while for the various signings and everything to fit into place, however. The season started poorly, with just two wins in the first ten games, including a 2-1 defeat at Carrow Road. A lot of this was caused by a lack of depth in the squad. George Burley wanted to sign a striker, largely because of a lengthy injury list that was keeping the physios busy: Scowcroft, Naylor and Sonner all had knee issues, while Mark Venus had a thigh strain, and Paul Mason had Achilles tendon problems. The only good news was that Gus Uhlenbeek was at least out of plaster after a broken leg.

Despite a 2-0 Coca-Cola Cup win over Manchester United, thanks to a brilliant display from Jason Dozzell – who had rejoined us after a spell at Spurs – and goals from Alex Mathie and Mauricio Tarrico, we were having a terrible time. The low spot came on 4 November with a 2-0 home defeat to Stockport County, who were then at their historical league high point (and would find themselves down in the sixth tier just over a decade later). Worse still, the attendance was less than 9,000.

In mid-November we beat Oxford 2-1 in the fourth round of the Coca-Cola Cup, which earned us another big home fixture against Chelsea. Although we would go out to them on penalties after a two-all draw, the bumper gates for that game (and the Man Utd tie, both of them over 22,000) were a financial godsend.

That month I sat down with George Burley to discuss getting him some extra coaching support. We wanted a senior man and chose our ex-player, the charismatic Bryan Hamilton, who was blessed with a quick wit and easy charm, and who knew how to lighten spirits whenever it was needed. After time at the helm of his native Northern Ireland and at various clubs such as Leicester, Tranmere and Wigan, Bryan definitely brought something different with him. After he left the following summer, former Man Utd defender Stewart Houston (who had worked alongside George Graham at Arsenal) came for six months, but when George was appointed at Tottenham, we really couldn't stand in Stewart's way, so he left too. We then went for John Gorman, who had been assistant to Glenn Hoddle at both Spurs and England, which was a masterful appointment – as indeed were all three – and contributed greatly to the leadership team that George had assembled, together with Dale Roberts.

The big squad news around that time is that we signed striker David Johnson, from Bury. He was diminutive, and definitely not the classic No.9, but he was clever, strong and a natural goalscorer. It felt like a real coup, and yet another inspired choice of George's. And it was partially financed by sending centre-half Chris Swailes in the opposite direction. David scored on his debut, a 1-1 draw at Wolves, and again the following week in a 4-0 away win at Reading.

It wasn't just his scoring potential, David felt like a catalyst for much better things to come. We also got Jamie Clapham on loan from Tottenham and, at the same time, George cleared out a few of the players on the sidelines, so Neil Gregory, Mark Stein, David Whyte, Andy Legg and David Kerslake all moved on. And Jason Dozzell left again, to join Northampton, a move that was questioned by some fans. Hard calls have to be made sometimes, and sentiment can't come into it, no matter how brilliantly a player may have performed previously.

After succumbing to Birmingham City on Boxing Day, we lost only once in the league across the rest of the season – a 2-1 defeat at the City Ground, which was largely down to the genius of Nottingham Forest's Dutch star, Pierre van Hooijdonk. And we gave up just five draws in that fantastic run, including a goalless one to John Aldridge's Tranmere Rovers, who featured John McGreal in their stingy defence.

Some of the highlights included the 3-2 victory at West Bromwich Albion, with Jason Cundy heading home a Jamie Clapham cross to grab the points right at the death. Then there was the 2-1 win over Man City, led by new boss Joe Royle! We were behind for nearly the entire game until Bobby Petta equalised in the 83rd minute, and Kieron Dyer clinched victory on the stroke of full time.

**A great month**
That match came in the middle of a wonderful February when we scored five times in three consecutive home games. On Valentine's Day, our future true love Marcus Stewart had put Huddersfield ahead with a memorable solo run, before Matt Holland, David Johnson (2), Mathie and Richard 'Bam Bam' Naylor hit back for us.

Ten days later Johnson grabbed a hat-trick in the 5-2 win over Oxford United, with Alex Mathie and Matt Holland also scoring (this after Matt had to stand in goal for a few minutes when Richard Wright had to leave the pitch for stitches!). And in between those two games, we climbed our own personal Olympus with a 5-0 demolition of Norwich – a sign of how much we had improved, as we had lost the reverse fixture. Alex got his own hat-trick in that one, and Bobby Petta also hit a brace as he terrorised the Canary defenders with his pace and skills on the left wing, while fellow Dutchman Gus Uhlenbeek was weaving his own magic down the right.

Petta and Dyer, who both gave us electric pace, were on the scoresheet again on the last day of the month, securing a 2-2 draw away to Sunderland in a red-hot atmosphere. After a single Matt Holland goal saw off Sheffield United (for whom a certain Ian Rush hit the bar), suddenly people were wondering if we could make the play-offs. They were left in little doubt as we set about winning every game we played in March (vs United, Charlton, Stockport County, Wolves and Reading), while only conceding a single goal and scoring nine.

That month also saw us secure permanent terms for Jamie Clapham. It took a bit of haggling with David Pleat at Spurs. They asked for £300k, I came back with a plan to spread the payments, and eventually we shook hands on four payments of £60k over 18 months, and another once he had made 30 appearances. Which of course he did. That was typical of how we afforded players in those days ... almost on HP ('hire purchase' for those not of a certain age).

That was a great bit of business for us, and Jamie fitted nicely into a team that was really hitting its stride, ending the regular season with five straight wins (Portsmouth, Port Vale, Bury, Sunderland and Crew Alexandra – 12 goals scored and just three conceded).

Despite not starting the season, David Johnson (father of Brennan, who recently made a high-profile move from Spurs to Crystal Palace) scored 22 times in all competitions, and our intrepid Scot, Alex Mathie, came through all his injuries to net 15 times. Matt Holland, Richard Wright and the tireless Micky Stockwell were ever-present in the league. What remarkable servants they all were for our club, with Micky deserving special mention after turning out 610 times for us (and a further 131 games for Colchester). What a career!

Being in with a chance of promotion to the Premier League earned us a relationship-building visit from Sky. So Jonathan Brill of (the now defunct) PR group Bell Pottinger, and the legendary John Bromley, the former head of ITV Sport, duly turned up and took me to Hintlesham Hall for a convivial lunch. 'Brommers', who had started his career writing reports on schoolboy cricket matches he had played in, was extremely good company and a well-known raconteur. My favourite story of his was of a travelling salesman in Kent who was looking for a pub for lunch. Seeing a sign that read 'a pie, a pint, and a friendly word' he pulled up and wandered in.

'Good morning, Landlord, can I have one of your pies and a pint, please?'

'Certainly, sir,' said the landlord, serving him.

As he was walking away, the salesman remembered to ask: 'Ah, landlord, I nearly forgot, what about the friendly word?'

'Oh, sir,' he says, beckoning his guest closer, 'I wouldn't eat the pie if I was you, sir.'

We would need all our reserves of good humour, as the play-offs against Charlton (one of those clubs we love to hate, and one that was later to become something of a retirement home for a lot of our best players) were a big disappointment.

The first leg at Portman Road got off to the worst possible start, with Jamie Clapham diverting a cross past Richard Wright. That was the only goal in what developed into a bad-tempered match. Charlton had come to be spoilers, with nine bookings in the game, and they had former Canary Danny Mills sent off. They won the second leg by the same score, but we could have few complaints.

Humph, humph, humph! So it was to be another year in the Championship, then actually known as the First Division.

That inevitably cued the usual chorus of grumbles disguised as questions, something that became all too familiar over the years. 'Well, Mr Sheepshanks, what is your reaction to that? Is this the end of the road for this team? You'll have to sell, won't you?'

Nor was my response much changed. 'Our resolve is redoubled,' I would say. 'Watch this space. We didn't come this far just to give up. We will learn from this and we re-emerge stronger.'

And so on …

## Chapter 17
# 1998/99: Third Time Unlucky

AFTER STARTING the season goalless in four consecutive games (three 0-0 draws and a 2-0 defeat at home to Sunderland), the mood picked up and we scored three goals in each of our next four games (three wins and a 3-3 draw away to Oxford).

One consequence of not being promoted was that we continued to be very short of money. We didn't sell until late August, when we accepted a bid for Alex Mathie from Dundee. I was desperately sad to see him go. Alex was a brilliant chap to have around the place. He had rotten luck with injuries, but still scored 47 goals for us in 133 games. We didn't have the money for new signings of note and, as our overdraft had grown to over £2 million, the bank became increasingly twitchy – and eventually worse than that. We had meetings with our bank manager at least once a month, and asked for an increased facility, but in the end they told us that we had to sell and reduce our debt.

We agonised over what to do, as we were playing well, and six nearly consecutive wins (marred by just a painful home defeat to Norwich) had lifted us to second in the table by early November. We really didn't want to weaken a very good squad.

Mauricio Taricco had become a huge favourite with the fans, and indeed with everybody at the club. Although born in Sardinia to an Italian father, he had grown up in Argentina. We had signed him in 1994 at the end of the John Lyall era, at the same time as Adrián Paz, a Uruguayan international, who we paid £900,000 for. Paz was a flair player who had his moments, but sadly flattered to deceive. He only played 18 times and stayed just half a season. Mauricio had been a bit of a punt at the time, and we had gone as much on his agent's promise of potential as much as anything else. It did rather seem for a time that Mauricio might be the same story as Adrián. I can remember thinking he looked like a fish out of water in September 1994 during a 3-0 home defeat by Bolton in the Coca-Cola Cup – as did another debutant that night, Claus Thomsen.

Claus went on to establish himself as a classy midfielder with us and got capped for Denmark. However, Mauricio never played for the first team again that season, instead going back to the reserves to learn all about English League football ... And he certainly did that!

Mauricio got his chance in the summer of 1995, after Micky Stockwell was injured in our pre-season tour in Finland. And what a gem of a player he was to become. After a few games into the season proper, there was an opening at left-back (he could play both sides) and he never looked back, quickly establishing himself as one of the first names on George Burley's team sheet. You always knew what you were going to get from him: a thoroughly combative and totally committed performance. He tackled ferociously for a relatively slight man, and would often tear down either wing to support an attack.

So when in late October 1998 the manager at Barclays told us that we had to reduce our overdraft, it was a really tough call. But, despite my protestations, they insisted.

The board discussed it all with George Burley, and we decided we didn't want to sell our strikers, Johnson and Scowcroft, or Matt Holland (who we had fought so hard to sign). Or anyone, in fact! So, we grudgingly concluded that it would probably cause least damage to the squad to let Mauricio go. We had young players who could come in from the academy to play full-back, such as John Kennedy, and there was also Frenchman Jean-Manuel Thetis ... so we reluctantly agreed to the £1.775m fee that Spurs were offering, a huge amount for a defender. We were to keep the deal on ice until after two big home games – West Brom that Saturday, and Wolves the following

Tuesday. We won each of them 2-0 and, of course, Mauricio was outstanding in both.

However, there was more drama waiting in the wings. In injury time against Wolves, Mauricio was tackled late, and viciously, from behind – I can see it all now at the far corner of the (then) North Stand end. It was a nasty foul. Mauricio crumpled like a sack of potatoes, and out came the stretcher. He was carried off to rousing applause. My heart had missed several beats by then. Would that mean the sale was off ... what could we do now? Sell a different player?

Of course, almost nobody else in the crowd had a clue what was at stake. As I left my seat in the directors' box, I caught the eye of Peter Archer, our bank manager (who had forced the sale). He said, 'I am sorry, David.' Which was, of course, meant well. But I recall angrily glaring back at him and saying something churlish that I deeply regretted after I had cooled down. He was just doing his job, and was a Town fan too. I was just so angry at being put in that position in the first place and then seeing what actually was a very good deal go up in smoke, thanks to what I saw as a cynical tackle.

The next day, I called David Pleat at Tottenham and asked him what he wanted to do. David is an honourable man who I have come to greatly admire. He behaved like a true gentleman and – to my enormous relief – said they still wanted to complete the signing; however, there would clearly have to be a pause for a medical assessment. After a couple of weeks it was clear that Mauricio would recover fully, and we agreed that Spurs would pay us half the fee immediately, with the balance a few months later when he had passed a full fitness test. Happily, this proved acceptable to the bank. So, panic over!

People obviously struggled to come to terms with selling Mauricio. They said he was a fans' favourite. Well, let me tell you, he was a chairman's favourite and manager's favourite too. Everybody loved him. Selling Mauricio was the worst.

I was recently reminded of this by Seán Salter, a name no doubt familiar to a lot of readers, who is blessed with an absolutely encyclopaedic knowledge of anything related to our beloved club (and much besides, as well as having a very sharp eye for a typo!). I am greatly indebted to Seán, who checked through the football sections of this book, and recalled the time – at the building where the supporters' club was based on Portman Road – that he told me how disappointed he was that I had sold his favourite player. Seán relates that I put my arm over his shoulder and said, 'How do you think I feel? He was my favourite player too?'

**Moving on after Mauricio**
Still, we had to move on. And we won our next match away to Barnsley 1-0, but lost our next home game by the same score to Bolton, with Bob Taylor – who would torment us that season – scoring in the 90th minute. The world felt a bit unfair.

The next week we were proud to host our first England U21 game at Portman Road, against the Czech Republic. England lost 1-0 but we were all thrilled to see Kieron Dyer, now a regular star in our first team, representing his country, while Richard Wright was called up to the full England squad.

The following week, Scowy scored a hat-trick for us to win 3-0 at Crewe and everything started to feel better again. It must be said that George's decision to give the captaincy to Matt Holland at the start of the season had been inspired. Matt led from the front and put in Captain Marvel performances week in, week out, not to mention getting nine goals from midfield that season. He grabbed a couple in the 3-0 victory over Portsmouth on Boxing Day, which followed a last-gasp win – courtesy of a Richard Naylor strike – at Sheffield United in a game that saw the debut of Titus Bramble. We then managed to lose three games on the trot, including going down 1-0 at home to Grimsby! Ugh.

However, George then pulled off what turned out to be a couple of master signings: we signed Fabian Wilnis from the Netherlands for £200k (that we had somehow cobbled together from the Taricco sale) and Jim Magilton on loan (initially) from Sheffield Wednesday. I recall doing the deal with Dave Richards (now Sir Dave), the Wednesday chairman, who was on the FA Board with me. We also signed Marlon Harewood on loan from Forest, a name we would unfortunately hear again a few years later when he lined up for West Ham in the play-offs.

We went down to Everton in the fourth round of the FA Cup to a single, comedy rebound goal – the ball hitting the post and bouncing back off Mark Venus to leave Nick Barmby with a tap-in. We then had a last-minute equaliser ruled out by Mike Riley (who later headed up refereeing at the Premier League). Still, we left with our heads held high and then embarked on an unbeaten run of seven games (including six wins), then a 3-2 defeat away at Crystal Palace, before another run of four straight wins, including trouncing Swindon 6-0 away, with Veno converting two penalties.

The only drawback was Kieron Dyer being badly injured at home to Watford. He carried on and scored with his 'good' leg before hobbling off, only to discover later that the other one was broken! What a player he had become.

Sunderland, spearheaded by striker Niall Quinn, were runaway leaders, but we were nip and tuck with Bradford City in the second automatic promotion place.

I remember thinking that it really was going to be our year. Jason Cundy came back to make the odd appearance in defence after a nightmare nine months out from a bizarre skipping-rope injury. And Jean-Manuel Thetis, the giant Frenchman, came and played his part in defence, which was much needed after we lost Mauricio.

In truth, and despite the loss of Taricco, we now had a strong squad with Matt Holland, Jamie Clapham and Richard Wright ever-present, and Tony Mowbray, Mark Venus and David Johnson all playing 40 games or more.

So we came to the penultimate game, needing to do better than Bradford to clinch automatic promotion. They were held to a draw by Oxford, but we went down 1-0 away at Birmingham. Still, maybe all was not lost. We were home to Sheffield United for our final game, while Bradford would have to go to Wolves, who were themselves challenging for the play-offs. We won 4-1, with Jim Magilton, James Scowcroft, Kieron Dyer all scoring, and Richard 'Bam Bam' Naylor coming off the bench to add another. Nowadays people would have been checking their phones, but back then they were glued to their radios – and there was great excitement early on because Bradford were losing and we were winning, meaning we would be up! That didn't last, and when Bradford went two ahead, we thought it was all over, until Wolves struck back towards the end. We just needed them to get another in the final ten minutes.

Needless to say, they didn't. But, as much as that day, when I look back over the campaign, one particular match still sticks in my mind: in mid-April, despite a club record of 26 clean sheets over the season, we somehow lost 2-1 at home to lowly Crewe Alexandra in front of an unbelievably frustrated 21,000 crowd. So, we had it in our hands at that point, but now had to make do with the play-offs.

## John Kerridge

During the season we had lost our director and great friend John Kerridge, who died suddenly at home. Although not particularly overweight, he had a large double chin that shook quicker than his head when he disagreed with something. He was a very wise owl, and would have made a great career coach – he had a real knack of being able to tap me on the shoulder and say, 'David, might there be another way of looking at this?' or some such remark that never caused offence yet always made me think. John had been a distinguished chairman of Fisons, taking them to extraordinary heights and into the FTSE 100 list of top companies in the UK. However, he never really clicked with the City analysts, and when the US Food and Drug Administration started finding issues with the INTAL asthma drug, then the criticism came thick and fast.

John was a proud man of Ipswich, and did great things for the town; for example, by sponsoring Ipswich Ladies Hockey. They became one of the top teams in the country, with Judy Wright (who would later become a director of the Samaritans when I was their patron) and England international Sandie Lister their talismanic captain and coach.

I had also enlisted John to become a non-executive director of Suffolk Foods, where he gave me and my brother Rick so much invaluable advice.

So John was a big loss.

We appointed another fine mind, diehard ITFC fan Richard (Lord) Ryder, to succeed him on the board.

## Sir Alf

Around that time we also heard the sad news about the legendary Sir Alf Ramsey, who had died at the age of 79 after suffering from Alzheimer's. What an extraordinary feat to take little old Ipswich to win the old First Division title in 1962 in our first-ever year at that level, and just five years after winning promotion from the old Third Division (South). He didn't do badly with England either.

Sir Alf was a very private man in his later years, preferring the company of his friends at Rushmere Golf Club to more formal occasions. However, I was fortunate to meet him on his occasional visits to Portman Road, when he always appeared immaculately dressed in his blazer and tie – which is how he is portrayed in the statue that stands proudly on the corner of Portman Road and what is now called Sir Alf Ramsey Way. The sculpture, the work of Sean Hedges-Quinn, was the result of a great fundraising exercise by the supporters' club.

Sir Alf's funeral in Ipswich was an extraordinary occasion when all the World Cup-winning players attended, and it was a privilege to meet them – so dignified, and heroes to a man. I was fortunate to get to know them all quite well over the years at the FA, at Wembley and various events, especially Sir Geoff Hurst, Sir Bobby Charlton and George Cohen.

## More play-off agony

So, the play-offs arrived, and in the first leg we went down to Bolton Wanderers 1-0, to a late goal in a tense affair.

The second leg was in front of a sellout 21,755 crowd at Portman Road (our capacity back then), and would have been absolutely riveting even for a neutral fan, not that there were many of those in a partisan and vocal crowd.

We scored early through skipper Matt Holland to level the tie on aggregate. But just before half-time, Eidur Gudjohnsen (the Icelandic international, who later played for Chelsea) fed their veteran striker Bob Taylor, making it 1-1 on the night. We hit back immediately and on the stroke of half-time, when Scowy set up Kieron Dyer to score from an oblique angle.

It stayed 2-2 on aggregate until close to the end. Then in the 84th minute, disaster struck. They scored from a deflection. Our hearts sank. However, not to be denied, the tireless Dyer managed to connect with a Fabian Wilnis cross, and his header looped over the keeper into the net. We were back on level terms. I remember leaping to my feet and yelling in not very chairman-like fashion, 'Kieron, you ******* little beauty.'

Kieron had a game of such authority and energy that night and, although their styles were very different, he influenced play in much the same way as Jim Magilton was to 12 months later. In extra time, Bolton, managed by the stirring personality Sam Allardyce, scored another when their Scandinavian duo, Jensen and Gudjohnsen, set the ball up for Bob Taylor to score again. That put them 4-3 ahead on aggregate, so we now needed two to win, since away goals counted once extra time began. Captain Fantastic, Matt Holland, gave us real hope by getting another four minutes from time, setting up a frantic finale.

But it was not to be. And again we were out on away goals. It felt so unfair! My *cri de coeur* was once more, 'Why should the away team in the second leg (which had therefore finished lower in the league, in Bolton's particular case a *full ten points back*) have an extra 30 minutes in extra time in which their away goals should count?'

I did my best to put a brave face on it, but how well I managed that I am not really sure. These days I am often reminding leaders in various walks of life that you can't really expect others to keep believing if you don't show your own unshakeable belief.

The same old questions were inevitably hauled out again, but this time the media focused on whether or not we would have to sell Kieron Dyer. I gave the same kind of answers as previous years, basically that we had proved we could bounce back from disappointments, and we would again.

'Okay, but you are getting a reputation for always missing out at the final hurdle.'

And the clock was ticking on the five-year plan …

# Chapter 18
# 1999/2000: on the Brink ...

ALTHOUGH I tried to put a brave face on it, I remember feeling completely down in the dumps for a while after that defeat. The Bolton tie had been our third play-off defeat in a row, and we had been 'nearly men' for too long. We seemed to have ended up as the bridesmaids far too often – as we had done even in the glory days under Bobby Robson. Yes, we won the FA Cup (1978) and then the UEFA Cup (1981), but in 79/80 we had finished third in the league, in 80/81 we were second (and really should have won it all) and in 81/82 we were runners-up again.

But we really had to focus our attention on the new season and how we could build on our all too frequent experiences in the play-offs and become winners.

One of the saddest things about it all was that I knew that we wouldn't be able to resist a big bid for Kieron Dyer. And nor, in all likelihood, would he, despite his immense dedication to the cause. That felt so sad. He hadn't just become a key player for us, he was on the verge of becoming an England star!

In the summer of 1999, and with the season not long over, I answered a call from Freddy Shepherd, the Newcastle chairman. I can hear his thick Geordie accent even now: 'Hello, David, how much will you be wanting for the boy Dyer?'

'We don't want to sell, but how much are you offering, Freddy?'

'Well, of course, he's not the finished article but I'll admit Bobby [Robson – now manager of Newcastle] likes him.'

'Good, so do many others ... how much, Freddy?'

'What about if we start at £5m?'

'Then it won't be a deal, Freddy – I told you there are others who are keen.'

'Alright then, £6m,' said Freddy.

This was a lot of money at the time for a player from outside the Premier League. 'Okay, Freddy, I'll talk to my board and come back to you tomorrow,' I said.

Which I duly did – we made all the decisions together. They knew, like me, that we had to sell, and left me to do the best I could.

I called next day and told Freddy we wanted £6.5m. In the end we agreed to £6m, with an extra half-million if Kieron was capped for England – which he duly was that same year.

The next day, West Ham chairman Terry Brown called and asked if £5m might tempt us. Ironically, Kieron would later move on to West Ham, for a fee understood to have been around £6m.

The money was transformative for us. George Burley was quite brilliantly building the nucleus of a strong team, with Matt Holland, Richard Wright, Tony Mowbray, Mark Venus, David Johnson and Jamie Clapham all playing 40 games or more in the previous season, and they were pretty much inked in on his team sheet for the coming campaign. Add new signings Jim Magilton and Fabian Wilnis, and our own James Scowcroft and Richard Naylor and, even without Kieron, there was much to look forward to ... and the new money in our coffers would enable us to add additional quality to this nucleus.

Our first two recruits were Jermaine (Jammer) Wright for £500,000 from Crewe, who, although a different player, George saw filling Kieron's boots. We also persuaded Tranmere (then a very competitive club) to sell their centre-half, John McGreal, for £650,000. Two superb signings!

We started the season in red-hot form – winning four out of five to leave us top of the table at the end of August. David Johnson bagged seven goals in five games, and he was playing so well that, despite his having represented Jamaica, the home nations were eyeing him up. DJ was indeed picked for the Wales squad, but injury stopped him going. And then Craig Brown, the Scotland manager, made overtures, only to discover that he was ineligible, so David carried on with Jamaica.

George Burley was deservedly voted Manager of the Month in August, but the autumn wasn't so good for us, either on or off the pitch.

We spent £800,000 more of our 'Dyer money' on Blackburn's England U21 full-back, Gary Croft. Almost immediately, he was caught by the police driving with a suspended licence. After an uncomfortable wait, he was sentenced to prison in December (for four months, as I recall), although he was let out – with an electronic tag – after six weeks in Hollesley Bay. We deplored his actions, both officially and privately; however, we took a long-term view (and an expedient one ... we had paid a big fee!) and supported him, particularly given his obvious contrition.

I decided to pay Gary a visit myself. It was the first time I had ever been inside a prison, and it was an eerie experience. Simon Milton had been along a few days before and prepared me for what to expect. Gary was actually in an open part of the jail, but it was, nevertheless, not particularly pleasant. We had 20 minutes together, he apologised to me for bringing embarrassment on the club, and I was glad I had made the effort.

Gary was given early release a few weeks later, and in mid-January he appeared as a sub at home to Swindon in a 3-0 win, the first-ever player to appear with an electronic tag. It was clearly visible through his sock, and all the papers carried a picture the next day.

What should have been the headline that night was that Micky Stockwell had scored what would turn out to be his final goal for us on his 601st appearance for the club. What a wholehearted player Micky was, and what a great servant to ITFC. Over the course of his career we saw him play full-back (and a marauding one at that!), tenacious midfielder and a diminutive, yet effective, striker.

But I am getting ahead of myself. On the pitch, our form as autumn turned to winter was rather hit and miss. There were injuries and DJ had an eight-game goal drought, but ironically a 'bore draw' at home to the Canaries seemed to catapult us back into form, and a fantastic run of 18 games unbeaten saw us climb up the table to second at the end of February 2000.

**Record signing**

As spring arrived, we got wind that Huddersfield might be tempted to sell their leading scorer, Marcus Stewart. This was hard to believe, given our rivalry and the fact that they were in the hunt for a play-off position themselves. However, George was keen and, after getting the board aligned, we decided to make a club record offer for him. The £2.5m we budgeted for would eat up much of what was left from the Dyer money, and it was certainly a big punt. However, when I entered discussions with my opposite number, Barry Rubery, it emerged that Steve Bruce, their manager, was very unhappy about losing one of their best players. Finally, and after a fair bit of haggling, we agreed a bonus of £250k if we were promoted. Marcus was then 27, but a record of 138 goals in 304 appearances for Bristol Rovers and Huddersfield spoke volumes about his talent.

This was a really exciting, statement deal. Marcus scored a wonder goal on his debut away at Barnsley in a 2-0 win (after Scowy had lobbed the keeper) and a week later got the winner at home to his old club, Huddersfield. We had bought a gem!

In part because of injuries to both Mark Venus and John McGreal, we then lost three out of our next four games, including – gallingly – going down 2-0 at home to Norwich. The only good thing I can say about that game is that it was a good managerial debut at the Canaries for our dear friend and former star player, Bryan Hamilton. By now, their owners Delia Smith and her husband, Michael Wynn-Jones, had become good friends and we had a photo taken in the boardroom afterwards with me smiling through clenched teeth.

Soon after that, I invited Delia and Michael round for dinner. When I told my wife, she said, 'You invited who? What on earth am I meant to cook!?' When the day came, Mona had hired a cook for the evening and the food turned out to be very moderate – so when Delia said, 'I'd be happy with scrambled eggs,' we realised Mona didn't need to get nervous over it. We had many more happy dinners (and plenty of wine) with them and their ITFC-supporting friends Matt and Sue after that, both with us and at their home near Stowmarket.

In late March we offered George Burley a new contract, and the first thing he did was to sign a young Dutch winger on loan. Martijn Reuser was a charismatic player with immense skill and determination, and though he lacked a bit of pace (sorry, Martijn), he could strike with both feet – and on his debut he chalked up the only goal of a tight match against Fulham in the 90th minute. So not a bad start.

The season built to a climax with a 3-1 victory in our penultimate game, away at Charlton (the eventual champions), with goals from Jim Magilton, David Johnson and another from Reuser. It meant that we had to win our last match, at home to Walsall, and pray that Man City lost at Blackburn. So another one of those games …

We took care of our part of the deal as Johnson scored twice as we beat Walsall 2-0. Things were looking good for a time as Blackburn took the lead and, amazingly, hit the woodwork four times. But in the end, Man City ran away with it as 4-1 winners. That meant automatic promotion for them, and condemned us to the play-offs yet again. For the fourth year on the trot! And, once more, it was Bolton that stood between us and Wembley. And a date with destiny.

So off we went to Lancashire for the first leg. It started grimly, and we were 2-0 down after just 25 minutes to goals from Dean Holdsworth and Eiður Guðjohnsen. Big Sam Allardyce and his assistant, Phil Brown, were beaming with delight. But in the 36th minute, Marcus Stewart struck a superb volley from outside the box that beat the Bolton keeper all ends up. Wow! And in the second half, Marcus did it again. I can remember him dribbling in the box, and we were there thinking, *Oh my goodness, he's going to lose it, come on, pass it*, but he didn't, and instead rounded the goalkeeper and drew us level. Wow! It stayed two-all – a score that probably left some people wondering whether it might have been better to stick with the away-goals rule that I had worked so hard to overturn.

As it turned out, though, things would actually work out very differently.

With a full house of 21,543 for the second leg, Portman Road was absolutely jumping, and you have to say the game lived up to every possible expectation. Bolton went ahead early on, before Jim Magilton (a man possessed that night) equalised from the penalty spot, only to see them grab another. Jim then made up for missing a second penalty by levelling again just after the break, but that only lasted a minute, and we were soon behind once more. Bolton were a big team and they were trying to muscle us out of it, and with us 3-2 down it was all blood and thunder. But Jim Magilton popped up again in the 90th minute after Tony Mowbray had skilfully guided a header down to him, and took us to extra time with just 50 seconds left on the clock. OMG!! It was actually the only hat-trick Jim ever scored in his 18-year career, and what a time to do it!

Thank goodness the away-goals rule had been scrapped by then, as yet again we would have been starting that nerve-wracking added half-hour at a disadvantage.

There was no time to reflect on that, of course, and when things got going again Jamie Clapham also scored from the spot – putting us ahead for the first time in the entire tie. By that point the Bolton players had begun to lose their discipline, with both Mike Whitlow and Robbie Elliott getting sent off, and I can still picture Sam Allardyce below us fuming away. Martijn Reuser, on as substitute, took full advantage of the disarray to thunder home our fifth, and clinch it 5-3 on the night, 7-5 on aggregate.

It was a match that seemed to have everything, and many present describe it as the greatest they have ever seen.

I very rarely went near the dressing room on a matchday – never beforehand and only occasionally afterwards. But I did this time. It would have been really very hard to resist.

We were going to Wembley! The emotions were running high, hearts were pumping, and there were tears of joy. The crowd ran on to the pitch. And the party began.

Yet we all knew we had to go and do it all again in the final, against Barnsley, in 12 days' time.

# PART FOUR

# Chapter 19
# A Scandalous Decision on Television Rights and an Unexpected Appointment

TO UNDERSTAND why winning at Wembley that day in 2000 was so very vital to us, and why the play-off final had become known as the 'most valuable game in football', we have to look back a few years, and to events, many of which I saw – and tried hard to prevent – at firsthand.

So for anybody who has been on Mars, or in the US, for the past few decades, it's worth explaining how football is run in England. The Football Association is the ultimate governing body of both the professional and amateur game and the national teams. However, it had delegated control of the professional game to the Football League, represented by four divisions, comprising 92 clubs.

That changed in 1992 when what was then the First Division broke away to form the Premier League, a decision largely driven by the big clubs seeking to control their own financial fortunes. Confusingly, the old second tier (and former Second Division) took on the 'First Division' name for a time, although it's now known as the Championship. That is now the highest division in the Football League, followed by the old Third and Fourth divisions, which have had various names, sometimes driven by sponsorship agreements, and are now known as League One and League Two.

The Football Association is habitually known as just 'the FA', whereas the Football League has now been replaced by the English Football League, from now on referred to by its acronym EFL.

The Football League meeting that took place at the Connaught Rooms in London on Thursday, 14 November 1996 holds a special importance in the history of English football, and indeed in my own personal story.

The meeting was called for the 72 clubs to hear presentations from Trevor Phillips (commercial director at the FA) and, representing the Premier League, Rick Parry, David Dein and Keith Wiseman. The purpose was to negotiate better TV and commercial returns for the Football League, as we were increasingly being left behind by the Premier League.

The FA wanted to make a play for taking the Football League under their commercial wing but that failed to gain traction. However, Rick Parry and his Premier League colleagues were offering to renegotiate television rights on our behalf, and to pay us 20 per cent of their combined rights going forward. This was a colossal deal. Several club representatives in the room pressed Parry to quantify what that equated to in hard cash terms. Understandably, in my view, he steadfastly refused to be drawn as they were still in negotiation with Sky TV and others. However, educated guesses put the value of the Premier League coverage alone north of £200 million, so 20 per cent would have been a minimum of £40 million a year to the Football League. This compared to about nine million that the League was getting at the time from ITV.

Private, non-binding discussions that a few of us had with the Premier League at the time showed that a figure closer to 25 per cent might well have been possible. Anyway, a vote was called at the end of the meeting and, despite the pleas for hard figures going unanswered, 71 out of 72 club representatives raised their hands to instruct their Football League board to continue negotiations with the Premier League.

About two weeks later – and after a difficult Ipswich AGM, which was followed by a live radio phone-in with worried supporters – I was standing in David Rose's office and noticed a breaking sports news story on the BBC teletext service, Ceefax. To our utter incredulity there was an announcement that the Football League board had finalised a new TV deal directly with Sky for £25 million a year, hailing it as a triumph!

I couldn't believe what I was seeing. This was in direct contravention of the decision made by the clubs. How on earth could this have happened?

**The clubs rebel**

It was outrageous. Somebody just had to stand up and do something. So I rang some prominent chairmen, including Ron Noades at Crystal Palace, Ian Stott at Oldham and Jonathan Hayward at Wolves. All of them were as shell-shocked and livid as me, and it felt to me as if there was a danger of it all being swept under the carpet. But we agreed to fight it, and to ask all the 22 clubs in our division for a £10,000 contribution towards a fighting fund to get legal advice, which we did, from law firm Herbert Smith.

The Football League board that had made the commitment with Sky was led by an independent chairman, Gordon McKeag. He was a good man, a solicitor and former chairman of Newcastle United. With him were two representatives each from the three divisions:

- First Division: Martin George (Leicester) and Bill Bell (Port Vale)
- Second Division: Terry Robinson (Bury) and Douglas Craig (York City)
- Third Division: Jimmy Hill (Fulham) and John Reames (Lincoln City)

They were all decent, honest and likeable men, and had clearly acted not only in good faith but also in what they felt was the best interest of the clubs. However, in my view, and that of nearly everybody present that fateful day, they had made a catastrophic error of judgement, the ramifications of which have shaped the game in this country ever since. It meant we had forever lost the opportunity to reconnect the financial fortunes of most professional clubs in the country to those of the Premier League sky rocket, resulting in an ever-widening financial chasm that for nearly 30 years has left the Football League clubs increasingly adrift.

It was a decision born of business naivety, and one that feels as scandalous today as it did then. In fact, the whole issue is extraordinarily topical. Rick Parry, the man who at that time was the Premier League chief executive, is ironically now chairman of the Football League, and has been in a prolonged dispute with his former employer in his quest for a redistribution of wealth for the 72 EFL clubs. That quest has included seeking government support, as well as the designation of a football regulator – and the recent appointment of David Kogan adds to the pressure on the Premier League, to the point that some kind of deal feels more likely than ever before.

My own view is that something really does have to be done, as competition in the Championship is distorted by the huge size of the two-year parachute payments paid to relegated clubs. Two seasons ago, we were complaining about the unfair advantage that Leeds, Leicester and Southampton had over us. But we managed to break the mould and pip Leeds to promotion in 2024. Now the boot is on the other foot, and Ipswich wouldn't swap their advantage for all the world. And that is the nub of the challenge.

The board that condemned the 72 Football League clubs to three decades of second-class citizenship was dominated by small-club thinking (four out of the seven being from the two lower divisions), and they just couldn't get their heads around the idea that our TV rights could go up from £9 million to well over £40 million. And they were simply not prepared to gamble a certain £25 million against the promise of something nearly double that and the possibility of much, much more. Added to that, there was a latent distrust of the Premier League from many of the smaller clubs.

That was not to say, of course, that Sky Sports and their deputy MD Trevor East hadn't been very clever in pursuing this 'divide and rule' approach.

What was inexcusable, however, was that the decision was made against the crystal-clear vote of all but one of the member clubs only a few weeks earlier. The ramifications have been enormous and have been felt widely throughout the EFL ever since. The Premier League had made us a very workable offer, even a generous one, but the board had essentially spat in their face. It was, quite simply, unforgivable in my book, a view that was shared by nearly everyone present when we met again later that month, and again for the EGM in December.

The precursor to the EGM was a non-statutory club assembly, at which Ron Noades, Ian Stott, Jonathan Hayward and I were appointed as a committee to lead the charge.

I was asked to open the case against the board. I remember being pumped with adrenaline. In those early days I used to perspire when under pressure, and had even taken to never removing my jacket. I used to get my suits made by a local tailor in Ipswich (the delightful Mr Sherwood), who had told me, 'Don't worry, Mr David, we'll put two studded holes under each armpit in your suit and that will let the air in.'

Although I had done plenty in life, I had never encountered anything quite like this, or anything nearly so public, so Mr Sherwood's vents were much needed. I don't remember my speech, nor did I keep a copy, but it seemed to work, as others came in behind me. I particularly remember a contribution from Bradford City's larger-than-life Geoffrey Richmond.

What made it all the harder was that sitting on the board were people I had always respected. As well as Gordon McKeag there was Jimmy Hill, the *Match of the Day* legend and ironically the man who had set the whole money ball rolling over 30 years earlier, when he led the Professional Footballers' Association (PFA) campaign to scrap the maximum wage. And here I was lobbying against them.

The next meeting, the EGM, was called between Christmas and New Year 1996 at the Landmark Hotel in Marylebone. Somewhat to our surprise, it didn't take very long for the entire board to resign.

I remember going into a private meeting to agree our next steps with the First Division chairmen. We had been so intent on inflicting board change as a penalty for their catastrophic decision that none of us had thought much about what to do next.

Noades and Stott were the best-known figures, but nobody seemed to be coalescing around them. And then, to my utter amazement, Ron proposed I should be asked to become chairman of the Football League! I hadn't been in the Ipswich role for long, and was only 44. To say it was a surprise is an understatement!

Following further discussions between the clubs, I was encouraged to take the role for two years with a remit to do three things: begin a modernisation process, find a professional CEO to run the league and find an independent chairman to succeed me within my two-year term.

What I didn't realise was that the position meant I automatically became vice-president of the FA and was appointed to its key decision-making bodies. This included sitting on the FA Executive Committee, the FA Council, the FA Cup Committee and the International Committee, which led to my attending all home England games and some away fixtures too.

This was all to be combined with my existing workload at Suffolk Foods and, above all, at Ipswich Town.

## Chapter 20
# Chairman of the Football League!

BY THE time I took the helm at the end of December 1996, the Football League – which had been founded in 1888 – was an ancient and respected institution, albeit one that was a little tired and short on imagination. It was also smarting from the desertion five years earlier of the top echelon to form the Premier League, though perhaps not as much as it should have been.

At that stage I am sure many were asking who I was and what my agenda was (again!). It started with the League's officers (what we would nowadays call the 'leadership team'), who could probably not quite believe what they had just witnessed. It must have felt like a coup to them, with me as the ringleader. What is more, they had all been heavily involved, complicit even, in the decisions taken by the old regime. However, I can only pay credit to the secretary, David Dent, and his assistants, the late Andy Williamson, and Glynis Firth. They were utterly respectful and correct towards me throughout – though, of course, while a strong agent for change, I was certainly no revolutionary. Indeed, among those elected to serve with me on the new board was one of the former directors, Terry Robinson, who became a great ally.

A series of issues, some of them distinctly thorny ones, awaited me, and would flavour my tenure in the post. Nothing I could put down in writing would do justice to the difficult nature of the protracted and sometimes bitter discussions that some of these things entailed. But here goes …

## Bosman

At that stage, British football, and indeed the game at a European and world level, was only just beginning to come to terms with the implications of the 1995 ruling in favour of a Belgian player, Jean-Marc Bosman, who had been prevented from moving to a French club.

The implementation of EU freedom of movement legislation led to sweeping changes that would revolutionise the transfer market, as any player could now leave for nothing once a contract expired, with no fee payable to his club. This had the immediate effect of players being offered longer contracts (which sometimes led to complacency) and also a tendency to renegotiate several years ahead of expiry. All of this favoured the players, leading to massive wage inflation and adding dramatically to both the power and wealth of their agents. With overseas quotas now quashed for European players, there was a huge influx of foreign talent, while several teams quickly found themselves overextended after trying to protect their squad assets.

When I took office, there was genuine concern that unless the authorities in Brussels and the various players' unions could agree a way forward, then the whole transfer system could be jeopardised. One of our chief interlocutors in this was the PFA, the world's oldest sports trade union. It's amazing to record that their CEO, Gordon Taylor (who I always got on well with), was already a veteran of 16 years in the role by then, and that he would continue in the post for over 20 more. He clearly didn't have a lot of incentive to retire, as he allegedly ended up on over £2 million a year, and was reputed to be the highest-paid union official on the planet.

Another membership group we used to converse a lot with was the League Managers Association (LMA), which was actually at pains to stress it was not a union. At that time their board read like a *Who's Who* of great managers, including David Pleat, Kenny Hibbitt, Brian Flynn and Alex Ferguson, before his knighthood. Howard Wilkinson, who won the league title with Leeds, had hatched the idea for the LMA back in 1991, alongside former England boss Graham Taylor, and was its chairman for 33 years. Their CEO was former

Notts Forest manager John Barnwell, who was later succeeded by Richard Bevan, and much of what he brought to the table involved improving managerial contract negotiations and compensation.

Our initial stance at the Football League was that we wanted three more years, until 2000, for the Bosman ruling to take effect, whereas the FA, Premier League and PFA were all pushing for it to come into force two years earlier, at the end of the following season.

We estimated the annual surplus value to Football League clubs of transfers at that point to be £14.5 million (basically the net amount the Premier League paid to non-Football League teams for their players, and obviously a risible sum seen from today's perspective). So in summer 1997 we decided to release a statement:

> It must be preferable that we try to reach a common collective agreement over the future domestic transfer system for the good of everyone in our game and that is exactly what we are endeavouring to do. Having said that, it is important to recognise the value of the market transfer system to the clubs outside of the Premiership and this is why the Football League has sought extra time to adjust. We are not seeking to frustrate the Premiership plans in this respect, but for understanding of our very different circumstances.

By October of that year, and with the effects of the Bosman decision still dominating the agenda at Football League board meetings, we had reluctantly accepted that players aged 24 and over would be able to leave on free transfers if their contract had expired, but that a fee would be due for those under that age, with the amount payable to be decided by tribunal if they were out of contract. That was a way of trying to help clubs protect the investment they make in training younger players, and indeed incentivise them to do more with their youth programmes.

But the differences of opinion between the Football League and Premier League over Bosman were just a small part of a wider rift …

## The tripartite agreement

That the tripartite agreement should sound like something from late 19th century diplomacy is perhaps only fitting, given that the creation of the Premier League had been a shot that was heard, and in many ways continues to reverberate, all around the football world.

As I appeared on the scene, nearly five years after the initial breakaway, the financial arrangement made to protect the Football League at the time of the Premier League's foundation was coming up for renewal. And the Premier League was keen to drive home its dominance, arguing that the £5 million yearly transfer to the Football League was determined by a fixed-term agreement that had now expired.

We at the Football League didn't agree, of course, and nor did the FA (the third group referred to in the 'tripartite' name). Discussion over the issue dragged on and, in one meeting in December 1997, Premier League CEO Peter Leaver informed us that the agreement was being terminated. He was a former barrister and strident in nature, so he also wanted to use the moment to understand whether the Football League would be restructuring, as the Premier League clubs would like to know what was beneath them! And most inflammatory of all, he posed the question: 'Do we think we can support so many commercial clubs?'

I restated our position, that it was a perpetual agreement, incapable of termination, and in a meeting the following month informed the Premier League that its 'notice' was invalid, and that 'without prejudice' dialogue was ongoing. There followed a heated exchange with Dave Richards of Sheffield Wednesday, who was representing the Premier League and would shortly become its chairman. He told me in his flat Yorkshire tone that the agreement would be dead by the summer.

Not long afterwards I received a call from Ron Noades to tell me that the Premier League would support a standalone First Division, which was itself a topic of heated debate. Noades was the chairman of Crystal Palace, who were then on one of the upswings of their yo-yo between divisions, although he would finally sell the club later that year after another relegation.

Given the nature of the whole relationship with the Premier League and the other issues we were dealing with at the Football League, I had reintroduced a PR committee, which included Chris Hull, our head of media relations, and Dennis Signy, a senior Fleet Street correspondent. Our agenda was clear: 'How can we, the Football League combat the marginalisation of the league by the Premier League?'

Nor could the political aspect be ignored. I had addressed the All-Party Football Committee at Westminster, which was actually largely made up of Labour MPs, this being just after Tony Blair's landslide general election win. I enjoyed their passion for the game, and became friendly with several of them, including Roger Godsiff (a big Charlton fan), Tom Pendry, Alan Keen (a massive Middlesbrough supporter), Jack Cunningham and Clive Betts from Sheffield – who, as I write, is still a serving MP.

I had already been selected to represent the Football League on the new Football Task Force set up by Tony Banks, the Sports Minister, and well chaired by his fellow Chelsea fan David Mellor. The committee secretary was none other than a young and likeable Andy Burnham, who was still a few years away from becoming an MP and is now, of course, mayor of Greater Manchester.

We had plenty of allies to our cause. One that comes to mind is John Dennis, whose Barnsley team had just got into the top flight for the first time after 99 years of trying! John was a genial fruit and veg wholesaler, and having both been in the food business, we developed a close friendship, often comparing notes on player deals.

Having just been to his first Premier League chairmen's meeting, John had rung me in June 1997 to vent his frustration at Peter Leaver's indifference to the Football League, especially compared to his predecessor, Rick Parry. In his gruff South Yorkshire tones, John told me, 'David, the Premier League don't need anyone else for anything. It's a case of sod the rest of them,' adding, 'Ken Bates [the Chelsea chairman] had a dismissive attitude and said, "Lovely to have you with us, enjoy your year."'

*On my first motorbike, a Triumph Tiger 200, in early 1969 as I can see the 'L' plate and I passed my test in summer 1969*

*A blast from the past! April 1971 leaning on the Toyota Corolla that Nick Deans and I made our temporary home to cross the Nullarbor Plain*

*Beside the road waiting for a ride in the Australian Outback, when I hitchhiked around Australia in 1971*

# The South African Government can afford to buy itself a good image

# But it hasn't got one

Not for lack of trying of course — the annual propaganda budget is near £2.5 million. But it has to cope with the Anti-Apartheid Movement

The Anti-Apartheid Movement — non-party, financed by private subscription and donation — has been active for over ten years in exposing what the South African Government wants to hide — the policies and practices of apartheid.

The Anti-Apartheid Movement makes sure the world knows that South Africa has become a fully-fledged totalitarian state; that there are:

- growing numbers of laws providing for imprisonment without trial — 90 days, 180 days, even indefinitely under the Terrorism Act.

- torture of political prisoners.

- increasing censorship of the press.

- enforced movement of unwilling populations — 900,000 Africans have been moved in the last 10 years, another three million are due for 'resettlement'.

- a high infant mortality and disease rate among Africans — half the children in the African reserve areas die before the age of five.

- starvation wages and restricted job opportunities for black workers.

- ever-growing expenditure on foreign military equipment and the domestic arms manufacturing industry.

- military and economic support for neighbouring white supremacist regimes in Rhodesia and 'Portuguese' Africa.

For only £1 a year, you can support the resistance to racism and harass the white-washers of apartheid. You can join the Anti-Apartheid Movement and read Anti-Apartheid News.

Send your £1, or more, payable to Anti-Apartheid Movement, to 89 Charlotte Street, London W1 (01-580 5311)

*Left: The anti-apartheid leaflet from 1970 after I joined the movement when I left school to join the protests in London. Right: The Lord's scorecard from Tuesday, 25 June 1963 — my first-ever Test match! With a veritable array of the cricketing greats of yesteryear*

*My dear father – early 2000s*

*A portrait of my ancestor John Sheepshanks, by William Mulready, from the Sheepshanks' Collection at the Victoria & Albert Museum, to whom he bequeathed 336 pictures, drawings and sketches. These included Turner, Constable, Landseer and Mulready on the condition that the public, especially working classes, should have the advantage of seeing the collection on Sunday afternoons*

*My wife Mona bedecked in blue and white before catching the ferry to Amsterdam for the UEFA Cup Final in May 1981, where we sat amid our 9,000 fans*

*Making my debut on the hallowed turf of Portman Road playing for a British Frozen Food XI against a formidable Tesco XI made up of several non-league players! I nearly managed 45 minutes before running out of puff! This was 1988. See how the stadium looks and the poor state of the pitch*

*As a young director in 1988 presenting man-of-the-match awards to Graham Harbey and Mich d'Avray. That is the North Stand (now Sir Bobby Robson Stand) behind us, all standing and segregated between home and away fans!*

*With John Duncan and Sergei Baltacha in the austere setting of the state offices of Sovintersport in Moscow, October 1988*

*With John Duncan showing off our traditional 'ushanka' hats at Portman Road, October 1988*

*My brother Rick in our Suffolk Foods days in the mid 90s*

*On tour in north Sweden, summer 1997*

*'This Is Your Life': with George Burley and Sir Bobby Robson as we present our club legend Pat Godbold with her 'This Is Your Life' book at the testimonial dinner we gave in her honour. Having "Mr R", as she called him, as guest of honour was the icing on the cake for Pat*

*Mona and I follow Sir Bobby Charlton into St Mary le Tower church, Ipswich for the memorial service for Sir Alf Ramsey in May 1999* (Credit: Newsquest)

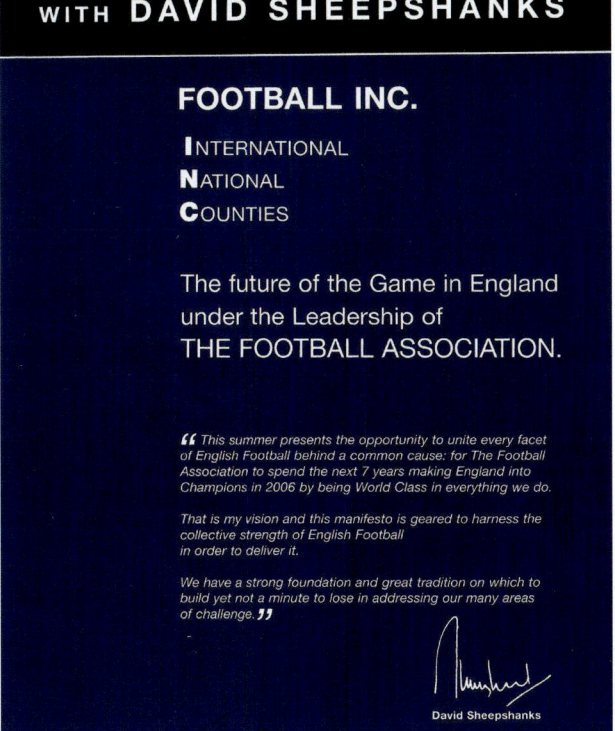

*My manifesto for the FA chairmanship, summer 1999*

*Royal Box hugging Matt Holland, play-off success, May 2000*

*The famous cover from the* Suffolk Magazine *in August 2000 after our promotion to the Premier League. Special make-up artists came to apply the mask, which was a nightmare to get off!*

John also gave me an indication of what Barnsley stood to make in what, in a sad confirmation of Bates's snide remark, was to be their only year in the Premier League:

- £3 million on 1 August
- £750,000 over the season – minimum of three games on Sky at £250k each
- £75,000 over the season – minimum of three games on the BBC at £25k each
- £1 million – Coca-Cola Cup and overseas TV
- Plus 145k per place ladder payment
- £5 million total to finish bottom
- And a parachute payment of £2 million if relegated

These were enormous sums back then – though completely dwarfed by the approximately £120 million guaranteed to the bottom club in the 2024/25 season.

How paltry the amounts we were dealing with seem now. I recall we had agreed a one-year deal for £53k per annum with Talk Radio (who, as well as owning 25 per cent of Channel 5, also empathised with our proactive aim to promote the Football League and its clubs). That was in addition to our BBC Radio 5 Live deal for £52k. On top of that, every club whose match was broadcast would get £3k per game. Which sounds like absolute peanuts today!

As far as television was concerned, that year all Football League clubs were invited to a Sky presentation and were told they hoped to feature all First Division (i.e. second flight) clubs twice a season. And in late August, I received a call from Robert Charles, a gentleman in what was otherwise a dog-eat-dog game, who had become head of sport at the then-new Channel 5 (and who, a few years later, would invite me to the Super Bowl in New Orleans). Robert wanted to see what they could do with the Football League. We had a chat, and I suggested he speak to Lee Walker, our broadcasting expert at the Football League. But I will never forget his speculative passing shot: 'And what are the chances of a Premier League II? We'd be very interested ...' I bet you would be, I thought.

Ever since it had become clear that the Premier League was going to be rather more than just a gimmick, there had been talk about the second flight, then called the First Division, becoming effectively a Premier League Mark II. Some even had a name for it, the 'Phoenix League'.

Needless to say, the lower tiers didn't like the idea of another breakaway one little bit. Although it was always a non-starter in my book, I believe that some chairmen at our bigger clubs pushed disputes over television and commercial fees much harder than they should have done, precisely to engineer just such a split. Some very vocal lower division chairmen became convinced that it was all a conspiracy, and that the First Division sides were being egged on by the Football League board to negotiate with the Premier League and that they would be cut adrift, none more than Paul Scally at Gillingham, who I actually got on well with, but was a prime agitator.

As Football League chairman, I was doing my damnedest to hold it all together. However, rumour, innuendo, distrust and bad blood were everywhere. Nearly all of it driven by money, power and fear.

In the spring of 1998, we held a succession of deeply frustrating meetings with the Football League clubs to try to hammer out a new decision-making framework that would respect the lion's share of value that the First Division clubs generated, while keeping the Second and Third Division clubs engaged, and the League together as a whole.

I tried to ensure that I would be seen as impartial by persuading each division to appoint their own representative committees. But, despite that, I constantly had to deal with mischievous rumours and reiterate that the First Division did not want to break away (although I knew some of them did!), and its members simply wanted to live within a reconstituted commercial framework that paid due recognition to the Football League's top division.

The, sadly, fairly widespread conviction that the board of the time (including me, of course) was only working to help the First Division was voiced at the meeting of all 72 Football League clubs by John Reames of Lincoln City (where he was chairman, and within the year would be manager too ... and a year after that would win the

Manager of the Month award). Douglas Craig from York City, who could be awkward to deal with, also said that he didn't trust the First Division and wanted a copy of their proposals. 'It is a naked attempt to get all the money and all the power.'

I wrote to the clubs in mid-April 1998 saying that the preceding weeks had been 'very trying ... with extreme views held and expressed on both sides', but that I was convinced that the 'best route forward was with a Football League not only intact, but together' and that 'the board have no evidence whatsoever of deals being done, having been done or ever being planned with any other bodies, however, any undermining of our authority now, quite apart from insulting individual integrity, would almost certainly jeopardise the future of the Football League as we know it'.

Interestingly, it wasn't just a breakaway that some were mooting at this time, and we as a board actually looked with a degree of seriousness at different league formats – having leagues of 12 teams, for example, with each side facing the other four times over the season. My notes remind me that the first reaction to this suggestion involved how supporters might react, which was quickly followed by us all wondering what Sky TV would think about teams playing each other four times a season. We were simply looking to deliver more meaningful matches and turning every stone to challenge the status quo. But it was soon clear there was no support for changing the structure.

The Bosman effect, meanwhile, had contributed to putting some clubs in a very precarious position, and sometimes we had to get involved. For example, Millwall at the time owed various sums to players, so the League had imposed an embargo on any new squad registrations until payments were brought up to date. We had a deposition from the Millwall lawyers arguing for an exception to be made and threatening a court injunction. That was typical of the kind of things that used to happen, with clubs regularly getting into financial difficulties. Brighton – a club for whom I have always had a soft spot – were in dispute with the League, and Bournemouth were facing a winding-up petition. How pleasant it is to see then that, as I write, both these south coast clubs are currently riding high in the Premier League and even challenging for a place in Europe. Good for them. It's a reminder that football fortunes are cyclical, and what comes round invariably goes round at some point, usually when most unexpected.

**The Coca-Cola Cup – victory in Europe!**
A place in Europe was exactly what was at stake in the prolonged battle we had over the Coca-Cola Cup. If you are reading this before 2027, then you may be more familiar with the competition in its latest incarnation, with sponsorship from Carabao. But in the past you might have known it as the Milk Cup (1981 to 1986), the Littlewoods Cup (1986 to 1990), the Rumbelows Cup (1990 to 1992), the Coca-Cola Cup (1992 to 1998), the Worthington Cup (1998 to 2003), the Carling Cup (2003 to 2012) or the Capital One Cup (2012 to 2016). Or, of course, the League Cup, which is how it had started out back in 1960.

The League Cup, in all of its guises, had always got on UEFA's nerves, which was precisely why it had been started in the first place. Football League's general secretary Alan Hardaker brought it in, at least in part, to give him more negotiating power with both UEFA and the FA. He even threatened to boycott the UEFA Cup unless the League Cup winner automatically qualified for continental competition. Curiously, in the first decade of its existence, two of those winners didn't actually get as far as the cross-Channel ferry, as they were from outside the old First Division – that included third-tier QPR, who had memorably come from 2-0 down to win the 1967 final.

In fact, there were no repeat winners in the first 13 years of the competition's history, perhaps a reflection of the fact that some of the big boys didn't take it as seriously as they might have. That is still the case now, you might say. And you would be right; the difference being that the resources available to the giants of the Premier League nowadays mean they can still win everything, even when fielding their reserves.

I can still hear the people from Coca-Cola telling me they wanted to see a return on their investment, and complaining that 'nobody seems to want to get out of bed to win it!' (and it was a distinctly weak Manchester

United team that went down to us at Portman Road the month of that October 1997 meeting). They also wanted to ensure that the final would still be held at Wembley, and were concerned that there wasn't enough marketing support, something we set about rectifying. But chief among the things Coca-Cola needed to even consider renewing their contract was for a place in Europe to be there for the winners.

There wasn't much doubt in my mind that UEFA wanted to free up domestic schedules so they could create more international club competitions that they could exploit. Indeed, at that time they were rather pointedly pushing for the Premier League to be reduced to 18 teams, and even threatening punitive measures. The Premier League didn't seem as bothered by a possible reduction as I would have expected, but was against having a second knockout competition at all. At a meeting in December 1997, I had to remind them of the £30 million a season their members earned from the cup, and even suggested the Premier League might want to do a television rights deal for the competition on behalf of both of us.

UEFA was also pushing for removal from the Coca-Cola Cup of guaranteed European qualification, which was at the discretion of the FA as its local member. That would have significantly devalued one of the Football League's prime assets, and deny even the dream of a European adventure to sides such as Oxford United and Luton Town, who had both won it over the preceding decade. We just had to do something.

After discussions with our trusted lawyer Richard Alderson, at Edge Ellison in Birmingham, it emerged that one of the possible routes was to take UEFA to court for abusing a dominant position. That was fairly extreme, and not something we would have wanted to do, but like all nuclear options was useful to have in my back pocket.

We also increased our political engagement, and enlisted the help of an MEP in Brussels, Mark Hendrick (that is 'Member of the European Parliament', by the way, as I so sadly now have to explain post-Brexit). I also addressed the football committee at Westminster, and kept Minister of Sport Tony Banks in the loop.

I was also regularly in contact with the FA, and managed to enlist the support of their chairman, Keith Wiseman, who told me, 'David, the word "fairness" is not in the UEFA dictionary.' Keith had initially echoed the Premier League's position on the issue, and the FA was also dead against getting into a major dispute with UEFA, wanting to stay in their good books for the 2006 World Cup bid.

So I called Sir Bert Millichip, a former West Brom and FA chairman, who was a senior member of the UEFA Executive Committee. He was an ally and supporter of mine, as an old friend of the Cobbold family at Ipswich. He said there had been a one-and-a-half-hour debate on the issue at UEFA headquarters in Switzerland, and urged me to go straight out there and meet their president, Lennart Johansson, who he was convinced I would click with. He then warned me to be careful of their lawyer, Alasdair Bell, and not to involve Graham Kelly, the FA chief executive. Kelly was a very able administrator; however, Sir Bert didn't want me to get sidetracked in FA politics. So, my starting point was to ring Gerhard Aigner, the UEFA CEO, to arrange a meeting in Nyon, on Lake Geneva.

Before that meeting I also spoke to Markus Studer, their head of legal affairs and deputy CEO, who came on strong and told me they believed they had a robust case. But he was clear that he felt football disagreements shouldn't end up in court, and the tone of the conversation changed when he asked whether we would withdraw our action if the European place was granted for the following three years. That felt like real progress.

So, six days later, on 29 January 1998, I flew out to Nyon with Football League secretary David Dent to meet UEFA's top brass, and agreed to do just that. Additionally, there was specifically no link during the three years to the number of clubs in the Premier League, which, of course, was beyond the control of the Football League anyway. It was agreed that, after that time, the matter would be reviewed by an arbitration panel, with the Football League invited to present its case. And the League Cup's European place has been retained ever since, I am pleased to say.

We then announced the news, trying hard not to sound too triumphant. However, it had been a real David and Goliath victory for the little guys. My press release that day ended: 'This is a very good day for the Football League and, I believe, for English football.'

And indeed it was. And, to be frank, after pushing through resistance on all fronts to confront UEFA over the issue, it was a brilliant moment for me personally.

### Will he or won't he ... a new CEO

By mid-1997 it had become clear that, although I was nominally chairman at both, I was effectively having to play the role of CEO at Ipswich and the Football League. David Rose (ITFC club secretary) and David Dent (Football League general secretary) were special people doing a great job, and up till then had been able to cope in their efficient, but largely reactive, styles. But these were challenging times at both organisations.

It had always been the intention to take on a chief executive at the Football League, and in mid-1997 the board agreed to instruct executive search firm Spencer Stuart. Our wish list for candidate qualities started with leadership, followed by commercial awareness, knowledge of the game, ability to read a room, good communication skills and confidence with the press.

Mine was never supposed to be a long-lasting appointment, and some people around the table felt we should take on a new independent chair first, so that he or she could be involved in the CEO selection process. That made sense on the face of it, but I resisted as I felt we were on a roll, and it was becoming increasingly clear to me exactly what kind of CEO we needed: somebody who would be transformative for the Football League. I felt best placed to lead that recruitment.

As to who might eventually take over my seat, politicians were at that stage the popular choice, including Richard Ryder, who was later to be on the Ipswich board and had recently taken his place in the Lords after retiring as a Conservative MP. Among the other names put forward were former Tory ministers Alistair Burt and Ken Clarke. My notes from the time say: 'One day a week for £25,000!'

The headhunters Spencer Stuart had a good track record in football, having recently worked for both Wolves and Sheffield Wednesday – who I noted were also in the market for a 'commercially astute CEO', which was not dissimilar to what our brief would be. We consulted with them and took the customary long-list-shrinking-down-to-short-list approach, starting off with over 100 replies to an advertisement on the front page of the appointments section of the *Sunday Times*. Spencer Stuart's inimitable chairman David Kimbell told me they included high-calibre people from the Virgin group, Holiday Inn and the Boots chemist chain. He highlighted someone called Scudamore, who had done well at Yellow Pages and now was running a good chunk of the Thomson newspaper group's US operations.

Richard Scudamore's candidacy turned out to be outstanding. So it was a major blow when, after the panel had interviewed him and agreed in December to offer him the job, he called me to say he would have to turn us down. I had been convinced from the day I met him that he was our man! Richard explained how sad he was to pass up the opportunity, but that he just couldn't afford to go against his employer – Thomson had essentially applied golden handcuffs. We were left wondering what to do next, as nobody else was quite at Richard's level.

We felt we couldn't go public with what had happened, and the delay led to unease and grumbling, including from Millwall chairman Theo Paphitis, who would later become a real pal, but was then – quite understandably – very vocal in his disappointment at the delay to an appointment.

March 1998 was a particularly trying month on several fronts, including the fact that the second-round interviews for the League CEO had proved unsatisfactory. But my mood improved dramatically one evening when the phone went. It was Richard calling from New York. He simply said, 'David, is there any chance that the CEO job might still be open?' My heart leapt, and I told him we were in the process of interviewing all over again. After a few searching questions to verify his position, I told him he would have to leave it with me.

I ran the whole thing past our nominations committee, and had to stake my name in assuring them of Richard's dependability, as they questioned his reliability and felt we had been left in the lurch earlier. I was convinced he was the right fit in every way: bright, charismatic, fun to be with – and he had even been a qualified referee in his younger years. He was perfect. Anyway, Richard flew over and we met in Le Suquet restaurant in London's Draycott Avenue to try to seal the deal. Happily, the selection panel all saw it the same way, and we hired him. I was thrilled. We had our man.

With Richard on board, we prepared for the Football League club summer meeting and 1998 AGM, including the key regulatory changes that we needed to push through to ensure that the top division would in future hold sway over the lower division clubs in all regulatory and commercial decision-making. This would be done by changing the composition of the Football League board from the previous two representatives from each division, to three representatives from the Championship, two from League One and one representative from League Two. There would also be a new commercial committee, heavily weighted towards the Championship, which would handle all future TV negotiations and would clearly prevent any recurrence of the board overruling the clubs.

When it came to the vote, we needed a 95 per cent majority to get the motion through 'on the day with consent to short notice', as they call it in legal jargon. Five per cent of 72 clubs is 3.6, and we knew that we had at least three 'antis' in the room. So, to get our 69 votes in favour, we had to ensure nobody else joined them. I led with the proposition, then Richard made a masterful speech, and between us we managed to carry the day.

It was hailed as quite a victory. Afterwards I bumped into Douglas Craig, the chairman of York City, one of the three rebels, on the hotel staircase (we were at Carden Park in Cheshire). Douglas was a proud Scot and was dressed in a kilt, with a *sgian dubh* (Highland dagger) in his stocking. I held out my hand and said, 'No hard feelings, Douglas, let's bury the hatchet.' He scowled and said, 'Aye, and I know where I would like to bury it!'

**Prince's Trust**
Something that happened earlier that day definitely helped to lighten the mood in the room. I had been asked by the Prince's Trust to introduce their work to the Football League, so I invited Tom Shebbeare (now Sir Tom) to make a presentation to the clubs. He brought along an 18-year-old from Manchester who had been on one of their programmes. The young man spoke of his experience for ten minutes, and melted the hearts of everyone present. Sadly, I can't remember his name, but he won universal applause and helped ensure an overwhelming vote to invite the Trust on board as a partner. I became a staunch advocate of the scheme, and was very proud a few years later to welcome Prince Charles, as he was then, to Portman Road to see our own Prince's Trust set-up, which was the first-ever to be domiciled inside a club.

Unfortunately, the Premier League didn't take long in spotting our great catch, and not much more than a year later they poached Richard Scudamore from us. Having been responsible for negotiating broadcasting and sponsorship contracts worth in excess of £5 billion, he stayed at the Premier League until retiring in November 2018. He remains a very great friend to this day, and someone who I admire enormously. It's never just about one person; however, in my view, and it was from close up, Richard played a huge part in making the Premier League the colossal commercial success that it is today.

**Moving into the 21st century: the Football League HQ**
I had been elected with a remit for modernisation, and I was determined to keep up the momentum for change. That included getting our headquarters moved out of the rabbit warren of tiny rooms in adjoining Victorian houses in Lytham St Annes, a seaside resort near Blackpool that had seen better days.

I faced plenty of resistance from people who considered it 'sacrilege' and insisted that 'the League has always been at Lytham'. Well, it hadn't, and in fact they had only moved there in 1960, when the old Sandown Hotel had been picked up for £11,000 and converted for a further £40,000. I am not quite sure what the money had been spent on, but what remained nearly four decades later was certainly not the base on which to build an organisation that needed not just to look forward but into the new millennium – which, being 1997, was very much on people's minds.

It was another difficult issue, and one that dragged on a bit. We eventually got Price Waterhouse (now PwC) in to look at the problem. They did a SWOT analysis (strengths, weaknesses, opportunities and threats) and came up with the idea of relocating to a new facility in Preston. Cue a new round of complaints, with some of the more senior staff arguing that 'very few people come to Lytham, so why the need to change?' Could they hear themselves? Others suggested we cut back on the sales office in London, and even the IT budget! The whole mindset was difficult to change, as the organisation obviously needed shaking up; however, nobody wanted to shake it. But I did.

My head said we should move to London, but my heart said we should create a facility – I liked the term 'operations centre' – somewhere accessible to all clubs, located in the Midlands or the north, with the marketing, commercial and PR functions down south, ideally in London. I got my way, and was very happy with the outcome, which meant that we were able to retain the key administrative skills, as the site chosen for operations was not that far away from Lytham.

The move eventually took place in 1999, after I had handed over the reins. Appropriately, it was indeed to Preston, which is where the league had initially been based, and where Preston North End had been the first-ever champions of England back in 1889.

Chapter 21
# Candidacy for FA Chairman

MY TIME as chairman of the Football League came to a close at the end of 1998, and as luck would have it the chair of the FA became vacant not long afterwards, following the resignation of Keith Wiseman. Keith denied any wrongdoing, but he was seen to be increasingly power hungry and had ultimately paid the price for a £3.2 million grant given to the Welsh FA, which some believed was a quid pro quo for support for England's attempt to gain a seat on FIFA's executive council. Graham Kelly also left as chief executive at the FA in the wake of the controversy.

At that stage, vice-chairman Geoff Thompson stepped up to head the FA Board as caretaker, with a full vote set for the annual FA meeting over the following summer. Being on the board, I had nodded through Geoff, an honest man and former magistrate from Sheffield. He was a safe pair of hands at a difficult juncture; that was unquestionable. But I came to see Geoff as being too much the champion of the status quo, when what was needed was a proactive approach to tackle the root of the problems that threatened to engulf us all. Geoff also led by consensus, or – as I saw it – the lowest common denominator approach. He very rarely ventured an opinion of his own, with 'I agree' being the most we tended to hear from him.

Above all, there seemed to be a real lack of direction, with Geoff all too keen not to rock the boat, and always intent on avoiding anything to upset the Premier League. He and Dave Richards were both 'Sheffield', and at times it felt a bit cosy between them.

I already had a fair bit of experience of the FA, as my Football League role had made me an ex officio vice-president. At the start it was before the FA even had what you could call a board of directors. Believe it or not, its full name in those days was still the 'Executive and General Purposes Committee'. It sounded like something out of a 1950s trade union.

One of the many issues the FA Board spent time looking at was how to develop the academy system. A lot was demanded of those hoping to get the top certification, and – as we were finding out at Ipswich Town – those requirements didn't come cheap. I recall that one of our major concerns was that the greater cost of the scholarships and training meant that bigger clubs would end up tying up more young players. Unfortunately, history has only proved us right.

Anyway, fresh from leading the Football League, my national profile was high, and I was encouraged to put my name forward by several colleagues, including former chairman Sir Bert Millichip. So I compiled a manifesto of all the things I wanted to do to improve the game, and went public with it.

'The Way Forward with David Sheepshanks' was a call to be 'world class in everything we do ... [and] harness the collective strength of English football' through a team effort in which 'everyone will have a role to play'. The main issues it identified were:

- tackling the problem of spiralling wages
- dealing with the growing problem posed by agents
- controlling the influx of foreign players (with the negative effect on our stock of home-grown players, and thus on our national side)
- ensuring England became hosts for the 2006 World Cup
- delivering the best chance for us to win that competition
- providing greater investment to county and schools football (including a call for a restriction on the sale of school pitches)
- reuniting the Football and Premier Leagues in negotiating television contracts

- creating a code of conduct that reinforced the idea of players being role models for society
- ensuring accountability and transparency through the adoption of a seven-year plan to implement these ideas and the modernisation process at the FA.

I also wrote to the FA councillors, using an expression that inadvertently pre-empted a campaign on the other side of the Atlantic: 'I wish to involve every single Member of Council with a new challenge – to help make England GREAT again! ... In conclusion, if you want more of the same then I know you will not vote for me.'

Needless to say, that shook things up a bit. Nobody had ever put together a manifesto before, and I followed that by hosting a launch event in the Langham Hotel in Portland Place, opposite the BBC. I then set about travelling around the country to visit every single one of the 91 members of the FA Council (with my friend, and former Suffolk policeman, Chris Cubitt at the wheel as I prepared for the next meeting).

I got a warm reception wherever I went, and much of the national press came in behind me. Paul McCarthy of the *Daily Express* said I was a 'powerful orator' with the capability of combining with then-England manager Kevin Keegan to give the FA 'a media-friendly, hugely acceptable public face'. *The Independent* reckoned I was the 'sort of dynamic, shrewd and smooth figure the FA needs to rebuild its prestige and influence at home and abroad', and put a smile on my face by quoting an unnamed ITFC employee as saying 'he has really turned the club around. He is popular and respected even though he has not spent millions on the team.'

Several journalists were quick to compare me to Tony Blair, back at a time when that was still a compliment. He had been elected two years previously, and although hindsight has not been at all kind to him, he was still riding a wave of pre-Iraq War popularity. 'Blair Flair could win David Job' read a headline in the *Daily Mirror*, which talked of an 'impressive performance' that 'looked like a bid for No.10, not No.16 Lancaster Gate'.

The comparison with Blair came with a suggestion that I, like he, may have been guilty of prioritising 'glitzy' style over substance, which left me wondering how much the people in Fleet Street knew about the hard yards I had put in at both Ipswich and the Football League. But all those play-off press post-mortems had left me with a thicker skin, and I knew from experience that if you needed to bring about significant change, then you had to make a strong initial impact. That was really the only off-note in the coverage, so I could live with it.

Indeed, the sportswriters generally welcomed what *The Times* called 'the opportunity to embrace modernity and professionalism', with Henry Winter in the *Daily Telegraph* saying the 'duel' with Thompson was seen as a 'professional versus amateur clash, as businessman versus blazer, a quintessential distillation of new versus old FA politics'.

Several highlighted the main obstacle standing in my way: the 'organisations which most need to reform if the game is to progress at all levels are the ones he [*i.e.* me] needs on his side to win election', in the words of *The Independent*, which went on to say that 'the FA Council, which is the electorate, needs to be neutered while the premiership, without whose support he has no chance, needs to have its financial dominance emasculated and its profligacy curbed'.

In a *Daily Express* article entitled 'Those in the Know Back Sheepshanks', Charlie Sale wrote that a 'more equitable distribution of TV money ... will not be an obvious vote catcher among the more self-interested Premiership bosses'.

Several journalists also wondered what would happen if Ipswich won promotion, as that would have meant me having to be elected by the potentially adversarial Premier League chairmen as one of their five representatives on the FA Board.

A week or so prior to the FA election, I had actually been given a slot to address the Premier League assembly at Stapleford Park in Leicestershire. But as it turned out, Geoff Thompson didn't want to say anything, and the chairmen decided that if one of us didn't speak, then neither should the other.

'Sheepshanks is denied his say,' grumbled Charlie Sale, who quoted a 'premiership insider': 'It's outrageous the way it's been worked in Thompson's favour. Clearly the [Premier League] clubs want the FA led by someone who will not be a threat to them.'

Despite that, I was reasonably confident when it came to the vote, which was part of the FA's July 1999 Summer Meeting at Carden Park, a golf hotel in Cheshire.

Geoff made a speech after dinner the night before the vote, which was followed by Leyton Orient chairman Barry Hearn shouting, 'Well, that has just won you another ten votes, Sheepy!' amid much hilarity throughout the packed room. An extraordinary and unusually bipartisan atmosphere grew around the bar as the evening wore on, with Barry (who became well known as a snooker, darts and later boxing promoter) walking around cheering 'Sheepshanks for chairman'. I clearly had my supporters. However, there were also groups sitting in corners who obviously had another agenda.

Geoff and I were invited to address the meeting before the vote. He showed himself to be the status quo man and, while no revolutionary, I was very much the opposite. There was polite applause for us both. It was hard to read.

In the end it was 53-31 to Geoff, with a few abstentions.

So I would have only needed a swing of 12 to carry the day. I sensed immediately that it was the axis of Richards, Bates et al. that had done for me.

Graham Kelly, the CEO who had resigned after the Wiseman controversy, summed it all up a few years later writing in *The Independent*:

> The council obviously preferred the safe hands of 'one of their own' to the gregarious and more outwardly ambitious Old Etonian Sheepshanks, whose printed election manifesto could almost have been produced by Saatchi and Saatchi. The council members – the octogenarians, the lieutenant-commanders, the majors, the representatives of the far-flung dominions – were, nonsensically, directors of

the Football Association Limited. Over the years many attempts at reform foundered on the rock of suspicion. Rational voices argued that change was needed, but when it came to the vote to install a more dynamic board of directors, there was always the worry that the whole sorry shooting match of privileges, perks and precious protocol might go up in smoke.

David Davies, later to become the executive director of the FA, recently told me that he thought it was all a case of 'typical internal football jealousy'.

I was only 46 back then and have learnt plenty of lessons since. Three in particular have come together in my mind over time.

*Lesson One*
I could almost certainly have fulfilled my ambition to chair the FA had I bided my time. Geoff Thompson had actually approached me ahead of the vote and asked me to come in with him as his vice-chairman on a joint ticket. With hindsight, I really needed someone to tap me on the shoulder at that point. A coach. A mentor. Someone like Frank Dick, who unfortunately wasn't around at the time. Being so committed to my agenda, I just couldn't see how it would work. So I turned Geoff down.

The world was very different back then. The first dot coms, and their 20-something 'disruptor' founders, were only just hitting the scene. Age and experience were deemed more important. And succession (at the FA anyway) was often not decided on merit or ideas, but rather by being the 'next person's turn' – and had I taken the vice-chair role, it very probably would have been my turn next.

*Lesson Two*
I was perhaps a tad naive in pursuing a national campaign. It certainly worked in terms of raising my profile nationally and I had strong backing from the national media; however, many of the council members (the

voters) were either not interested in what the media thought or, worse still, were actively antagonised by newspaper headlines. Producing a manifesto was unprecedented, and it quite simply unnerved too many of them. I was absolutely right to have visited all the councillors in person, but that was probably all it would have taken.

*Lesson Three*

Know your enemy! Ken Bates of Chelsea was at the height of his power and influence, and when it suited him he could be just plain rude.

To give Ken his due, he would usually tell you something to your face – he was of the 'I'm no backstabber, I come through the front door with a hatchet' brigade. And when I saw him, he had told me he wouldn't support me. I actually got to know Ken better when serving on the board to create the new Wembley, and give him credit for his vision of a world-class stadium with much more and better space (than Stamford Bridge!) and also both high-end and also more traditional terrace-style food and entertainment. So you had the choice of champagne and caviar, or pie and a pint.

Ken's good friend, Dave Richards of Sheffield Wednesday, was a difficult man to read, seemingly a friend and ally to your face, but – on occasions – a different kettle of fish behind your back.

I simply hadn't understood how these two, in particular, would seek to undermine me and become enemies. Maybe I was too trusting. Perhaps I could have pre-empted much of it directly.

So, given this, I think that just about all of the Premier League representatives voted against me, although I don't know how many exactly. They saw Geoff as somebody who had worked out alright for them so far, and who – with due respect to him – was unlikely to represent a threat to them.

In truth, I have loved the FA, and even had a passion for its work, believing with every bone in my body that I had what it takes to lead it if we were properly to represent football for everyone, not simply the elite. The strapline from my campaign had been 'Football for

ALL!' – which ironically the FA later adopted. And, of course, it was that which upset the blinkered self-interest of the Premier League. Quite simply, they were determined to control the agenda.

# PART FIVE

# Chapter 22
# The Wembley Showdown

FINALLY, FIVE seasons on, we were to have a shot at being the bride rather than just the bridesmaid, and to make our five-year plan come true in the most glorious way possible. Of course, automatic promotion would have been preferable for the nerves, but to get a chance of winning at Wembley – if you knew you were going to win, you would take that every time! So, after all those defeats in May over the previous campaigns, and all those nightmare 'well, Mr Sheepshanks …' interviews, now it was time to put it right.

Although none of us felt any kind of complacency, I had a private conviction that it was our turn. Needless to say, I never admitted to that publicly – how many chairmen and managers do you see saying idiotic things that just pile pressure on the team, and basically doing their opposite number's team talk for them! So there was none of that, even though inside we were feeling very determined.

George was every bit as resolved as any of us, and knew we would most likely be without key striker James Scowcroft, who was injured in the second leg against Bolton. That would be very tough on James, a local man, a very good guy and a key player, having scored 15 goals for us that season.

Off the pitch, the most pressing issue was planning the ticket sales. Our success had really captured the imagination locally – this being the first trip to Wembley since the Bobby Robson era – so there were many more who wanted tickets than we could supply.

It was a lovely problem to have, but was a nightmare for directors, players and staff alike, as all our friends were asking for favours.

However, Paul Clouting, Bill Leggate and the team at the ticket office handled it brilliantly, basing it heavily on loyalty through season tickets and regular away travel. And in the end, I think we got it pretty much right.

The other thing that happens in May–June is budgeting. Most clubs know which division they will be playing in by that stage, but we didn't – and the vast differences in our plan A and plan B was a reflection of the sad, and ultimately destructive, gulf that had opened up between the Premier League and the rest of us. Excitement was reaching fever pitch as the big day loomed. This was, after all, the most valuable match in football, one that nowadays gives the winner about £200 million over two seasons.

So, with the stakes so much higher this time, the cup fever of 1978 was being relived in our own era.

I often went to stay with the team before away games, and decided I should do so again, but only for the night before the match. They had headed for a secluded spot by the Thames, near Windsor.

I don't remember much about dinner, it certainly wasn't a late one. However, I do remember the morning of the match, and watching David Johnson having a fitness test in the grounds. We were already without Scowy, so to lose David too would have been a hammer blow. As it happened, he passed – but only just – so would start the game (although, as we know, he didn't last and was replaced by Bam Bam). Even so, just having him there at the outset was definitely a psychological boost for us all.

I was asked by George whether I would like to say a few words to the players during their pre-match lunch. I have absolutely no idea what I said, but many years later Jim Magilton told me it was good, so whatever it was it clearly didn't spoil things.

Leaving before the team, I was driven to the ground on my own, and got there in time for the buffet lunch in Wembley Hall. That no longer exists, having been pulled down along with the rest of the old stadium. Indeed, our play-off was the last competitive club game to be held in one of the most iconic of sporting venues. Another club game, the Charity Shield, was played there later, but that wasn't considered competitive – though readers old enough to remember Billy Bremner of Leeds and Liverpool's Kevin Keegan going at it after being sent off might not consider that the season opener was ever exactly a friendly!

So this was six years before the new Wembley opened; six long years, I can honestly say, having gone through the experience firsthand. With all the finals in between played in Cardiff.

**Finally ...!**
Upon arrival, someone gave me a buttonhole of blue and white roses or carnations – I don't remember which. To say I was nervous as we approached kick-off was a big understatement, although I didn't drink any of the wine that was being offered around. I have been to so many play-off finals since and, while great fun for the neutrals, the stakes are just so high for the participants. I recall we had done a deal with Barnsley so that the losers would take the winners' share of the gate receipt. It was less than one million pounds, as I recall, and peanuts compared to the Premier League revenues the winner qualified for, but definitely a way to sweeten the pill down in the real world a division below.

When kick-off time arrived, Mona and I headed for the Royal Box, where we were next to the CEO of our sponsors Nationwide, and the very colourful Football League chairman, Peter Middleton (a former monk, who had succeeded me in the role 18 months earlier). Sitting on the other side of them were our great friends (and adversaries for the day) John Dennis, the Barnsley chairman, and his wife Chris.

Richard Scudamore, who had just become CEO of the Premier League, and his wife Catherine were there, as were my parents and three brothers and, of course, my children (Sophie and Tom, then aged 13 and ten).

The stadium was a veritable sea of Ipswich blue and Barnsley red, and a cacophony of sound. The nearly 37,000 tickets allotted to each club contrasts with the FA Cup Final allocation where the two finalists only get around 30 per cent of the seats each (then just under 25,000), with the rest going to neutrals from clubs up and down the land. So, the play-off finals not only have more at stake financially, but they are also far more partisan.

The noise cranked up even further as the teams strode out, and it's hard to describe the mixture of pride, excitement and nerves all wrapped up together that I felt at that moment. I was delighted to see James Scowcroft behind George Burley, leading our boys, albeit in his team suit, given his injury. He had been voted our Player of the Year, so it was doubly sad for him to be missing out, but George – and all of us – wanted him to feel included.

The Town fans were confident, as we had beaten Barnsley 6-1 at home early in the season, and 2-0 away in February. But this proved to be a much tougher game, and was different from the outset.

Although David Johnson went close in the opening exchanges, it was Barnsley that drew first blood after just six minutes. Craig Hignett hit a long-range shot that dipped at the last moment, bouncing down from the underside of the bar and hitting our keeper, Richard Wright, on the back and bouncing, agonisingly, over the line.

However, on 28 minutes we were level. Jim Magilton crossed for Tony Mowbray to climb high and head home for 1-1. We were starting to get on top, but just before half-time Craig Hignett somehow got himself between Richard Wright and the ball, and Richard was judged to have pulled him down. We all said our prayers, and our magnificent 'one of our own' keeper responded by saving Darren Barnard's penalty! So we went in for the break still level, somehow. I can't remember anything about half-time, other than that everyone in Wembley Hall was nervously finding different ways of saying both teams were still in it, everything was still to play for, etc.

I was sure we could move it up a notch, even though David Johnson had gone off injured to be replaced by Richard 'Bam Bam' Naylor. Richard was another home-grown player who had come down from Leeds to join our academy. He was a quiet man off the pitch, but hard as nails on it. I had got to know Richard quite well before becoming chairman, largely through the aquarobics sessions and vicious rugby water polo we used to play together.

George's half-time team talk must have been laced with a bit of magic, as now Bam Bam came to the party, latching on to a flick by Marcus Stewart in the 52nd minute ... and six minutes later Marcus Stewart headed home Jamie Clapham's curling cross; 3-1! Yes, we were nearly there. Could we relax? Could we hell! This was Ipswich, after all! Our fans were tempting fate by singing in expectation, and in the 78th minute Tony Mowbray was adjudged to have tripped Geoff Thomas in the box, and that man Craig Hignett duly scored from the spot. So 3-2, with 12 minutes left.

We had a let-off when their No.9, Neil Shipperley, had a goal-bound header acrobatically saved by Richard Wright. Cue George Burley's decision to send on our Dutch winger, Martijn Reuser. In the final minute of normal time, hey presto ... Bam Bam fed Reuser near the halfway line, he sprang the offside trap and hared towards goal and with great skill let fly from 25 yards ... and bang, it was in the top of the net!

'Naylor ... he's stabbed it through. Reuser is ... onside ... Reuser. Premiership! Done and dusted for George Burley. Nails bitten to the quick, but elevation now surely, assured.'

Ahh ... it still sends shivers down my spine. We were 4-2 up and practically into stoppage time. I really don't know how much was added, as it was all such a blur as the final whistle blew.

That blur and the ecstatic high continued through the ceremonies. Needless to say, our fans were in full voice and, sportingly, many Barnsley supporters stayed on to watch proceedings. I shook hands with legendary cricket umpire Dickie Bird, and was also greeted by Sir Michael Parkinson, another Barnsley follower – both of them now sadly no longer with us. They were so generous in defeat, and among many messages received none was kinder or more eloquent than the handwritten note I got from Michael.

I remember going down to the pitch and doing a jig before heading for the changing rooms to congratulate George, his coaching team and all the players. I was greeted by Jim Magilton, who managed to soak me with a mixture of champagne and bath water. But I did manage to escape the fate of referee Terry Heilbron, who had already changed into a smart suit after what was actually his last game before retirement. He got thrown into the bath!

We had already decided that I would travel with Mona, Sophie and Tom on the VIP coach and not with the players. I took calls all the way and did interviews with Radio 5 and other media, both local and national. We were greeted by fans and banners on the bridges across the A12 as we made our way to the Suffolk Show Ground, where my predecessor, John Kerr, and others had arranged a marquee for us, it being only two days before the Suffolk Show opened.

I was still high as a kite. And I swear not a drop of anything passed my lips. It was pure adrenaline ... and my golly, how we partied! It went on long into the night. The karaoke microphone got heavy use, especially from Jim Magilton and Marcus Stewart.

Next day I woke up to see myself being interviewed on breakfast telly, and calling it 'the best day of my life'. I can still remember Mona's face at that remark.

Two days on we were received in Ipswich Town Hall, preceded by an open-top bus tour around the town with tens of thousands turning out to cheer the players. They really deserved it.

Life in sport has taught me that moments like that are all too ephemeral, and if you let yourself get carried away, then you will invariably come down to earth with a crash. So although it was a great summer bathing in the bliss of finally having shaken the monkey off our back, at the same time I kept on reminding myself to keep my feet on the ground. Premier League, yes, but the mission now was to stay there ...

## Chapter 23
# 2000/01: Even More than We Could Have Hoped For

ONCE THE sheer euphoria of what we had achieved at Wembley finally wore off, we were soon back at our desks handling the serious side of running what was now a Premier League club.

It didn't matter that the bookies had made us favourites for relegation, as we knew we had a good manager and a good team, although we did try to be realistic by budgeting for 17th place; that is, to stay up. Psychologically, that felt important.

We were quickly in negotiation with Richard Wright's agent, Jonathan Barnett, to try to thrash out a new contract. Despite the fact that Richard was adamant he wanted to stay, this took some doing as Jonathan kept digging his heels in. It was a reminder that it's the commissions earned from moving players, rather than negotiating higher wages, that makes agents most of their money.

We also signed Martijn Reuser on a permanent deal for £1m, and a few weeks later George Burley identified Icelandic defender Hermann Hreiðarsson as a possible recruit. He had played in the top flight for both Crystal Palace and Wimbledon. All was not well there and we had not one, but two protracted negotiations to get our man. The first was with legendary Wimbledon chairman Sam Hammam, a Lebanese businessman and a smart negotiator, as was his brother, Ned, with whom I had to do part of the deal. Eventually, we agreed an ITFC record fee of £4.5m. Then there was the small matter of the player's terms. Hermann's agent was an Icelandic lawyer, Ólafur

Garðarsson, who was a nice man, and a straight shooter, but he drove a hard bargain for his clients. The first lesson from this was never to be in a hurry on a deal – obviously, if the other party smells it, then the price hardens. Fortunately, in this case, Wimbledon wanted the cash as much as we wanted the player. Yes, we were paying a lot but we could afford it, and Hermann was to be our single, high-profile signing and turned out to be worth every penny.

What a phenomenal signing he proved to be. A gentle giant off the pitch, he transformed into a tenacious Norse warrior on it. The fans soon christened him 'Herminator' as he marauded up and down the pitch. He could play left-back and wing-back. Or centre-half, which is where George played him in his early games as a replacement for the now-retired Tony Mowbray, before he moved to left-back, or left-wing-back.

Our capacity as an all-seater stadium was still 22,500, and was to stay that way until we could justify building more. So immediately we were promoted we decided to push the button on constructing a new Churchmans (or South Stand). With the added upper tier we would increase capacity to 26,000 by early spring 2001.

But for now, the 37,000 who had travelled to Wembley simply wouldn't fit into Portman Road. So, Paul Clouting, our excellent commercial director, worked with the ticket office to come up with a membership scheme, with the emphasis on rewarding loyalty.

We'd had 3,600 season ticket holders when we started on our five-year plan back in 1995; that number had increased to 10,000 the previous campaign and now, in the Premier League, we would have to introduce a cap. We thought long and hard and finally went for 16,000. After allowing for 2,000 away supporters, that meant we would have 4,000 seats to rotate among the people who were now buying club memberships, which would allow them to come to one in every three or four home games.

One really difficult issue I had to address almost as soon as we were promoted involved our CEO Howard Wells. Howard had an impeccable track record after running the Sports Council in Hong

Kong, the National Sports Centre at Bisham Abbey and, more recently, Watford FC. We had brought him in during January, as I recall, to allow me to be more strategic and less caught up in the day-to-day stuff. I remember the board members asking me if I was sure, but I had been so overworked that I really felt I needed the senior administrative help. Sadly, it didn't work out, and I felt every bit as immersed in the detail as before. It was an incredibly difficult call, but after conferring with the board, call it I did. At the end of his six-month probation, we agreed to part ways. It was doubly hard on Howard, given that we had just been promoted, so he was now a CEO of a Premier League club. I can only say that he accepted it very professionally, and we managed to keep it amicable.

In my current leadership coaching world, with Vistage UK, we often talk about the importance of 'leaving well' or 'being a good leaver'. The world is a small place and you never know when you will meet people again, or friends of their friends. Howard left well and it's to his credit and says everything about the man.

I had stood down from the FA after promotion, since I had been there by virtue of my Football League position. But I was kindly invited to go with their delegation to a friendly match in Malta in June 2000, to watch Richard Wright make his full international debut. As it turned out, Richard had a nightmare. He conceded two penalties, the first of which cannoned off the post on to the back of his hand and into the net. But he managed to save the second, which came late in the second half, which meant England saved a major embarrassment by scraping home 2-1. Richard was retained as third-string keeper in the Euro 2000 squad.

## Puncturing United's air of invincibility

When it finally came to the big domestic kick-off, we were away to Spurs at White Hart Lane and, although Mark Venus scored the opening goal, Richard Wright gave away another (!) penalty and in the end we lost 3-1. It wasn't really a match to set the pulse racing, but three days later we played one that did just that. It was our first home fixture back in the big time, and we were to host Manchester United ... with David Beckham, Roy Keane, Paul Scholes, Ryan Giggs et al. It was a sellout, of course, and Portman Road was humming with anticipation from well before kick-off.

When Fabian Wilnis ran through from the right towards Churchmans and thumped his shot past their showman goalie, Fabien Barthez, the stadium absolutely erupted. And Fabian's celebratory jig so caught the eye that an artist friend of mine, Tim Fargher, painted the scene and captured it for eternity.

We set about pummelling United, with Barthez forced to make an amazing save from David Johnson. However, they weren't to be denied and David Beckham scored a trademark free kick to equalise. 'George Burley's side punctured the air of invincibility that has built up around Sir Alex Ferguson's men, to make a major impression on their return to the top flight,' wrote the BBC.

It was a night to savour. I remember Beckham being the only United player to stay behind and sign autographs for all the fans who had queued up. I had met David a few times with England, and he always looked to give something back to the game. He was very good like that. Years later, Mona and I were invited to a summer ball at 'Beckingham Palace' in Hertfordshire. We went with ICAP founder and City grandee Michael Spencer and his wife Lorraine, and David and Victoria were very friendly and welcoming. We danced the night away to Robbie Williams playing live. What an eye-opener that was – but we enjoyed it, and it was lovely to be asked.

The next home game was against Sunderland, and this time Titus Bramble scored to give us a 1-0 win. We were up and running! And my new PA, Anne-Marie Hutchinson, a Geordie and Newcastle fan, was doubly happy.

I fell very ill at that time with deep vein thrombosis, DVT, and spent a week in an oxygen tent and on a drip in Ipswich Hospital. I thought I had asthma, but actually so-called 'shower' emboli had invaded my lungs. All was well in the end, but I was left with a vulnerable chest. That meant I had to sit out a few games, but came back to see us draw 1-1 at home with Arsenal – Marcus Stewart for us, while Dennis Bergkamp scored from Thierry Henry's blocked shot.

The Arsenal game was memorable for another reason. My dear late godson James (who sadly died of cancer during Covid, aged 37) came to the game with his parents, my cousins Charlie and Belinda Cox, née Sheepshanks. James, who had been born with all sorts of complications, actually lived a much longer and happier life than doctors had originally feared. Nevertheless, while he was slightly stunted in his growth and with a mental age of a younger boy, he brought enormous joy to his family and friends. I was a very proud godfather. James loved his football and didn't see any reason why he couldn't support not only his local St Johnstone in Perth, but also Celtic, Ipswich and Arsenal. I made an exception for the dress code in the boardroom for James, who proudly wore the Ipswich shirt that I had just given him.

Arsène Wenger (a true great of the game – and an absolute gentleman) was one of the very few managers who would come up before lunch to greet both his and the opposing directors. On this occasion, I took James over to meet Arsène, one of his heroes. 'Hello, James,' Arsène said, 'I see you are an Ipswich supporter.' 'Yes,' replied James, immediately dropping his trousers to the floor, revealing a pair of Arsenal boxer shorts, 'and really an Arsenal fan underneath, Mr Wenger!' Much laughter ensued, and I am pleased to say that Arsène recalled the story with great amusement when I saw him at an event recently.

The season got better and better – we won 3-0 at Everton as part of a streak of seven wins and two draws, only interrupted by a disputed Alan Shearer penalty that gave Bobby Robson's Toon Army (with Kieron Dyer in their ranks) a 2-1 win over us at St James' Park. That was in front of 50,922 fans, the biggest crowd to have watched one of our games for over 20 years. It was wonderful to play against our old maestro, Sir Bobby. Except for the result, of course.

We beat Charlton 2-0 and then won 1-0 at Coventry after George Burley urged us to attack, and Fabian Wilnis duly nodded in an injury-time winner. Then came a 3-2 win away at Manchester City

– which sounds strange to write these days. It was a result that took us to third in the table, and we had actually gone three up through Marcus Stewart, twice, and Hermann. Francis Lee, their former chairman, was not a happy bunny! It got even better a few weeks later when we beat Liverpool 1-0 at Anfield after Marcus Stewart waltzed round their keeper, Westerveld, to score a brilliant solo goal. Meanwhile, George found striker Alun Armstrong available for £800k from Middlesbrough, so we snapped him up.

By now George was thinking that David Johnson might be surplus to requirements and we knew that his hometown team, Nottingham Forest, were keen, so the Armstrong deal was good business.

Although we went down to an Ole Gunnar Solskjaer double at Man United, we came back from two down to earn a 2-2 draw at Chelsea in our Boxing Day match three days later, as Marcus scored a late one to wipe the smile off Ken Bates's face!

Starting in the autumn we also had a fabulous run in the League Cup, then in its Worthington Cup incarnation. We clocked up wins over Millwall, Arsenal and Coventry before Titus Bramble cleared off the line at the very end to earn us a 2-1 extra-time victory over Manchester City. In the semi-final we took a tight first leg 1-0 at home to Birmingham through a Marcus Stewart penalty – which was probably harshly given against our former player Danny Sonner.

We also won our early January FA Cup match at Morecambe 3-0 in front of the *Match of the Day* cameras with Jon Champion commentating, and a crowd of nearly 6,000. Everybody at Morecambe could not have been friendlier, and I remember their half-time pies were the best!

But back to the League Cup semi-final second leg. We arrived at St Andrew's to be greeted by the 'Porn Kings', as they were known by some, the publishers David Sullivan and David Gold, together with their MD, Karren Brady (who all later moved to West Ham). The now Baroness Brady greeted me with a copy of her latest steamy novel! We were favourites, with a goal advantage from the first leg and with Marcus Stewart in hot goalscoring form. So we fancied our chances. But our hearts sank when we saw the pitch. It was an absolute quagmire. The kind of muddy bog I remember seeing at Derby's now-demolished Baseball Ground back in the old days.

Trevor Francis, sadly recently deceased and a tremendous striker in his day, was their manager, assisted by our very own Mick Mills. Trevor had been a finesse player, but he appeared to favour brawn over brilliance in his team selection. They were a big, strong lot, and they simply muscled us out of it. It was two-all on aggregate at 90 minutes, so we went to extra time and they went ahead, then there was a freakish bounce in the mud bath and they scored again. It felt like a travesty, and I recall doing something I very rarely ever did, which was to go down to commiserate with George and the team. I wanted to try to pick them up after the two cup defeats.

We then lost to Leeds at home, with Marcus Stewart harshly sent off, and to a Thierry Henry goal at Arsenal away, before getting back to winning ways against Everton with goals from Matt Holland and Alun Armstrong.

At this time we came close to signing Hassan Kachloul from Southampton. We were really excited. A Moroccan international, he was a charismatic and extremely skilful wide player who scored goals. He was available on a free transfer and agreed to join us, before, at the very last minute, John Gregory persuaded him to go to Villa. Humph and double humph!

Still, we kept on winning ... mostly ... and finished above Villa!

## The South Stand opens, and we welcome back Bobby Robson

We opened part of the new South Stand for the Liverpool game in April, raising our capacity from 22,500 to initially 25,000. It's now named after Sir Alf Ramsey, of course. On the subject of great past managers, Bobby Robson came to town with his Newcastle side and got a huge ovation. It was his first competitive return to Portman Road, and I can remember my legs tingling with excitement. We won 1-0 with a Stewart penalty after Nobby Solano (their popular Peruvian) was red-carded, and climbed to third in the Premier League with just five games to go.

We won three of them, drew one and lost one. But even that wasn't enough to hold that place. In the penultimate match we beat Man City at home 2-1 on a really tense night. Their gifted Bermudan Shaun Goater got the first on 74 minutes ('feed the goat, and he will score' as their then-manager Joe Royle used to say). Matt Holland equalised four minutes later before Martijn Reuser headed in to clinch the three points in dramatic fashion. We had therefore relegated Man City, who only 12 months earlier had pipped us to automatic promotion.

Their chairman, David Bernstein, made a generous and moving speech of congratulations a few minutes later in the boardroom, which was warmly applauded on all sides. I later worked with David when he chaired the FA, and always admired him for his sense of sportsmanship on what was a miserable night for them.

Of course, another irony was that 18 months later we would ourselves be relegated, and appoint Joe Royle.

Our captain fantastic, Matt Holland, played every one of our 38 games in what had been a truly memorable season. Goalie Richard Wright was superb throughout, Marcus Stewart scored 21 goals and Hermann Hreiðarsson had proved a gem of a signing – he was an inspirational warrior of a player. As well as those four, Jim Magilton and Jermaine ('Jammer') Wright were nearly ever-present, and Alun Armstrong scored eight times in 21 appearances after being signed mid-season.

We had done it with minimal outlay on new players: Hermann, Martijn, Armstrong and later Chris Makin. So the squad that got us promoted was essentially kept together, with David Johnson being the only player we sold, to Forest for £3m. George had picked up David when he was pretty much unknown, and he had gone on to be a fabulous player for us, scoring 62 goals in 158 games, so it was sad to see him go.

After his exploits, George was deservedly named Carling Premier League Manager of the Season and also Manager of the Year by the LMA.

All in all, it was a quite phenomenal season for a newly promoted club, and huge credit is due to George and everyone in his team. We had to pinch ourselves that this was really happening; however, the *esprit de corps* was palpable to anyone who saw us that season. It's such a precious commodity and – as we discovered to our cost the following year – all too easy to lose.

We also won the Fair Play League, while Alan Ferguson was voted groundsman of the year. And it didn't stop there as we were also awarded programme of the year, and I hesitate to say it, but I was even voted chairman of the year by *FourFourTwo* magazine!

At the end of it all, *The Guardian* end-of-season review proclaimed: 'George Burley was a managerial sensation, they scored goals from all over the pitch (so much for an "uninspiring" midfield), and won the hearts of the country.'

The article also included a beautifully pithy – and refreshingly honest – assessment of the journalists' own shortcomings as pre-season pundits, not that they had been alone in doubting us: 'What we got wrong: The lot.'

## Chapter 24
# 2001/02: the Pros and Cons of Europe

WITH THE South Stand finished, the board decided to bite the bullet and press 'go' on the project to build a new North Stand (now the Sir Bobby Robson Stand). This was a big call, and a decision taken after much soul-searching by the whole board as to feasibility. In the end the view was that if we didn't do it then, many years might pass before we could. So with our finance director presenting all sorts of scenarios that demonstrated affordability, we decided to build it.

Another very important development was the completion of the investment at Playford Road, with the purchase of extra land that gave us about 35 acres in total and space for nine pitches as well as the 60 x 40-yard indoor dome.

We had always believed that we were better than relegation candidates, but never that we could qualify for Europe in the first year back in the Premier League. I had set a target of three to five years in my mind for that. But in Europe we were, and we gave it a good crack. And boy, did we enjoy it!

The games were played on Thursday nights, shifting some of our league fixtures to Sundays, and began with Titus Bramble grabbing a late equaliser at home after Torpedo Moscow had led for most of the game. Mona came along as we and a thousand or so supporters headed off to Russia for the return leg, and what an extraordinary trip it was, seeing Ipswich Town fans in Red Square.

The Russian police were unnecessarily jumpy, and probably thought the friendly Suffolk folk were the English hooligans they had no doubt heard about. I even had to come to the rescue of one group who were in danger of being arrested for taking a flag into Red Square, something that was strictly forbidden.

We had a fantastic time in the city, including an unforgettable tour of the Kremlin – which is actually full of gold and crystal, priceless pictures and various other artefacts.

Come the match, Mona and I were separated from the rest of the directors and entertained to caviar and all the trimmings with leading politicians, before being seated on throne-like chairs with waiters behind us. It felt like being part of the Politburo. And the trip was rounded off with a win, through Finidi George and a Marcus Stewart penalty, taking us through 3-2 on aggregate. The Russians weren't happy!

Next up were Helsingborg, and again we were at home for the first leg. It was a great occasion at Portman Road, and I invited the UEFA president Lennart Johansson to open the newly built South Stand for us. England manager Sven-Göran Eriksson attended, along with many other dignitaries. The match didn't quite live up to it, but the goalless draw at least meant we hadn't shipped any away goals for the return trip. When it came to the second leg, we went behind in the opening minutes, but charged out after half-time and beat them comprehensively 3-1, with a goal from Hermann and two from Marcus Stewart.

After the game, John Motson and I joined hundreds of the 2,500 Tractor Boys who had made the trip in a packed Harry's Bar. Superfan Carl Jennings recently reminded me that I was hoisted up shoulder height and crowd-surfed around the celebrating mass, to much delight but agony for me the following day!

### A career in politics?

While in Sweden, and after a warm-up call from party chairman David Prior, I was distracted not by one, but two calls from no less than Conservative leader Iain Duncan Smith, asking me to consider standing for them in the Ipswich by-election, which was caused by the sudden death of Labour MP Jamie Cann, who I liked. It was a marginal seat, and they were insistent that all their research showed that I had enough local backing to stand a very good chance, and I have to say I was tempted. I made some enquiries and talked to various people I trusted. In the end I was swayed by David Mellor, who thought I would win the seat but warned me that all my charity and community involvement meant I was effectively already doing what an MP does, but that I would be frustrated by spending the following ten years in opposition (in fact, the Conservatives got back to power in 2010, but he wasn't far off). So, after much agonising, in the end I rang Iain and thanked him profusely for the faith he had shown in me, and explained that it hadn't been on my agenda before, and with an important job to do at Ipswich Town I felt I had to decline.

Looking back at it, I am reminded of something Enoch Powell once said: 'all political lives, unless they are cut off in midstream at a happy juncture, end in failure, because that is the nature of politics and of human affairs.' If that is true, then thank goodness I never went through with it. While not having any regrets, it's certainly something I will always wonder about. However, it was unquestionably a major crossroads.

The draw for the next round came out and, guess what, it was Inter Milan! The first game was deadlocked until George Burley brought on substitute Alun Armstrong, who had been doubtful for the game after suffering a stomach virus. His late bullet header from a Jamie Clapham cross duly handed us a win to take to Italy. Bottom of the Premier League, and yet we had confounded the pundits by beating one of the top teams in Europe.

The return leg, on 6 December, was a very different story. Christian Vieri grabbed a hat-trick, and the strength in depth at Inter was made clear when he went off to be replaced by Brazilian superstar Ronaldo. We didn't have a good game defensively, and Armstrong's penalty was no more than a consolation as we went out of the competition 4-2 on aggregate.

So we had a bit of a humbling on the night, but our 9,500 travelling fans made me very proud. I have a great memory of standing in the Piazza del Duomo on the morning of the match in a sea of blue and white. I don't think the people of Milan had seen anything like it, nor have they since! There were a lot of rustic Suffolk accents in evidence, and one old boy came up to me and said, 'Diavid (as I have always been called by most fans) yer see that there loit on toppa that there spoire …'

'Yes,' I said.

'Well, oive been wunderin ow do yer reckon they change the loit bulb when it's brerk?'

The San Siro was far from full, but the away end was. The Italian police held them back when I went to applaud them, so they sang, 'Shit ground, no fans.' I loved it.

Our continental adventure was a wonderful ride while it lasted. But as it turned out, the European experience was all too much, too quick. Culturally. Financially. Organisationally. In just about every possible way, it was an experience that would test us beyond our limits. When I reflect on it all now, that extraordinary first year back in the Premier League took its toll. And getting into Europe, while fantastic for the fans and for all of us in so many ways, was also the catalyst for so much that went wrong.

Something I often find myself saying as a professional coach is that you really have to learn from experience, both your successes and mistakes (I find it helps to put the positive part first). Taking time to look at what you have got wrong sounds obvious, of course, but there are times when everybody needs to be reminded of it. So, looking back at it all over the years, I would say there were three areas where the Europe factor hurt us:

## 1. Overextension

Being in Europe unquestionably pushed us into buying more, and more expensive, players than we would otherwise have done. We felt we needed a bigger, better squad, and creating it was a distraction. Finidi George and Matteo Sereni behaved professionally, and I am not implying anything detrimental to them, but signing them was undoubtedly a mistake (especially the latter). I doubt we would have gone for either had we not been in Europe. Myopic over-expansion caused by temporary success is a common problem in business, and precisely the error we had fought so hard to avoid the previous year. Now we had fallen into that very same trap.

On reflection, the arrival of two outsiders probably caused splits in the dressing room with the players who had put the hard yards into getting us back to the top flight. It's not as if we hadn't tried to inculcate Finidi, Sereni and others into the club culture, because we had. But whatever we did, there may well have been an us-and-them feeling towards these culturally different, big-money foreign imports.

George Burley was really excited about signing Finidi, and he had a tremendous home debut, scoring twice in the 3-1 win over Derby, but apart from occasional glimpses (once away at Villa, I recall), I am afraid other clubs before us had had the best of him. He was only 31, but simply didn't have the legs any more.

There was plenty of speculation as to how old Finidi really was, as supposedly passports didn't get issued every year in Nigeria when he was growing up. A few years later when Joe Royle became manager, he said to me, 'Chairman, if Finidi was 31, then I'm ten stone!' It was probably all very unfair, but made me chuckle, as only Joe could!

We needed to sign a goalkeeper after Richard Wright had left us for Arsenal (for £3m). That had been a deal we wanted to resist, but it was clearly a bigger club and the salary was much better than we could offer. His agent was always difficult to deal with, but I didn't begrudge Richard the opportunity, and in those situations it's hard to hold back a young man pursuing his career at the top. That said, looking back, I don't think we would have been relegated if Richard had stayed one more season. I know we can't pin it on just one player in a team game; however, in my view the side was significantly destabilised by the change of keeper.

Sereni was recommended to us by Sven-Göran Eriksson's assistant, Tord Grip. We had actually lined up Mart Poom, Derby's

Estonian keeper, and a £4.5m fee had been agreed. But just as we were about to clinch the deal, Mart got injured, breaking a bone in his hand. We had also signed Norwich keeper Andy Marshall; however, George Burley wasn't convinced he could excel at this level.

So George flew out to Italy to watch Matteo, and came back saying that he was our man. So we did the deal. Again, with the benefit of hindsight, we hadn't done enough due diligence for such a big signing. However, time was against us.

These were not so much signings that went wrong, as ones that never went right. And as we became more desperate towards the end of the season, other new arrivals only exacerbated the problems. On top of that we weren't to know that the market would collapse a year later, so that we wouldn't even be able to get our money back.

## 2. Complacency

The second negative factor was complacency. The feeling that we had already made it. I have thought about it a lot and often ask myself to what extent that came from us at the top. Certainly, we were all thrilled; however, as a board we were also realistic. Whereas we had budgeted to finish 17th the previous season (i.e. to stay up), we decided, after much debate, to budget for 12th place in our second year, which we believed would be consolidation after overachieving in the first.

In early July I left for a month's family holiday to the US and Australia. But the week before returning home, I got a worrying call from Alesha Gooderham. She had been an amazing support as PA, bringing extraordinary energy and intellect to everything we did. So brilliant, in fact, that we promoted her to head up PR as head of communications, another role in which she excelled. The media suddenly became much more amenable, so well did Alesha host and build good relations with them.

'You can't get back here quickly enough,' she told me. 'Everyone is walking around with their heads in the clouds. They think they're all superstars.'

It wasn't everyone, of course, but she certainly got my attention.

I talked to George when I got back, and suggested I address everybody after training one day. I told them about my trip Down Under and we discussed the brash cockiness of many Australians in sport (the late, great Shane Warne being the best example), contrasting it with arrogance. I urged them to realise that people would be ready for us this time, and that we were all going to start equal bottom, on zero points. The message was: self-belief, *Yes!* Arrogance or conceit, *No!*

### 3. Fixture congestion

The third, 'European', factor was simply the distraction of the additional games. They were such fun, for players and supporters alike. But after beating Derby County in August, we didn't win another Premier League match until 22 December.

In that time, though, we managed to win three UEFA Cup games, and had those been Premier League fixtures, we would have been comfortably safe at the end of the season.

The win that finally ended our domestic drought, 2-1 away at Spurs, lifted the mood just before Christmas. Come Christmas Day itself, Pablo Couñago and Sixto Peralta had no family to go to, so Mona and I invited them to us for a traditional festive lunch. We had bought Pablo, an U21 international, from Celta Vigo in Spain. He turned out to be a special young man, although at that stage still one for the future. He went on to score 35 goals in 122 appearances from 2001 to 2005, and another 26 goals in a second spell with us from 2007 to 2011.

Sixto had also joined us over the summer, on loan. A young Argentine midfielder, he quickly buddied up with his fellow Spanish speaker, Pablo.

Christmas Day with the two of them and all our family was delightful. They even had a glass of wine or two with their turkey, which got me worried that they would underperform the next day.

But though clearly in a good mood, they were professionals. On Boxing Day, while Pablo didn't play, Sixto did, and scored as we beat

Leicester 2-0. The week before we had been rooted to the bottom of the table, but the Tottenham game started a run of seven wins in eight games (including completing the double over Spurs, just three weeks after the reverse fixture). By 2 February, when we won 2-1 at Everton, we were suddenly 12th.

I remember it all too well, as I had been invited by Robert Charles, then controller of sport at Channel 5 (and an Ipswich fan), to go to New Orleans to watch the Super Bowl. It was the St Louis Rams (the massive favourites) against the New England Patriots, featuring a little-known quarterback called Tom Brady. That was to prove a lesson about taking anything for granted in sport, one we were ourselves about to experience.

The weekend included the obligatory steamer trip on the Mississippi. And on board, who should I come across but Man United CEO David Gill. 'Well done,' David greeted me. 'You've won at Everton, you're 12th and that must make you safe.' Or words to that effect.

But the 2-1 win at Goodison Park proved to be the high-water mark for us. I got home the following week to watch us being walloped 6-0 at home by Liverpool. They were rampant! It was a humiliating experience, but they really had an extraordinary team, and three days before had beaten Leeds 4-0 away as well.

Being out of the FA Cup (having gone down 4-1 at home to Man City in the fourth round), a quirk of fixture scheduling meant we then had nearly four weeks to stew over that defeat without a game. The team went on a training camp to Cyprus to break it up a bit. But a three-and-a-half week hiatus was too long.

We had 12 games left to play, so surely we would be fine. Or so we thought.

**The storm clouds gather**
Well, we weren't. We only won once, drew three times and lost eight of them, including going down to a solitary Ruud van Nistelrooy goal against Man Utd in the penultimate game. 'It takes a lot to rile

the Ipswich fans, probably the most phlegmatic in the Premiership,' commented *The Guardian* on the atmosphere at Portman Road after the Dutch striker had taken an obvious dive in the area, only to get up and score the ill-gotten penalty himself.

We were duly relegated on the final day, going down 5-0 at Liverpool. Our fans had travelled up in their thousands and treated Anfield to a great demonstration of gallows humour by singing, 'We're going to Grimsby, we're going to Grimsby, you're not, you're not ...'

On the flight up from Cambridge (with local firm Suckling Airways), the terrible feeling of foreboding that had been afflicting me for weeks seemed to peak. I couldn't bear it. We were to be confronted by the perfect storm, and one I felt powerless to stop. It wasn't just me that felt that way. The directors, coaching staff, all of us knew things were going to get very tough. It would become like being sucked into quicksand, and I repeatedly had that ghastly image of the boy sinking in the scene from *Lawrence of Arabia*.

My mood wasn't helped at all by the cavalier way in which some of the players got on the plane after the Liverpool game. Senior, proud members of the squad such as Matt Holland, Jim Magilton, Mark Venus and Hermann Hreiðarsson were all miserable and recognised the gravity of the situation. Whereas others, who will remain nameless, got on board laughing and joking, as if they didn't give a damn. That was proof of how fractured the culture had become.

I felt sick. As I had done since the dreadful 4-1 defeat at Bolton. How had we turned into such a pushover since that first Liverpool game? We had won seven of the previous eight, for goodness sake.

So what lay behind this gut feeling of impending doom? The answer was that it was becoming increasingly clear that the forces that govern the commercial side of the game were aligning against us. With a 31 August transfer deadline being implemented for the first time, I could already see the disaster waiting to happen, not just for us, but for all three relegated clubs. Being put on a time limit left us between a rock and a hard place. In previous years, if you went down, you could trade your way out of difficulty without any arbitrary deadline, just as Coventry had done the year before. Now the teams facing the drop would have to sell within three months, and every buyer would know that they were in the box seat.

And we simply had no trump cards left to play.

## Chapter 25
# 2002/03: a Perfect Storm

ALTHOUGH WE had obviously begun planning for various scenarios months earlier, on relegation we set about reorganising our finances in earnest. As we had known all along, it all depended on what we could get from selling our top players, as the newly prevailing economics for relegated clubs meant that the Premier League parachute would most likely be nothing like enough to bridge the gap in revenues. We suddenly faced a massive shortfall.

In ordinary circumstances, without the arbitrary August deadline, we would have found plenty of value in the transfer market, but that value was artificially depressed by the time constraint, and the situation was further complicated by the fact that some of our best people simply did not want to leave.

Meanwhile, our two most expensive players, Matteo Sereni and Finidi George, were sitting on huge contracts, but with massively depleted values compared to the £9m we had paid for them. With hindsight, the cost of those two signings alone did for us. It was our call, not theirs, of course, so I am not apportioning blame, but nobody could have predicted that, after just one year, their value would have fallen to zero.

The summer was all too short, but as it progressed we managed to sort out a deal to sell Marcus Stewart (very reluctantly) to Sunderland for £3.25m, which is what we had paid for him. In a different market, and given his scoring record in the Premier League, that would have been double or more, and was only half what Kieron Dyer had gone for three years earlier. While I was writing this book, we heard the terribly distressing news of Marcus's battle with Motor Neurone Disease. Marcus is – as is well known – a great guy, and he has stayed close to former team-mates and ITFC colleagues, myself included, after retiring from the game. We wish him the very best.

In addition to Marcus, that close season saw the departure of Titus Bramble to Newcastle for £5m (thanks, I think, to Bobby Robson) and later Jamie Clapham to Birmingham for £1.5m.

Losing every one of them hurt. But still it wasn't enough.

We also had an offer from West Brom for Hermann and Matt, which we were very reluctant to accept. However, the decision was made for us, because both players point-blank refused to leave. Although we really needed the money, having top guys like that wanting to help us get promoted again was actually a real boost to morale.

In the end we managed to get Sereni off the wage bill by sending him on loan back to Italy, to Brescia, where he would play with no less than Roberto Baggio, which was probably the highlight of his career. We couldn't get a fee for him anywhere. He was damaged goods.

French winger Ulrich Le Pen also left on loan, for Strasbourg. We had only signed him (for £1.4m) in desperation, but he got injured 12 minutes into his debut and that was all he ever played in the league. At £2,000 a second he must go down as our worst-ever signing! That probably isn't fair on him, but it certainly never worked, either for him or for us, and his Wikipedia page says somewhat laconically: 'it is assumed that he and his family never really settled in England'.

And then there was Finidi, who nobody wanted either. Eventually, Real Mallorca took him back on a free transfer. He would make 14 appearances for them, without scoring, before retiring at (allegedly) 33. It had been another financially disastrous signing.

Ironically, given the role that the Europe factor had played in getting us relegated in the first place, one of the few good pieces of news at that time came when we learnt that our fair play record meant we had qualified for the UEFA Cup. Again! Yes, it would crowd the fixture list, but we felt the additional revenue would prove a very welcome addition to our depleted coffers.

## Saying goodbye to George

Our pre-season in Denmark was the first time I saw firsthand that all might not have been right in the camp between manager, coaches and players. Nevertheless, we started the league season winning 2-0 away at Walsall, and then thumping Leicester 6-1 at home (they had been relegated alongside us, and the result was rather fortunate, I seem to recall). Even before that, the bookies had made us favourites to bounce straight back up, so we were in optimistic mood.

However, things went sharply downhill at that point. We had beaten Luxembourg part-timers Avenir Beggen 1-0 away and 8-1 at home, and followed that with another two-legged UEFA win over Sartid Smederevo of Serbia. But domestically we only took five points from the next six league games, culminating in a dismal 3-0 defeat at Grimsby.

Things were not right. I would hesitate to say that George had 'lost the dressing room', as the saying goes; however, I had seen a lack of respect for him from some of the squad when we were in Denmark that I didn't like at all. Especially since he only ever wanted the best for his players, staff and club.

But that night in Grimsby it became clear to me that a change needed to be made.

I remembered how, right at the start, and with both of us young in our posts, I had told George that I would back him to the hilt, until the day that I couldn't. And I had backed him ... but now that fateful day had sadly come.

So, upon our return, I called an emergency meeting of the directors. Nobody felt good about it, but they unanimously concluded that we would have to part company with George.

I met him next day around 5pm, in his office. He was clearly shocked. We'd had seven pretty amazing years together. Years with plenty of heartache, but also of triumph through adversity, and times in which he had supported me, as well as the other way round. And we had more than fulfilled our dream together, not just in getting into the Premier League, but for European football too. What made it much harder was the fact that we had awarded him a big contract the year before after finishing fifth in the league, a contract we were now completely unable to fulfil.

It was one of the hardest things I have ever had to do. I had never sacked a manager, and Ipswich had never been a 'sacking club' like some are – even more so these days with the amount of money involved. In fact, here, for the record (and excluding caretakers) is the full roll call over nearly half a century up to that point (during which time Britain had 11 prime ministers, incidentally):

| Alf Ramsey | 1955–1963 |
| Jackie Milburn | 1963–1964 |
| Bill McGarry | 1964–1968 |
| Bobby Robson | 1969–1982 |
| Bobby Ferguson | 1982–1987 |
| John Duncan | 1987–1990 |
| John Lyall | 1990–1994 |
| George Burley | 1994–2002 |

Unlike some of the ruthless sackings you read about today where the new man is installed the very next day, suggesting it has all been done behind the existing manager's back, we hadn't chosen a successor. So we decided to put Tony Mowbray in charge while we collected our thoughts as a board.

The minute you make a change like that, you are bombarded with applications from all the out-of-work managers, and hounded by agents working for people who are already in a job.

The board discussed possible candidates. Everybody thought highly of Tony Mowbray. However, there was a strong feeling that, given our predicament, we needed experience. So Joe Royle and Mick McCarthy were at the top of the list.

I called Joe and he agreed to come over and meet with us. I also spoke to Mick. He was delightful, and flattered, but had only just left the Ireland job (after the famous altercation with Roy Keane) and felt that he needed a longer break.

Years later, Mick McCarthy did finally become our manager, which, with all due respect to the others, was the best appointment that Marcus Evans made during his tenure. Mick and his wife Fiona became good friends of ours at that stage, and would often come over for dinner. We have even met up for golf over the summer in Portugal a couple of times, and had some great fun on his boat in Portimão.

At the press conference when he was later appointed at Ipswich, somebody asked Mick his opinion of Roy Keane, given that he was taking a position that Roy had held a few years earlier. By all accounts, there was a pregnant pause before Mick famously said, 'Opinions are like arseholes, we've all got them but some are best not aired in public.' At least, that is how it was told to me.

Mick was the master of one-liners, and I will never forget what he said when he was asked about his expectations for recovery after being appointed Wolves manager: 'My initials stand for Mick McCarthy, not Merlin the Magician.'

Classic Mick. What a great guy! He proved an excellent manager at Ipswich, as he and TC (Terry Connor, his assistant) really got the club sorted out. In terms of league performance, we hadn't done much more than flirt with relegation over four years of Keane and Jewell, but he got us into the play-offs in 2015 against Norwich, after assembling a very competitive team. And on a shoestring budget, something unbeknown to the outside world, since by then Marcus Evans had reined in his spending.

I stood with our fans at Carrow Road that day, as I was denied a place in the directors' box by Marcus's man Ian Milne, and his colleagues. How things had gone downhill, I reflected, when I saw them stride into the Norwich boardroom before the game (Delia Smith, good friend that she is, had kindly invited me). My chum Alex Dolbey and I proceeded to have a ball in the stands (other than the result, of course, 3-1 to them), where I received the ultimate, and very humbling, compliment of being hailed 'as one of our own' by the Town fans. I was enormously chuffed, as being Suffolk raised and an Ipswich diehard nearly all my life, I am proud to say I am just that!

Anyway, getting back to 2002, Mogga (aka Tony Mowbray) did well as caretaker, but the results just wouldn't come. We beat Sheffield Wednesday 2-1 in his first game in charge, but then lost to Reading, drew with Burnley and lost to Gillingham, which always felt awful.

So, we appointed Joe. The larger-than-life character that is Joe Royle immediately lifted the mood. He is a terrific man with great stature and presence, blessed with a devilishly funny, very Scouse sense of humour.

We hit it off from day one, as he did with the rest of the board, the players and, most importantly, the fans. People loved him. It was impossible not to. We got to know him and his wife Janet very well, and I am still close to his son Darren, who is now CEO of Oldham Athletic. Oldham are one of Joe's old clubs, of course, and they always used to beat us on that darned plastic pitch of theirs at Boundary Park!

We also played another round of the UEFA Cup against Liberec of the Czech Republic that we drew on aggregate 1-1, but lost on penalties. That was probably just as well, as somehow the magic of the previous season's UEFA ties was missing.

The mood wasn't helped by the tragic news, in early February 2003, of the death of Dale Roberts. A tremendous guy who was liked by everyone who knew him, Dale lost a courageous battle with cancer at the age of 46, having been a confidant and number two to George Burley throughout his managerial career. It was so desperately sad, not least for his dear wife Cheryl and their sons Mark and Tommy.

Back at Portman Road the struggle to raise funds continued, with endless meetings with Barclays and Norwich Union (our two main creditors) and prospective investor-supporters. In normal circumstances we would have sold some players and moved on, as we had in the past.

But these were not normal circumstances.

**The darkest day**
All the clubs outside the Premier League had been boosted a couple of years earlier by the creation of a joint venture mainly run by Carlton and Granada, who owned several licences on the ITV

network. In 2000, ITV Digital, which had originally been named ONdigital, pledged to pump £315 million into the Football League. The operation was plagued by piracy and low viewing figures from the outset, so that by 2002 it was thought to be losing up to £1 million a day. It went under, and the money promised to the clubs never materialised, plunging many of us into crisis.

On 10 February, the darkest day of my career, we had to admit defeat in our efforts to refinance the club without the protection of being put into administration, and our advisors felt we had no option but to do so. I put out a statement explaining that relegation, the demise of ITV Digital and the introduction of the new transfer window had made our situation much worse, depressing the transfer values that we would otherwise have been able to expect.

I continued:

> We deeply regret this action and the pain that will be felt by creditors and suppliers, including many that are local and of long standing. If there had been a better alternative then we would surely have taken it. The directors have a clear legal responsibility to protect the interests of all creditors ... and absolute responsibility to guard and protect the livelihood and future of this Football Club, for shareholders, employees, supporters, stakeholders, the people of Ipswich and our community at large, which this action is also designed to accomplish.

It was just ghastly, and gut-wrenching at a personal level. I simply couldn't stand the consequences for those creditors who had lost money. It was little consolation for them that I and other directors had lost lots as well. What a truly terrible day it was. A legacy of that time is that I simply cannot abide the mention of the word 'administration' or 'administrator' in any context, even, for example, the phrase 'football administration', and go out of my way to avoid ever using or hearing it. It just makes me shudder.

To their eternal credit, the board of directors stood shoulder to shoulder with me. I was ready to resign, and asked around for advice as to whether I should or not. What I heard back was that I very probably represented the best chance of guiding the club to recovery, and that there were no other credible individuals or groups waiting in the wings.

After a day or two of soul-searching I decided I would speak publicly on the matter. I concluded that the first thing was to go on to the pitch at half-time in our next match to apologise and take full responsibility for what happened. At the same time, I tried to give a message of confidence that we could work together to recover.

There were some boos, understandably; however, the vast majority of the crowd applauded, and I took that as a vote to carry on with all the energy that I could muster.

The second thing I did was to call a meeting in the Town Hall, where I fielded questions from the audience of 500 or so, along with Derek Bowden, who was going through a baptism of fire as our recently appointed CEO. It was never going to be an easy night, but at least we had nothing to hide. And the reaction was broadly supportive.

We had grasped the nettle and confronted the issue. And I remain convinced this is the right way to handle difficult situations like this. There is a great quote, the first part of which comes from Aristotle: 'Nature abhors a vacuum, and finding one fills it with poison and drivel.' The point is that if people at the top go silent, then others will start to make it all up, and then things can end up anywhere.

We took a lot of advice and appointed Nick Dargan of Deloitte as administrator. It was his duty to realise income in the best way he could. I have to say that Nick handled our difficult circumstances very professionally, even when he had to make hard calls.

Inevitably those hard calls included bidding farewell to some of our favourite players, and equally inevitably they went for far less than they were worth. We were forced to sell Darren Ambrose to Newcastle for what I recall was only £1m. It felt insulting, a travesty, farcical even. Then farce turned to tragedy when Hermann went to Charlton for £900k, which was another gross undervaluation. He was in his prime, so Charlton had another steal, and normally the fee would have been in excess of the £4m that we had paid for him.

With all this happening in the background (or, more accurately, foreground and centre stage), what Joe Royle achieved between November 2002 and May 2003 was nothing less than remarkable. From near the bottom of the table, he took us back to seventh by the end of the season, and we missed the play-offs by only four points. Joe's efforts were heroic.

Gates held up, averaging 25,500, with Pablo Couñago getting 20 goals. The charismatic Spaniard developed a great love for the Tractor Boys, a feeling that was wholeheartedly reciprocated by all the fans. He was among the scorers in my favourite game of the season, on 18 April 2003, when we beat Portsmouth 3-0. Martijn Reuser and Tommy Miller got the other two, in front of 29,396 – just short of the new, all-seater record set against Nottingham Forest the previous match. That felt like confirmation that we were all reading from the same page, and with us exiting administration at the end of May, we began efforts in earnest to get the club back on an upward trajectory, and felt we could approach the close season with at least a degree of optimism.

That close season also included a huge honour for the club, and indeed for the town, when we staged a full England international against Croatia on 20 August. This was back when the new Wembley was still being built, and the games were distributed around the country. It was something I had lobbied for at the FA as hard as I felt was appropriate, and it was wonderful to see us win 3-1 (Michael Owen, Frank Lampard and a David Beckham penalty), with Kieron Dyer coming on as substitute. A crowd of 28,700 turned out and everything went smoothly, thanks to sterling work by everybody, in particular Derek Bowden, Paul Clouting, former club secretary David Rose and his successor Sally Webb.

## Chapter 26
# 2003/04: Joe Wheels and Deals

I ALWAYS felt that the previous season's upheaval had been our responsibility as a board, even if we had been dealt a very tough hand. But it had become clearer than ever that we had to engage with our shareholders and loan note holders to build a stronger financial base. So in September 2003 we launched a share issue with the aim of raising up to £5 million.

On the pitch, Joe Royle had shown just what a master dealer he was during the close season, bringing in five good players on free transfers: Wimbledon goalkeeper Kelvin Davis, who would go on to do great things for us, as would Shefki Kuqi (who joined from Sheffield Wednesday in September), and also Drissa Diallo from Burnley, George Santos from Grimsby and Chris Bart-Williams from Charlton. Alan Mahon came in on loan from Blackburn, as did Matt Elliott from Leicester later in the campaign.

On the negative side we saw Matt Holland go to Charlton for £750k, another ludicrously low sum, but Matt – much as he loved ITFC – wanted to play in the Premier League, and he still had a lot to offer. Mark Venus left on a free transfer to Cambridge, while Thomas Gaardsøe went to WBA for a pittance. These were yet more previously unimaginably low values, caused by the 31 August deadline that nobody in football had done enough to anticipate, or predict the effect of. Nor had anything been done to protect the victims, particular the relegated clubs – Leicester, Derby and ourselves. All three of us ended up in dire financial straits, and it was little comfort, and all too late, when the Premier League later decided to increase the parachute period up to four years.

Despite all this, on the pitch it was beginning to feel as if we were building a strong team again: Fabian Wilnis, Chris Makin, John McGreal, Tommy Miller, Pablo Couñago, Alun Armstrong, Martijn Reuser, Jermaine Wright, Bam Bam Naylor and Jim Magilton all remained from the previous season. Plus there were the newcomers and, of course, our own graduates from the academy – Darren Bent, Ian Westlake, Dean Bowditch, Matt Richards and Lewis Price.

The mood was only enhanced when Joe named Jim Magilton, whose passion made him a natural leader, as club captain to replace Matt Holland. Jim openly embraced the 'one team, one dream' approach I had championed, and I was very touched recently when he told me that it was a vision which had 'resonated throughout the dressing room and among the supporters'. Which is exactly how it should be. It is the spirit that defines us, and one to be preserved at all costs.

Joe took the team for the customary pre-season trip to Sweden where we played Mjällby and Trelleborgs, and also crossed the water to Helsingor in Denmark (known to an English audience as Elsinore in *Hamlet*). We won them all.

However, the league season started disastrously, and we picked up just two points in the first six games. That left us bottom, but we followed it up with eight wins in nine, and there was certainly no lack of goals. In fact, we scored a bucketload (84), with Darren Bent getting 16 and Shefki Kuqi, Tommy Miller and Pablo all bagging 12 each. The problem was that we conceded lots as well (72), the third worst in the division. The 6-4 home win over Crewe Alexandra in January seemed to sum up the entire season, while my personal highlight was a 6-1 win over Burnley.

We finished fifth, and in the play-offs again – beating West Ham at home 1-0, but then losing 2-0 away. That cued yet another round of 'well, David – what will you do now, you'll have to sell again … is this it …?' and so on. It was like a broken record.

## Selling Suffolk Foods

At the same time, I was beginning to hear some off-notes in the music coming from my own business, which Rick and I had founded back in 1989.

I was an out-and-out salesman and always proactive, so from the outset we had won a lot of national accounts for our mayonnaise, which we made in two, five or ten-litre printed buckets for the catering sector and sandwich/salad manufacturers. At our peak, we would end up producing 400 tonnes of mayonnaise a week for clients across the UK and abroad. Those clients included several around the West Country and in London, where we started doing business with another old Starfish customer, Oli Leatham of Leathams Larder.

Oli became a good friend and introduced me to Julian Metcalfe, who then had two outlets of what he hoped would become a new concept in sandwich shops. So, literally from the outset, we became mayonnaise and sauce ingredient suppliers to none other than Pret a Manger, staying with them on the journey as they became a national name. That journey included creating a whole series of bespoke products, including their famous 'secret sauce', which was developed along with Julian and his food scientist, Nellie Nichols.

Reaping the rewards of all the earlier business development work, Suffolk Foods developed at such a rate that in the mid-1990s we were making enough to move from Rendlesham and to convert a large shed-type facility at Martlesham Industrial Estate into a specialist mayonnaise factory. We also qualified for the BS 5750, which essentially ensures that 'you say what you do and do what you say'. It's a brilliant control process, as long as you make the system work for you – and not you for it. The 'BS' (British Standard) tag was later dropped for 'ISO' (from the International Organisation for Standardisation), the same accreditation system we introduced at Portman Road.

A few years earlier we had added the extra experience with the arrival on the board of John Kerridge, a colleague of mine at Ipswich Town, who was then chairman of Fisons, a FTSE 100 company. He was a wise old owl, always insightful and thought-provoking until his untimely death. I learnt a lot from him about being a non-executive director. John refused a director's fee, but instead accepted a small share option.

By 2003 things seemed to be flattening off, with sales up but profitability down, so my brother Rick and I became engaged in lots of discussions about the way forward. After starting out with a remit that covered the production side, Rick had taken on more and more of the overall running of the firm while my attention had expanded to embrace ITFC, the FA and other responsibilities. So he was keen to buy my majority share out and, given my other commitments, I was amenable to that. But a few months later we concluded it was better to sell up entirely, so we opened negotiations with Billington Foods from Liverpool, who had made a play to acquire us.

The sale went through in the summer of 2004. I know Rick was disappointed at the time, but shortly afterwards he started the process that would end up with the creation of Stokes Sauces. They had a bit of a bumpy start, but the firm is a massive success today, so great credit to him – and now my daughter Sophie works there too!

**Suffolk Community Foundation**

Another distraction at this time was my growing involvement in a project that is still very dear to my heart. A couple of years earlier I had been approached by Richard Middleton, who had been running Ipswich Community Voluntary Services (ICVS) to see whether I would be interested in supporting a new community foundation for the county.

It was a concept that came from the US, where philanthropy is far better established and supported, and proof of this is the hundreds of community foundations all over the States. The idea is simply to create a focal point locally through which people can donate and support a whole range of local causes that might otherwise struggle under the radar. That means lasting endowment funds can be created to support future generations. As things gathered pace, we increasingly found that people wanted to give in their own lifetime so they could enjoy seeing their funds make an immediate difference. Donors of over £25,000 could name their own fund, and have a say to ensure the money went to their favourite causes, while smaller amounts went into a generic fund, which our grants team would channel to the areas of most need in the county.

In the early days we were boosted by Lord Lieutenant Tim Tollemache holding a drinks reception for us at his Helmingham Hall home. Lord Tollemache and his wife Xa, a brilliant garden designer, would host all kinds of charity events, including what became our annual Suffolk Dog Day, which attracted over 6,000 people with their dogs. Within a year or two it had grown further, raising our profile and relevance in the local community, and about £50,000 of unrestricted reserves – so, money that could be used at our discretion.

There was a funny moment at Helmingham a few years later when Danny Dyer, who claimed to have relatives in common with Tim going back four centuries, visited for the ancestry programme *Who Do You Think You Are?* The Hall really is one of the most impressive places in the country to approach – the drive runs through a beautiful deer park and ends at the moated residence. As Danny arrived, he was captured wondering, 'Who's the geezer with the drawbridge?'

On a much more serious note, one of the things the foundation would go on to do was to administer a memorial to the six women killed by Steve Wright. Nigel Pickover, the editor of the *Ipswich Evening Star*, approached me to join a campaign called 'Somebody's Daughter', which raised £20,000, with the idea being to create a refuge centre to help vulnerable girls break drug habits. I was joined as a trustee by Liz Harsant (a splendid lady who is now a county councillor), Rev. Paul Daltry, Rev. Peter Townley from St Mary Le Tower Church, and our then-MP Chris Mole, and was pleased to be involved and do my best for them.

Anyway, by late 2004, we were plucking up the courage to register the Suffolk Community Foundation as a charity and, to raise some core capital, we held a dinner in London for 200 of the county's wealthiest and most influential people. We had secured the use of the splendid Goldsmiths' Hall through another peer, Roger Cunliffe, who is a member of the City of London livery company that owns it. The evening was a stunning success, raising just under £200,000 to help kickstart our new Suffolk charity. These things don't organise themselves, and everybody in the county owes a debt of gratitude to Simon Loftus (chairman of Adnams at the time), David Barclay (who had recently retired as director of Barclays), Clare, Countess of Euston (later to become Lord Lieutenant herself), Terry Hunt (editor of the *East Anglian Daily Times*), Clare Howes, Claire Horsley, Canon Graham Hedger, Fiona Mahony and others involved in those early days.

That cash gave us the confidence to appoint Stephen Singleton as our first full-time, professional CEO – taking it over from Claire Horsley who had selflessly done it as a volunteer from the outset. Simon Loftus, our first chairman, then suddenly decided to retire, and muggins me was asked to take it on.

As if I didn't have enough on my plate …

# PART SIX

## Chapter 27
# 2004/05: Punching Above Our Weight

WE ALL knew this season was going to be huge for us, particularly because our finances would be stretched, as we no longer had the Premier League parachute payment to rely on.

We got back to having summer concerts at Portman Road, which was no hardship from my point of view, as it included Elton John (with James Blunt as his warm-up act). Mona and I went to visit Elton in his dressing room (in the Bobby Robson Suite) where he had a wardrobe that was about 20 yards long, with countless changes of outfits (most of them outrageous, even by his standards!). I have always admired Elton, having met him on numerous occasions at Vicarage Road watching his beloved Watford. To think that I first saw him on stage in London in 1973, and he is still performing 50 years later. When I met his drummer, Nigel Olsson (another amazing performer), he showed us his secret to playing long concerts – he wears a golf glove on each hand!

The good news among the financial gloom was that we had Joe Royle as our manager, and he not only continued to be a master wheeler-dealer in the transfer market, but also an inspirational leader. His wonderfully infectious sense of humour quickly draws people to him.

Joe used to say leadership was all about 'kidology' – essentially kidding people to believe they are better than they really are! It worked for him and, although it's not quite how I would describe the technique, I can say that in my experience management of any description often involves encouraging individuals and entire teams to believe in themselves and how good they can be. Even to believe that they can be better than they think they can.

And that was something Joe did brilliantly. It's as the inimitable Bill Shankly once said: 'A lot of football success is in the mind. You must believe you are the best and then make sure that you are.'

Joe pulled off another coup in attracting a new leader to the club in Canadian Jason de Vos, on a free transfer from Wigan. Jason was a tall, commanding centre-half, and an absolute boss on the pitch! Joe also identified Darren Currie, for whom we somehow scraped together a fee of £375k, who came from Brighton. Darren was a very skilful winger and became a crowd favourite – perhaps he lacked a bit of pace, but he was full of trickery and he could deliver some great free kicks and corners. We also brought in the experience of midfield enforcer Kevin Horlock, who was out of contract at West Ham.

These players replaced some of our favourites, such as John McGreal, who went to Burnley, Jermaine Wright (Leeds), Martijn Reuser (who went back to the Netherlands), Chris Makin (Leicester) and Alun Armstrong (Darlington). Marcus Bent came back from loan, and we managed to sell him to Everton for £450k.

The season kicked off with a home win over Gillingham, a draw with Forest and a close defeat, 3-2, at George Burley's Derby. But then came four wins on the trot, and shortly afterwards an 11-game unbeaten run with only a loss at Stoke between them. We were on our way, and looked a force to be reckoned with. Joe Royle had paired our home-grown striker Darren Bent with Shefki Kuqi, and they proved to be a potent strike force. Darren – who had formerly combined with namesake Marcus as the 'bent double' strike force – was another favourite 'one of our own', and Shefki was quickly adopted by the fans. He was a genial and gentle man off the pitch, but a giant in every way on it. Built like Iron Man, he developed his own swallow-dive celebration for when he scored. Which was plenty! Shefki got 20 goals and Bent 19, helping us to the verge of automatic promotion.

I will always say we should have been promoted, and I really think we would have been had it not been for an injury to Shefki in our home game with Leicester on 12 February. We were a few points clear at the top at the time, and we won 2-1, but Shefki clashed with the formidable Dion Dublin and came off worse, suffering a bad knee injury. Despite having brought Jamie Scowcroft back on loan in the January window, and bringing in the very experienced David Unsworth at left-back, we drew the next game and then lost the next three. That included a defeat away at our promotion rivals Wigan, a game Shefki was rushed back for. But it was too soon, and he wasn't at his best.

Those results meant we slipped from the top spot. However, next game we got back to winning ways by thumping Nottingham Forest 6-0, my favourite game of the season, with Shefki scoring, along with Richard Naylor (now playing central defender), Ian Westlake and Darren Bent, while Tommy Miller got a brace.

At the end of a season it's your accumulated points total that matters, so it's impossible to say which particular game had cost us. We certainly had plenty of opportunities, but once more had simply not taken them.

Now we were in the play-offs yet again, for the second year running against Alan Pardew's West Ham, who had finished 12 points below us in sixth. That made us favourites, although we knew we would be without David Unsworth – who we signed on a 93-day loan. We had realised the implications back in February, and it had been a toss-up whether to wait a week, or to play him in a tough away fixture at Sheffield United. But play him we did, meaning he wouldn't be available for the play-offs.

Joe and I had to have strong words about this. I had told him explicitly that 93 days was the maximum we could sign him for, so it was a matter of whether he wanted him then or for the play-offs. It's easy to judge in hindsight, and I think Joe made the right call to go for automatic promotion with the best team he could. It was only when we were in the play-offs that he intimated to the press that it

*Summer 2000 – with George Burley introducing the inspirational Hermann Hreiðarsson, our record signing at the time, to the media*

*In happy times with George Burley. This shows the newly built Sir Alf Ramsey Stand and the North Stand (before the Sir Bobby Robson Stand was built), 2001*

*Enjoying Red Square, with Mona before our epic UEFA cup tie against Torpedo Moscow*

*Being interviewed on the pitch with fans in the background at San Siro stadium, Milan (Credit: Warren Page)*

*All dressed up with Sven-Göran Eriksson, 2002*

*Showing our handprints in Planet Blue with 'Big Joe' Royle, 2003/04* (Credit: Warren Page)

**THIS DOCUMENT IS IMPORTANT AND REQUIRES YOUR IMMEDIATE ATTENTION.** If you are in any doubt as to the action you should take, you should immediately consult your stockbroker, bank manager, solicitor, accountant or other independent financial adviser duly authorised under the Financial Services and Markets Act 2000.

This Form of Acceptance ("**Form**") should be read in conjunction with the accompanying offer document dated 22 August 2003 (the "**Offer Document**"). The terms and conditions of the Offer Document, as defined and contained in the Offer Document, are deemed to be incorporated in and form part of this Form. Unless the context otherwise requires, the definitions contained in the Offer Document also apply to this Form.

If you have sold or otherwise transferred your ITFC Shares, please pass this Form, the accompanying Offer Document and reply-paid envelope as soon as possible to the purchaser or transferee or to the stockbroker, bank or other agent through whom the sale or transfer was effected, for delivery to the purchaser or transferee. However, as the Offer is not being made, directly or indirectly, in or into the United States, Canada, Australia or Japan, such documents must not be forwarded or transmitted in or into the United States, Canada, Japan or Australia.

The Offer is not being made, directly or indirectly, in or into the United States, Canada, Japan or Australia and neither this Form of Acceptance nor the Offer Document are being mailed or otherwise distributed or sent in, into or from the United States, Canada, Australia or Japan and persons receiving this document (including custodians, nominees and trustees) must not distribute or send them in, into or from the United States, Canada, Australia or Japan. Doing so may invalidate any purported acceptance of the Offer. Further details relating to Overseas Shareholders are contained in paragraph 6 of Part B of Part IV of the Offer Document.

# Form of Acceptance, and Authority

## Recommended Offer

by

## Ipswich Town plc

for

## Ipswich Town Football Club Company Limited

Acceptances of the Offer should be despatched as soon as possible, and in any event, so as to be received by 3.00 p.m. on 15 September 2003

---

### ACTION TO BE TAKEN TO ACCEPT THE OFFER

- To accept the Offer, complete this Form on page 3 by following the instructions and notes for guidance set out on pages 2 and 4.
- Return this Form, duly completed and signed and accompanied by your share certificate(s) and/or other document(s) of title by post or by hand during normal business hours to Capita IRG Plc Corporate Actions Department, The Registry, 34 Beckenham Road, Beckenham, Kent BR3 4TH, **as soon as possible** but, in any event, so as to **arrive no later than 3.00 p.m. on 15 September 2003**. A first class reply-paid envelope for use only in the UK is enclosed for documents to be lodged by post.
- You should complete a separate Form of Acceptance for each different designation under which ITFC Shares are held. You can obtain further Forms of Acceptance by contacting Capita IRG Plc (telephone: 0870-162-3100)
- If your share certificate(s) and/or the document(s) of title are with your bank, stockbroker or other agent, you should complete and sign this Form and arrange for it to be lodged by such agent with the relevant document(s).
- **Please read Parts A, B and C of Part IV of the Offer Document, the terms of which are incorporated in and form part of this Form.**
- If you hold ITFC Shares jointly with others, you must arrange for all your co-holders to sign this Form.
- A Form which is received contained in an envelope postmarked in the United States, Canada, Australia or Japan or otherwise appearing to PLC or its agents to have been sent from the United States, Canada, Australia or Japan will not constitute a valid acceptance of this Offer.

If you have any questions as to how to complete this Form, please contact Capita IRG Plc (telephone: 0870-162-3100)

*The share offer we instigated in September 2003 to raise funds for Ipswich Town after the financial disaster of relegation in 2002*

*Wolves v Ipswich Town: feeling disconsolate after a defeat. You can't win them all*

*Father and son: Tom is an avid Tractor Boy to this day*

*Shefki Kuqi doing his trademark swallow dive after opening the scoring in a 1-1 draw at Elland Road in April 2005, with Pablo Couñago in the background*

# Wealth divide close to breaking point

**TALKINGFOOTBALL**

**DAVID SHEEPSHANKS**

Premier League were offering us 20 per cent of the combined total of Premier League and Football League broadcasting deals. Of the 72 clubs, all but one had voted to pursue talks with the Premier League. It was a decision that was made with the best intentions but one that will go down in history as one of the worst decisions in football history. The chance to reconnect the Premier League to life below may never come again.

With the encouragement of others, I led

*One of the several articles I wrote for* Daily Telegraph *'Sport' in the late 90s/early 2000s*

*Walking pitchside pre-match at Portman Road, with director of comms (and later CEO of the community trust) Terry Baxter behind me, September 2006*

*A memorable tribute to Sir Bobby Robson at the BBC's Sports Personality of the Year in December 2007. The great man is surrounded by Sir Alex Ferguson, Gary Lineker and so many of his Ipswich, England and Newcastle players. I felt humbled to be invited to join them*

*The great man is given a hero's welcome on returning to Portman Road in May 2008*

was my fault, as he had wanted Unsworth to be available! Even so, minus David Unsworth, we went to Upton Park full of optimism.

As it turned out, West Ham were brilliant in the first half and went two-up in 13 minutes. Jason de Vos had a tough afternoon, and it felt as if we were on the ropes. Nigel Rennie (a superb referee) had a game to forget as well – pleasing neither manager! However, we were nothing if not resilient, and we bounced back through an own goal, before Shefki equalised for 2-2. So it was on to Portman Road for the second leg, with honours even and our tails up.

Surely we could make it this time. I was so utterly desperate for us to make it, if possible more than ever before. Given what had happened after getting relegated three years earlier, this felt like the time to restore some honour and also reset the club's finances. And if we were promoted, those that had lost money in administration would have got a welcome dividend. We had blown what looked like automatic promotion only weeks earlier. So now ... please ... come on guys!

There were over 30,000 of us crammed into Portman Road the following Wednesday. Pablo Couñago was out injured, and Joe made two changes with Drissa Diallo and Kevin Horlock dropping to the bench for Darren Currie and Matt Richards. The first half was tight and nervy. But after the break and with everything still to play for, Marlon Harewood tore past Matt down our left side and crossed for Bobby Zamora to tap in. Ten minutes later the two of them combined again, and with exactly the same result. So 2-0 to West Ham, and we were out. Again.

## A silver lining

There was one piece of silver (or *silverware*) lining to the cloud of the play-off failure: we won the 2005 FA Youth Cup, beating Southampton with a last-minute goal at Portman Road in front of a crowd of nearly 15,000. The match was over two legs – we had drawn 2-2 away to a team that included Gareth Bale, David McGoldrick (later to play for us), Theo Walcott and Adam Lallana. Our own star

Owen Garvan was out ill, but 15-year-old Ed Upson came off the bench to score a rocket that won it for us at the end of extra time. Lots of people in that side went on to play for our first team, notably keeper Shane Supple, Danny Haynes, Liam Trotter, Garvan and Billy Clarke, who was also out injured. I was really thrilled for all the staff at the academy, Bryan Klug in particular. This was a triumph against all the odds, and one that was achieved with far less resources than Southampton had at the time.

Staying on a theme of youth development, around then we also set up a community outreach programme by establishing partnerships in Newmarket (with the horse-racing school) and in Oulton Broad (for sailing). As with our football centre at Portman Road, local schools were invited to identify the children who might be 'lost' in some way, and maybe struggling for self-esteem or a sense of identity, and we would take them into after-school classes once or twice a week. Those would include play sessions and coaching in football, riding or sailing, according to the location. It was a huge success and quickly became fully subscribed, with many teachers and parents telling us what a difference it had made to their children's self-confidence and inner happiness.

Right from when I used to charge around the country calling on customers in my food business days, I have always enjoyed visiting our peers. That was especially true when it came to community schemes run by other clubs, something that is now widespread (and is regularly featured on *Match of the Day*), but which was then in its infancy. So a small group of us spent a fascinating day visiting the Tottenham Hotspur Community set-up. The people there saw themselves as builders of the future, forging partnerships with ethnic associations and other local groups – in government, education and law enforcement. What the Spurs people were pushing for was more accessibility, affordable ticketing, support to ensure girls and racial minorities felt included, visibility and interaction with the players, and a culture that was lived by everybody at the club, from top to bottom. Just the kind of thing we were trying to do at Portman Road.

In the summer of 2005 I was very chuffed to be made a deputy lieutenant of Suffolk (as indeed I remain today). It really meant a lot to me, as it's the most special of counties, a place without pretentiousness, with no airs and graces, and people who are almost universally friendly. We have less rain, more sun and the best football team in the land!

As a result of that appointment, I took on a few local roles, such as becoming patron of Ipswich and East Suffolk Samaritans, and president of Citizens Advice Ipswich – both roles I have been proud to carry out for 20 years now. And as a deputy lieutenant, I also represent Felixstowe at important civic events in the county, such as Remembrance Sunday.

The previous year I had received recognition for services to the community from an unexpected source, when I was given an honorary doctorate by the University of East Anglia. I actually only accepted after a lot of soul-searching, and had initially declined the award as it might not have felt quite right coming so soon after all the ills that had befallen us, and our creditors, at Ipswich Town.

## Chapter 28
# 2005/06: Living Within Our Means

SO WE had been condemned to another year of scratching and scraping our way to having anything like a competitive team. That meant we would again be forced to sell some of our top players, people we really liked – both on and off the pitch – like dear Shefki (who ended up at Blackburn) and our own Darren Bent. To make things worse, Darren's agents were Jonathan Barnett and David Manasseh, who had already proved quite a handful when Richard Wright went to Arsenal a few years earlier.

Football agents come in for a lot of bad press, and that is sometimes justified as they can have a disruptive effect on key players. However, I have always found that you ignore them at your peril, and it's far better to try to work with them. They are a fact of life and can sometimes actually be a stabilising influence, strange as it may seem. If you treat your players right, as we always tried to, then their agents see that and help keep their clients' feet on the ground. Much like business generally, it's a matter of respecting each other's position and interests, and keeping good communication channels open. If something really has to be said, or a tough decision made, then I liked to adopt an approach known as 'radical candour'.

That is actually the title of a great leadership book about the importance of honesty and being straight with people. The extremes either way just don't work – 'obnoxious aggression' and 'ruinous empathy' as the author (Kim Scott) calls them. Now that I am a leadership coach, I regularly have to explain to people that they are not doing anybody any favours by beating around the bush or prevaricating.

This new season was clearly going to test me and all of us at ITFC. It was a constant and continual struggle to improve the club's financial outlook.

I had a difficult meeting with Joe about players and what we could afford. So Darren Bent duly went to Charlton for £3m (ugh! ... not again ... they were rapidly becoming the ITFC old boys). I remember Richard Murray, their chairman, ringing a few years earlier when we were relegated and confiding in me that if it had been them, they would have been in the same boat we were – which was scant comfort at the time. Kelvin Davis went to Southampton for £1.25m. I hated selling him too, he was a good man and a top keeper. And then Tommy Miller, Pablo, Drissa Diallo and Jimmy Juan all left on free transfers (with no buyers to be found), as well as several younger players. It was another major purge to give us at least some room for manoeuvre.

In came Sam Parkin, a highly rated striker from Swindon for £500k (a big investment for us in those days, but he got injured early on and never really did it for us), Nicky Forster on a free from Reading (who did well) and midfielder Gavin Williams for £300k from West Ham. And then there was a diminutive (and delightful) full-back from Spain's Liga 2 named Luis Castro Rodríguez, who was always known as 'Sito'. We also recruited a young Canadian winger, Jaime Peters, who had potential. To this we added home-grown youngsters from the academy – Danny Haynes, Billy Clarke, Owen Garvan and Liam Craig, all aged 17 or 18.

It wasn't quite like for like. The new faces I felt would, at least, make us competitive, but it certainly didn't feel like a squad that would be challenging for promotion. Still, with the Premier League parachute money now expired, we simply didn't have the financial muscle.

So our focus off the pitch very much remained on money, and how to generate more resources.

## Looking for development opportunities

We formed an investment committee to look at any possible opportunities, wherever in the world they might lie. One of the possible money-spinning options that was coming to prominence for clubs like ours at that time was pairing with a casino, the gaming business then being viewed ripe for expansion in Britain. It was an option we looked at seriously enough for me (together with my opposite numbers at Watford and Gillingham) to be invited over to Las Vegas as personal guests of legendary gambling mogul Sheldon Adelson. And he certainly meant business, as all three of us were given the high-roller treatment together with massive suites on the top floor of the Venetian hotel. When I walked in I had to ask why there were so many scantily clad women all over the building. Imagine my surprise when I was told that they were hosting the world's largest pornography convention!

Back home, Holly Bellingham, who ran a very successful medical liability insurance group, had already joined us and it was a nice two-for-one deal, as her husband – and business partner – Simon Turner was just as keen on the club as she was. We came up with interest-bearing loan notes as the best way to raise funds, and both Holly and Peter Cohen invested significant sums in them, as did several other supporters. By then we had built several larger executive boxes in the Britannia Stand (we had a major deal with the Britannia Building Society at the time, now it's back to being the West Stand). Big supporters Kevin Britton and his wife Jacqui, as well as Rodney Brody, were among those who helped us out by taking out long-term contracts on the new boxes.

Club CEO Derek Bowden was doing a tremendous job working on our finances. As part of that effort, he and I met with James Hehir, the Ipswich Borough Council CEO (and thus our landlord), to discuss the possibility of developing part of the practice pitch, maybe with a five-storey mixed development and perhaps a small hotel. James – who died in 2009, aged just 61– was a very forward-looking leader, and he was clearly interested, as he could see the potential upside for both the club and the town.

Derek, finance director Anna Hughes and I also met with Michael Anderson, who had contacted us with a view to investing. He had made money in the pharma industry in the US, and previously had some involvement with Crystal Palace. But there was something Derek and I both felt uncomfortable about. In return for a seat on the board, he wanted to invest through both cash and loan notes. These were significant six-figures sums that were certainly not an amount to be sniffed at back then. He actually transferred the first part to us; however, after further investigation, we as a board unanimously decided not to accept his money, and we returned the funds. I think we got that right.

Some time later I found out Anderson had invested in Gillingham in support of Paul Scally, a relationship that endured for several years. It's a matter of public record that Michael later successfully fought extradition to the US.

In the spring of 2006 some of the trustees began to ask who actually governed the ITFC Community Trust. Was it them as trustees, or the club itself? The perception was that the club still saw the trust as a department of the club. I agreed that we needed to address that; however, it did feel like a bit of a power grab by one or two of them, as clearly the trust wouldn't have come into existence without the club. It meant the two organisations had to liaise very closely. I had unfortunately created the problem by having so many independent trustees appointed, which was a mistake ... Or was it!? This all resurfaced in a more strident fashion when Marcus Evans acquired the club, and would lead to a major rift, at which point the number of independent trustees became a major plus, as it prevented Marcus from controlling the charity. In the end they reached an impasse, and depressingly he eventually closed the club's community arm. The trustees left and created a new charity called Inspire Suffolk. This whole affair, which happened after I was no longer at the club, was such a crying shame.

Budgeting for the following season involved forecasting attendance levels. The leadership team went for a prudent 22,500 average gate, but new ticket office manager John Ford said it would be 24,300. It actually turned out to be 24,251, so full marks to him!

We were helped in all this when, in October 2005, David Rose returned in a part-time matchday capacity, having retired as club secretary after an astonishing 40 years with us. He had started off back in 1958, at a time when Alf Ramsey had been combining the role of secretary with managing the team. You will find that the board meetings of that era were written in David's elegant longhand script! We had given David a testimonial dinner the year before when, although Bobby Robson couldn't attend, we had World Cup winner Alan Ball and also Ken Friar as our special guests. Ken is a legendary figure at Arsenal, where he was once chief executive, and where – despite being in his 90s – he still turns out as a matchday boardroom host.

There was a lot to do in the close season, and our agenda in summer 2005 included a general redecoration of the academy offices, investment in IT, new gym equipment and new floodlights for the pitches at Bent Lane and the Playford Road academy.

We also had a big review at the academy, to work out how we could build on the FA Youth Cup win. The decision was made to concentrate our attention on the U14s and U15s, to keep away from the media and to close our satellite in Brentwood so as to focus more on Suffolk. We also decided to create a surgery, much like the ones that MPs run, for parents of academy players to discuss their hopes and fears about their sons' welfare, development and progress, or lack of it.

I had a not-dissimilar session with Joe, where we came up with the 'Time for Generals' programme. We wanted to emphasise how we would build on strengths and work on our weaknesses, how we could challenge underperformance, work out what we had learnt and what we could do better. It really taught me a lot, including things I still put into practice in my work as a career coach.

In July, we had our annual barbeque party at Glemham Hall (the Cobbold family home, which as I write has recently been put up for sale). Absolutely everybody at the club was invited – together with their partners – as well as people from the supporters' club, media, local government and commercial backers. There were over 200 of us, and we always had a steel band. It was a great way to get everyone together, and it was nice to see just how good the players were at mixing. When I heard the event had been stopped a few years later, it felt symbolic of the club beginning to lose its heart and soul.

Also that summer we had two more concerts at Portman Road promoted by Stuart Galbraith, including Neil Diamond (who I love, and was fantastic). REM came a month later, with The Zutons and Idlewild supporting them. Neither was a sellout, but they were great nights.

The sad thing was that nowhere in sight was there an Ed Sheeran. We continued to cast high and low in search of new investors – including in the US; however, the Americans hadn't yet acquired the appetite for English football they have now.

In January 2006 we just about scraped £150k together to sign Alan Lee from Cardiff. He was a No.9-style big striker who had caused us lots of problems when he was playing for Rotherham. Joe was keen on him and it felt a very good deal. Prozone analysis described him as being 'in his prime at 27. Big Strong. Goalscorer.' That would do nicely, so we gave him a two-and-a-half-year contract, and it turned out to be a super signing. He scored 34 goals in 109 appearances – the only blot on his copybook was that after we sold him to Palace he went on loan to Norwich! In 2013 he came back to join our academy coaching staff, still lives in the area to this day and is now a fully inducted Tractor Boy.

My other memory of Alan is from an end-of-season dinner, when I had to join him on stage to sing 'Wonderwall'. I am a big music fan (my bath/car performances are much enjoyed – by an audience of one!); however, Oasis are not really on my list, so I had to ad lib badly to keep up.

Meanwhile, back at Portman Road, the season was coming to a very disappointing end. You have probably already worked out that it was a rather forgettable season, as most of this chapter has not been about anything on the pitch. Anyway, we limped over the line, with five of the last six games ending in defeat, to finish 15th.

### A very hard call – end of the Royle era

Joe Royle, who I still think the world of, appeared to have lost the 'fire in his belly'. It was evident in all sorts of ways. He used to make veiled criticisms of the board, and he was open in his opposition to investment in the academy (a minimal outlay in the broader scheme of things, and one that was vital for our future). It felt a bit like a mini blame game – all of which could have been overlooked, but the bigger issue was that a plan for the future was missing.

I met with the entire board, and there was a reluctant unanimity that it was time for change. Everyone liked Joe and respected him enormously; however, our new financial realities meant that we had to look for skills commensurate with our status.

In truth, Joe was a fabulous, top-class manager, but he could only really deliver if he was allowed to work his undeniable magic in the transfer market. He had charmed and cajoled, inspired and kidded to get the best out of players. However, in the end the body language simply didn't lie. We all knew that money was tight and that the relegation parachute fund was over. It was now a different kind of game we were playing. Joe once said that in the end he was 'juggling dust'. We had to get the best out of what we had, and down in the bargain basement there was precious little scope for Joe's expert wheeling and dealing. He knew that, and he knew that I knew that. Sad as it was, our time together was coming to a natural end.

Joe and I met for lunch in a pub near the docks, the day before he went back home to Ormskirk for the summer. As we sat there, we went all around the houses talking about the disappointment of the season, but somehow I couldn't manage to pull the trigger. I was guilty of 'ruinous empathy'.

He left and I went home, thoroughly disgruntled with myself for fudging it. So I rang him later that evening and said I thought we had some unfinished business. I suggested meeting him halfway between us at Crewe. We both knew the deal …

I caught the early train to London and then up to Crewe, where we had arranged to meet in a small restaurant I knew across from the station. Having travelled all over the country for so many years for both football and my food businesses, there was hardly a large town or city that I didn't know my way around.

Joe was sitting there waiting for me, and we went through the motions of having lunch. I said that I hadn't been entirely candid in the conversation the day before and that I felt we had reached the end of the road together. He knew. We finished on a few 'what might have beens', none more so than the consecutive play-off defeats and Shefki's injury (when we had been running away with the league). I knew we would have done really well under Joe in the Premier League, but it was simply not to be.

We walked back to the station and he came with me to my platform. The train came in and we hugged and blubbed. I mean real tears. Both of us are emotional men, and we have genuine warmth and affection for each other. Just as well there were no camera phones or social media in those days!

Joe (together with his wonderful family) and I are still close to this day, and I often reflect on what would have happened had we been promoted, as we should have been, and how well he would have handled the big transfer budgets and operated in the top flight.

**Jim wows the room!**

The phone started ringing just as soon as I got home from Crewe. Agents and managers galore were calling and writing to put themselves forward. The board agreed that Derek Bowden and I should interview a longlist of candidates, and that we would then whittle it down to a shortlist of three for the whole board to meet and interview.

I sought out the opinions of various people in the game I was close to, including David Dein, vice-chair at Arsenal (we had sat on the FA Board together for many years), Graham Taylor (ex-England manager, and a wise man), FA technical director Trevor Brooking, leading journalist Henry Winter, Terry Robinson (another stalwart of the League and FA whom I had grown to respect greatly), and legendary commentator John 'Motty' Motson, another dear friend (and secretly an Ipswich fan, though I think he also supported Barnet and his son's team Derby, among others).

I also consulted Bobby Robson, when I rang him to ask if he would consider becoming ITFC president, which he was delighted to accept.

I made a longlist of possible candidates including Tony Pulis, Mick McCarthy, Colin Calderwood, Ian Holloway, Nigel Pearson, Martin O'Neill, Terry Butcher, Frank Yallop, Tony Mowbray, Phil Parkinson, Avram Grant, Martin Allen, Eric Black and Laurie Sanchez, not all of whom were available or interested.

For the sake of privacy, we did the first interviews at my home. But two of those who ended up on the shortlist became a matter of public record: Jim Magilton and Nigel Pearson.

Nigel, who was obviously the more experienced of the two, interviewed brilliantly. We got on really well, and he was very calm and articulate, thoughtful and well reasoned about his approach and plans. At the same time, he was desperately keen to get the role and to do well for us. While I couldn't discount others, I have to admit that after I met Nigel I was convinced that we had found our next manager.

Jim, who was conscious of his lack of track record, had at the outset asked me, 'If I apply, will you take my application seriously?' and went on to explain that he had never been so serious about anything. That was a mark of his passion, and it came as no surprise to see him coming across as a charismatic and infectious leader. What was more remarkable was his masterful grasp of everything that needed to be done to turn us back into being a force again. He wanted to bring in Bryan Klug as first-team coach, and Steve Foley, as well as Jonny Bickers (who now does data work in Aussie Rules) as performance analyst. So they had some important bases covered.

When it came to the second round of interviews, our director Roger Finbow kindly allowed us to use his legal offices at Ashurst in the City. It was easy walking distance from Liverpool Street station – and away from prying eyes.

We were now a large board of ten, including Holly Bellingham and Peter Cohen, the CEO of PHS Cleaning Services, which had twice been sold to investors and bought back again. That gave Peter, who is a delightful man and massive Town fan, the capital to put into the club.

The first candidate to attend will remain anonymous. He was very good and accounted for himself well. As it happened he had been offered another job that very day (which he had told me about, but we both decided he should still come).

We allocated an hour for each of them, and the second to appear was Jim Magilton, along with Bryan and Jonny, who operated the slides. The candidates were asked to make a ten to 15-minute presentation of how they would go about the job, before taking questions from the directors and asking any of their own.

Jim absolutely wowed everyone in the room. It felt as if there was an electric charge hanging in the air as he left. And from that point on, it was basically his job to lose.

So although Nigel presented very well and professionally, and everyone knew he was an excellent candidate, they had already made their minds up. The mood cooled rather, and it didn't matter how well he made his points, they just fell flat. I felt incredibly sorry for him.

When he left, the directors all turned to me saying, 'Well, there's really only one candidate,' almost suggesting there had been no need to bring the others! They did, however, state very firmly that they thought it would only work if I stayed very close to Jim as a mentor.

If there is a lesson to be found from the whole experience, it was this: always interview someone twice, and ideally away from your office. I have found that in most jobs it's skill that is the prerequisite, but you don't always learn much about that in the first interview. It's the person we want to know about – their ambitions, character, values, temperament, resilience under pressure, sense of humour, what they think about certain things, and what they do and don't tolerate. Above all, you have to work out how likeable they are. Will they fit in with our culture here? The trick, I have found, is to use deep-dive, open questions.

Later that day, I had the sad duty of having to ring the unsuccessful candidates. Disappointed as he was, Nigel was the perfect gentleman that he has always been. He is one of the managers I have admired the most over the years.

The much happier duty was to make a call that began, 'Jim, you know I promised you that if you applied, I would ensure it would be taken seriously. Well, guess what, you've won!'

He was ecstatic!

# Chapter 29
# 2006/07: Jim's First Year – Learning on the Job

THERE WAS a huge amount for Jim to do. Not the least of which was setting out the ground rules as to how we were going to work together. I was very clear that I would in no way want to interfere with player selection, training, etc., but I was going to be visible at the training ground and we were to have a weekly one-to-one meeting – just me and him.

But the first thing on Jim's list was to tell me that he was going to hang up his boots, at least in terms of turning out for the first team. That felt right, as he really couldn't expect to play at the top level, and manage too. The next thing was to review the player/football budget, and try to make the best of the limited room for manoeuvre he would have to work in. And alongside that was the player and staff bonus scheme.

Jim told us he wanted to focus on performance, and came out with a great line: 'Some people grin and bear it. Others smile and change it.' He had this way of saying things like that, in his animated Irish accent. He also asked whether he could retain Watt Nicoll as an advisor/mentor to help him. Watt is certainly an interesting character. Formerly a folk singer of some renown, he had restyled himself as a motivational guru. I was slightly dubious, I have to say – but it can be lonely at the top, especially when you are new to a big role, hence the value of a personal coach, which is what I have been working as for the last ten years. And that was why Jim had chosen Watt.

To be effective, it has to be someone independent of your authority, whether in the office or at home. The consequence is that they are non-judgemental, and are not weighed down by conflicts of interest, meaning they can be someone you can trust with your inner fears or concerns. So I went with it.

**Exploring the options**

We had another pop concert on 3 July 2006, with Rod Stewart supported by The Pretenders. It was the third time Rod (a former Brentford triallist, and a massive footie fan, of course) had played Portman Road and, as ever, he was fantastic.

Back in the early 90s he had done consecutive nights backed by Joe Cocker and Status Quo. That was quite a billing, and it's hard to believe that neither sold out. In fact, I seem to recall that on that occasion Ipswich Borough Council had underwritten part of the risk with the promoter, and had to give away/heavily subsidise nearly 10,000 tickets on the second evening. But we were certainly trendsetters in giving the people of Suffolk some great nights out.

At the beginning of August we were approached by local property developer Mike Rockall after an introduction by Stephen Fletcher, who had run Bidwells in Martlesham for many years. Mike wanted to build us a new stadium outside town, not far from the A12/A14 intersection. Of course, that would have been heresy for most fans; however, I was of the firm view that we needed to examine everything before rejecting it. That would clearly have been dynamite news, so we kept the whole thing tightly under wraps.

Firstly, any such move would enable us to completely refinance the club. Owning the freehold would mean we could attract investors, significantly reduce debt and build new academy and first-team training grounds, as well as generating new opportunities (such as putting up residential and/or commercial space around the stadium). We were looking at a 2011/2012 build, which would include the creation of a new railway station. But we would need to put together a long-term project and think in terms of a 50-year masterplan for the club. It all sounded very attractive. However, I had major reservations as to the feasibility of it all and, even if it was a goer, whether Mike was the right partner.

In particular, we would have to be really convinced by – and invested in – our partners, including Mike, and their ability to deliver. We agreed to continue to investigate the possibilities and to research more on what other clubs had done, or were doing, Spurs and Southampton, for example.

While it was a huge opportunity, Derek and I became increasingly cautious on three grounds: firstly, timing was poor and public support fragile; secondly, Norwich Union would have had to be brought in – and we were doubtful that would happen; and thirdly, to take it to the next stage, we needed much more than a 'deal in principle', which is what Mike was offering at that point.

So for the sake of prudence, we poured cold water on the idea, though without entirely dismissing it.

Other stadium issues were also to the fore around that time. When I met with Watt Nicoll he told me in no uncertain terms that the first-team dressing rooms were 'stale, sterile and not conducive to high performance' and that the 'corridor was like an entrance to a morgue'. He was quite right, unfortunately. We had forgotten about it and let it drift. It just hadn't been a priority. So we arranged for redecoration and some motivational pictures, etc.

Watt also had a line I very much liked: 'Be careful that the toes you step on today are not attached to legs that support the arse you may have to kiss tomorrow!'

Meanwhile, Derek, Anna and I called a meeting of the directors to discuss our refinancing efforts. We explained that the club needed a minimum of five – and preferably ten – million pounds to relieve debt and add to the player budget. I said that if we couldn't find a suitable individual, then we would have to create a consortium of investors who could one day become the owners. That all sounds sensible, of course, but back then there were simply not enough supporters with significant financial muscle to actually make it happen.

So we looked at the possibility of selling shares (the club, albeit very undercapitalised, was at least stable and viable by then), and considered how we could leverage the value of the Playford Road training ground. We made it clear that the land itself was definitely not for sale, but it would be a valuable asset when it came to attracting future buyers or investors.

In the weeks going into 2007 I put my address book to work, and must have made over a hundred calls to every HNW (high net worth) and UNHW (ultra-high net worth) individual that we could come up with. They were people in Suffolk, Essex, London and further afield. Wherever we had to go and whatever we had to do. We needed that investment.

Getting Holly Bellingham on our board had been a seminal moment for the club, and an immense statement considering how things had always been up till then. Let's not forget that women hadn't even been allowed in most boardrooms just a few years earlier, although some teams did lay on a 'ladies room'. There had already been trailblazers such as Rachael Heyhoe Flint (the former England cricket captain, who was at Wolves) and Karren Brady (first at Birmingham and then West Ham), but when our finance director Anna Hughes also joined the ITFC board, that made us the first club to have two female directors.

And we had another woman in a senior position in Sally Webb, who was now really established as club secretary. So that was a great personal satisfaction. I have always tried to get as many women as possible sitting at the high table and involved in the decision-making process. And I simply cannot understand companies that don't.

At around that point, David Rose retired again after doing a stint supporting Sally, and in his honour I should recount the episode when David was asked by an unhappy senior player why he had been dropped to the reserves. 'Well,' replied David with characteristic wit, 'I expect it is because we don't have a third team.' I was honoured to be asked to give the funeral eulogy for David in September 2024, and included that story. He was a very special, but also a very modest, man who was an oracle on all things Ipswich to those of us who served on the board. We had been very lucky to have him, and we all treasure his memory.

## Jon Walters – a bright spot

We got a string of good results in August and September of the new season, but they were sandwiched on either side by three straight defeats – including a 5-1 home drubbing by Nigel Pearson's WBA. And the season went on a bit like that. During the January transfer window Jim told me he wanted a right-back and had identified David Wright at Wigan, who he thought we could get inexpensively. He was also looking at getting Mark Noble on loan from West Ham, which came through, but David Norris at Plymouth turned out to be too expensive for us at the time, as was David Healy, an Ulsterman like Jim (and Northern Ireland's all-time leading goalscorer). There was also the intriguing possibility that we could re-sign crowd favourite Pablo Couñago, which eventually we did. On the way out would be Darren Currie, Dean Bowditch, Jaime Peters, Sito and Scott Barron.

The first weekend in January is synonymous with the FA Cup third round, and that year we had been handed a potentially tricky away tie with Chester City. It was a lovely crisp and sunny day, made even brighter by coming across Larry Carberry outside the ground, along with his son and grandson, all supporting us. A Liverpudlian full-back, Larry had played in Alf Ramsey's 1961/62 league-winning team. A charming man and real gentleman, he always tried to come down to our players' reunion dinners.

We huffed and puffed our way through a 0-0 draw, a great result for Chester (captained that day by Roberto Martínez, later the Everton and Belgium manager), and one that earned them a replay and a valuable share of gate receipts to look forward to at Portman Road. The thing that really stood out from that day, however, was the performance of Chester's centre-forward, one Jonathan Walters. Although he didn't score, he absolutely ran his socks off, and looked a cut above the rest.

We did some research. Supposedly Jon had had some problems off the pitch early in his career at Blackburn, and then at Bolton, while still being very highly rated. From 2003 he spent four years or so drifting through moves to Hull, Crewe, Barnsley, Hull again and then Scunthorpe and Wrexham, before ending up at Chester – for whom he had scored nine goals in 26 games.

What we were hearing was that Jon was the real deal, a pedigree player who would thrive in the right environment and with good coaching support. He played well again in the replay (won by a single Matt Richards goal). Jim Magilton liked him. So did Bryan Klug, and also chief scout Steve McCall. We desperately needed a striker, and Jon was a bit different as he could play wide as well. After talking through what we could stretch to, I walked out to bat to see what deal we could come up with. Chester were very short of money and their directors had told my colleague Roger Finbow how desperate they were at the Portman Road replay. In the end I managed to agree £100k fee plus £50k based on appearances, £50k on promotion, plus 20 per cent of any profit we made selling him on. We were delighted.

It was a gem of a deal, and Jon gave us his all from day one! He would become a star player, scoring 32 goals in 146 games between 2007 and 2010 (when he got on the wrong side of a certain Roy Keane!). He went on to score another 43 goals for Stoke in 226 Premier League games, and 14 for Ireland. All in all, not a bad spot for £100,000! Well done to him, he is a thoroughly nice guy who I was lucky enough to meet again when he was standing for the PFA, where he worked before becoming sporting director at Stoke. I wish him only the best.

However, February 2007 left further relegation as a distinct possibility after one of the worst months in club history: we didn't score once, lost all four league games and went down at Watford in the FA Cup fifth round. It wasn't the best backdrop to the meeting that Derek, Anna and I had with Alex Musson of Riverhill Partners, who we had engaged to help us pull funding together. We looked at firms such as Seymour Pierce and Panmure Gordon, and various hedge funds, including Och-Ziff, while there was also an American investor mentioned (Andy Appleby, who later bought into Derby County). It was concluded that we should reconvene once Riverhill had met with Norwich Union.

At the academy, we agreed to draw up 'The Ipswich Town Way' showing our values, which would be used as a screensaver and put on posters around the building. We also decided to assemble the best examples of persistence leading to eventual triumph. It's funny to reflect that we were talking very much the same language that the club is using again now with 'Run Toward Adversity' from the Arizona Public Safety Personnel Retirement System (as I write, still part of a now wider investment group in the US-led club ownership structure). That is just my kind of approach, and an example of 'culture eats strategy for breakfast'-type leadership. Of course, strategy is important but it's a waste of time if you try to activate it on shaky foundations. In other words, if you haven't got the right people in the right places, and they haven't bought into the culture, then you are building on shifting sands.

We were also determined to introduce high-tech video analysis. This is less than 20 years ago we are talking about, but it already seems extraordinary to say that now.

Fortunately we managed to turn things around in the league and prevent any last-minute scrambles to avoid the drop, and a one-all draw at Carrow Road helped ensure we would at least finish ahead of Norwich. The same score in the next game sent Leeds down, with the players forced to leave the pitch towards the close because of a pitch invasion, before being brought back on for the final minute. We ended in 14th.

Still, seven wins in the last 12 fixtures meant we could at least see some green shoots appearing.

## Robin Sheepshanks RIP

However, the end of the season was overshadowed for me by the death of my father on 25 April. The previous evening all my direct family had got together to have a drink with him – my mother, brothers, Mona, and also Rick's wife Anni. He was up and dressed, but very frail, being at an advanced stage of bone marrow cancer, or myeloma. I had driven him and my mother to his old school reunion at Eton three days earlier, and you could tell he had kept himself going for it. That particular evening he was very gentle and loving towards everyone – not descriptions we would normally have associated with him, although he was always a very kind man. I think we all feared the worst, not least because the two years he had been given to live in 2005 had already expired. I hummed and hawed about going to London for an FA Board meeting the following day, but the Macmillan nurse assured me he would most likely be with us for a little while yet. The next morning I caught the early train, but as I got to Wembley I had a quite extraordinary sense of foreboding that something had happened or was going to happen. The meeting started, and about an hour and a half in, my phone rang. It was Rick.

Papa had had a stroke that morning. So I made my apologies and ran for the train, getting there around 4pm. He was conscious, but had lost his gag reflex, and the horrible sounds that condition creates can be very disconcerting. The family had been around him all day, so they left me to lie on the bed and talk to him. He was fully conscious but struggling. I told him I loved him and what a wonderful father he had been. I think he heard me, but he didn't *do* fuss. These were things you couldn't really say to him, the upright, stiff upper lip, military man that he was. But he was as caring as he was principled.

After an hour or so I went home, a five-minute walk away, to get changed. Believing all was stable, my brothers came with me, and we talked about preparing ourselves for the worst. Suddenly we got a call, and they rushed back ahead of me and Mona. I got there five minutes later and he had just died.

I had always dreaded his death, but I knew I had to hold it together. He'd had such a profound influence on all our lives. I was devoted to him and admired him greatly. I was even said to look a lot like him.

I equally always dreaded seeing a dead body and never had until that moment. My mother and all the family were understandably in bits, yet somehow I couldn't cry. I often wonder whether I would have cried had I been there right at the last. His dying words were, 'I am so exhausted.' He was 81.

The remarkable thing is that, despite him leaving this world, I still continued to try to make my father proud, even well after he left us. A lot of people have told me they feel the same way about their parents after they have died.

My father died the same day as Alan Ball.

## Chapter 30
# 2007/08: Under New Ownership

DURING THE close season I had a crucial meeting with Bryan Klug, who I had worked closely with at the academy and who was now Jim Magilton's number two, to discuss coaching. He came up with a line I thought was so good that I wrote it down: 'There isn't a footballer at this club who doesn't believe that we cannot get better.'

We talked at length about how to embed *performance coaching* at the first-team level, and *development coaching* throughout the entire club, and came up with a programme. In a typical week, Monday to Wednesday would be taken with development, while Thursday to Saturday would be game preparation.

So, on 26 August 2007, I took my seat alongside nearly 20,000 others to watch our boys take on Crystal Palace. Sitting next to me in the directors' box was Jim Magilton, an arrangement we had decided upon as a way to keep him from putting the players under too much pressure. He had such high standards, and while there was plenty of encouragement, there were times when Jim just couldn't stop himself criticising them. A couple of times every game his blood would boil over, and I would have to tap him on the leg to cool him down. It probably came, at least in part, from having so recently having been down on the pitch himself – indeed, Jim continued to turn out with the reserves, where he felt his influence could help the younger players.

Jon Walters scored in the 72nd minute of the Palace game, which earned me an enormous bear hug from Jim. Owen Garvan, Jason de Vos, Alex Bruce and Jon himself were all immense, while Neil Alexander made a great save as we put in a tremendous defensive performance, meaning we hung on to keep the three points, and go top.

It was my 29th wedding anniversary, so the celebratory dinner tasted even better with the delicious Rioja brought over for me by Pablo Couñago's agent.

Away at Watford a few days later, I was proud to see our fans put on a great show, with an entire end of the ground heaving with blue and white. Watford had just been relegated, and the trip was a reminder of the riches that had flooded the top flight since we had left the promised land a few years earlier. They had staff running around all over the place, and everything about their new stand, tremendous hospitality and facilities all smacked of money.

We were greeted by their chairman Graham Simpson, who had become a friend over the years (and is now running Simpson Travel, who specialise in letting luxury villas in the Mediterranean) and CEO Mark Ashton – yes, the very same man who is now in charge at our beloved ITFC! Also present was the legendary John 'Motty' Motson, who was not known for hanging back when the wine was flowing.

These occasions are often revealing. That day we learnt that their wage bill was £13.5 million, which is a pittance today even for a relegated club, but was double ours at the time. Unfortunately, it showed. They had quality all over the pitch and I remember thinking that their massive Nigerian centre-half Danny Shittu looked as if he was fed on raw meat and ought to be playing American football! We conceded after just six minutes and went on to lose 2-0. They went top, and we slipped to fifth.

It was a similar situation a fortnight later at WBA, who were also still benefitting from Premier League parachute money. Just about the only good thing from the game, in which we squandered chances and lost 4-0, was hearing a story told by their director and former sports reporter, Jeff Farmer. Apparently, the then-chairman of Mansfield Town had once rung Johnny Cobbold to ask to buy a player, at the request of their manager and former Ipswich player Peter Morris. Patrick Cobbold was late for a meeting to discuss the deal, which had annoyed Johnny. So when the Mansfield chairman rang to talk, Johnny assumed it was a spoof by his brother, and let rip with a string of four-letter invectives. Whether or not the transfer went through, history doesn't relate.

We turned things round in the next match, against Coventry, where at half-time we paraded the Suffolk County Cricket Club players, who had just won the Minor County Championship. By then we were 3-0 up and cruising, running out 4-1 winners with a brace from the irrepressible Pablo Couñago. It had been an opportune game at which to host Inga Lockington, our Danish mayor, who inexplicably was later denied citizenship post-Brexit after having lived here for over 40 years.

The goalless draw against Barnsley was enlivened by the visit of the new bishop, who presented some awards and delighted my mother, who I had invited along specially. She loved bishops!

At the home game against Scunthorpe, which was to be the last before the change in ownership, we hosted legendary striker Ray Crawford, our first-ever England international. He won his caps in the early 60s, when he and Ted Phillips were scoring goals for fun to make us league champions under Sir Alf Ramsey. We won 3-2, with a late Tommy Miller goal moving us up to fifth in the table. Not bad for a team that was supposed to be skint and with a rookie manager.

### Searching for a buyer

Nevertheless, by 2007 we were increasingly coming to the realisation that if we were going to find a major investor who could transform the situation, then we would have to go public somehow and widen the net beyond the Ipswich family. We had tried everything over the previous few years, working through all our own contacts, with various finance groups and, of course, our wonderful fan base, many of whom had invested in support of the cause.

It seems extraordinary to be writing this in the current climate, where there are any number of big investors – especially foreign ones – who want to buy into a club like ours, sleeping giant that we were.

Yet, while we had received various expressions of interest, there was never anything substantive. So one day I called Henry Winter, at the time the senior football correspondent at the *Daily Telegraph*, and asked him whether he would consider writing an article on our situation, and fortunately he felt there was enough public interest to warrant it.

In August that year, a few days after publication, I received a call from a PR guru working for Marcus Evans. Whether Henry's article was actually the trigger for that I will never know, but Marcus had already been looking at a few clubs – with Southampton and Derby among them, I believe, and probably others besides.

We met at Marcus's office near Marble Arch, ironically in the same building that had previously housed the Premier League. It was a luxurious, top-floor set-up, unlike the lower floors, where he had installed rows of telesales girls and admin people running an empire that extended to over 50 offices and employed 3,000 staff around the world. Marcus had started out publishing trade magazines, and – in his own words – stumbled into hospitality when producing programmes for golf tournaments, where companies had some hospitality included with their adverts. He then acquired rights from numerous international tournaments that hadn't seen the full potential of the corporate entertainment market.

The Marcus I know is a very private man, and I have respected that, although it did seem a bit strange that the company should bear his name. He even had his own box at Portman Road, separate from where I and the other directors sat. But whereas an extreme aversion to being photographed may have saved him some harsh treatment from fans of all persuasions, it inevitably ended up piquing the interest of the media, who ultimately got hold of a shot of him. As I know only too well, running a football club is like living in a goldfish bowl, and it's very difficult to escape that.

Looking back on everything that happened, the local media were suggesting that we were in dire straits and had no option but to sell the club. That simply wasn't the case. Hard work and the great generosity of our fan base meant that the situation had been steadied, and in fact we were just about to announce a profit, so we could definitely keep going, albeit with little to no flexibility. We were saddled with significant long-term debt, and certainly didn't have any financial muscle. Even so, by December 2007 we were in a play-off place and going well with Jim Magilton at the helm.

The problem was that football was increasingly becoming a big-money game, and had we not done a deal with Marcus, living within our limited means would – over time – almost certainly have resulted in a weaker squad, and with it deteriorating results and unhappy supporters. We had spent five years looking for a major injection of capital, and there had been talks with a Thai consortium, research done for us by Riverhill Partners, and plenty of rumours about David Sullivan – who was exiting Birmingham City and would shortly buy into West Ham, where he is still the owner. But these investments just didn't materialise, leaving Marcus as the only serious game in town. We had explored every avenue, and we felt he was the best bet to take the club on in this costly new environment, in which we as directors simply couldn't compete. We would have far preferred to keep ploughing on, but we felt – as supporters and stewards – that we owed it to the fans to see the club recapitalised and refinanced to a level that it had never been before in its entire history. This was our rationale.

And we certainly did our homework. Although we didn't find a lot, the ITFC board undertook extensive due diligence once the seriousness of this new approach had been established. There was a lot of understandable speculation as to Marcus's background and motives for acquiring us, especially given that he was actually a Chelsea fan, and that his only link to Suffolk was that he had briefly owned a cottage in Walsham le Willows. What was on record was that the previous year Marcus had made a failed bid, worth over £750 million, as I recall, for the Trinity Mirror Group. He was also rumoured to have pledged a seven-figure sum to Nick Clegg's Liberal Democrats. Disturbingly, we gathered that he did not 'do corporate governance', no more than merely complying with the statutory number of board meetings. Evans was evidently a 'command and control'-type boss who didn't delegate much. So far it had clearly worked exceptionally well for him. But he called all the shots.

That was undoubtedly a concern. However, as our discussions continued, Marcus and I began to develop a relationship, even a good one, I would say, despite how different in style and outlook we clearly were.

There was much local speculation around the terms of the deal. The most important thing was that, after negotiating with Norwich Union and Barclays (our principal lenders), Marcus bought the debt, lock, stock and barrel, and our terms precluded him from ever selling the club with any liability for that debt, though he has rejected the widely held belief that there were considerable tax planning advantages to be derived from the transaction.

There were also those who thought it was all merely a vanity project. But Marcus is a businessman, and I believe he had sensed the potential profit in the deal, not least from getting a slice of what he believed – correctly as it turned out – would be a significant increase in the value of TV rights. The even bigger prize would, of course, have come with getting back into the Premier League, and his spending in support of his early managers is evidence of that.

However, what nobody could have foreseen was that the parachute payments for relegated teams would grow tenfold or more in just a few seasons, making it ever more difficult to compete against heavily funded yo-yo clubs. Which probably explains why he stopped investing. And although he continued to pay good wages, when key players were sold it was only a question of time before we ended up seeing the effects on the pitch, all of which led to our unbelievably depressing relegation to League One.

**Ironing out the details**
I managed to persuade Marcus that he would be best served by allowing the shareholders to retain their stake, and he generously

allowed us to structure the deal so that they retained 15 per cent of the company through the vehicle of Ipswich Town PLC (although he would effectively own about a third of those shares as well). I was determined that the people who had so selflessly come to our rescue in our hour of need a few years earlier would have the chance one day to earn a dividend on their shares, if – as we had to believe – the takeover would result in a boost to our fortunes on the pitch.

Little did we know that, despite significant investment on Marcus's part in the transfer market, and with the exception of one season when Mick McCarthy got us to the play-offs, the next few years would see a steady decline in our league fortunes. So, regrettably, no dividend ever resulted. Nevertheless, I still commend Marcus for allowing the supporters to retain a stake, as I remain of the view that it was the right thing to do.

Getting to that point, and ironing out the details of the deal, inevitably took a few months and countless discussions. Some of those were actually very technical, and I ended up having to learn legal terms such as 'drag and tag', which is a device to protect shareholder rights in the event of a buyout offer. Fellow director Roger Finbow was an enormous help, both with legal advice and facilitating use of Ashurst's Liverpool Street offices for meetings out of the public eye.

In late September, I visited Marcus at his lovely London home, and the following week our directors were invited to his offices. He was relaxed and created a very good impression. 'My heart is as much in this as it is in my entire business,' he told us. At lunch a day or two later, Marcus told me that he was easy to work with and that he would invest more if necessary. We also agreed that neither of us liked surprises.

Just such an unwanted surprise occurred in early November, when upon arrival at Bramall Lane for the Sheffield United game, I was greeted by Derek Davis of the *East Anglian Daily Times*. 'Can you confirm that David Sullivan has been thwarted in his attempt to make an offer for the club?' Derek asked. 'No,' I replied, and left it at that.

I rang our communications chief, Terry Baxter, to alert him there was bound to be a story in the next day's paper, and sure enough there was a piece about Sullivan. So I spent the morning on the phone calming Marcus, our directors and others.

A couple of days later, Richard Scudamore, by then CEO of the Premier League, came to stay (to support his team, Bristol City, who we beat 6-0!) and his account of the exponential growth in revenues reminded me of quite how much ITFC needed some serious money to get back on the big stage. The Premier League's initial £40 million turnover after breaking away in 1992, Richard explained, had become £140 million within five years, and by 2007 was up to nearly a billion pounds! We really were being left behind.

**A stressful few weeks**
The last few weeks before signing were full of angst, as I agonised over the deal. Had we weighed everything up? Is there anything we had missed? Could we get better terms by employing some brinkmanship? Were the loan note holders being properly treated? Above all, was it the right thing to do?

There was a bit more wrangling; for example, over the number of non-executive directors to be left on the board. Marcus wanted only one, and had proposed Kevin Beeston, a relative newcomer who had run Serco, among other companies, and had been incredibly helpful and supportive to me throughout the negotiations. That meant waving goodbye to Holly Bellingham and Peter Cohen, who had invested heavily, as well as Roger Finbow, Richard Moore, Philip Hope-Cobbold and others who had been the backbone of the board for many years. The carrot was that anybody who wanted to stay on as directors of the PLC could do so as, although owning just the rump of the club, the PLC would remain and give the shareholders something to treasure, even though it only equated to a net ten per cent of the capital. And we were also pleased that Marcus had agreed to give Jim Magilton a new two-year contract.

The news of the deal was released on Monday, 3 December, with the boardroom packed for a press briefing that went on for an hour and a half. I spoke afterwards to Nigel Pickover, editor of the *Ipswich*

*Star*, who said he remembered me telling him years earlier that I would stay on after the administration crisis and deliver a brighter future for the club. 'And now you have,' he said. 'This deal would never have happened without you.' It was unlike Nigel to hand out compliments, so that was much appreciated!

The move was generally welcomed, and *The Guardian* would later write of Marcus, and the deal:

> His purchase of Ipswich Town, one of the few clubs still intrinsically linked with its historic local owners and a last bastion of the oak paneled boardroom brigade, was welcomed by most fans, who recognised the need for new investment after the club over-reached itself on its last incursion into the Premier League.

The day after the media briefing we took the train to London to meet with Marcus and explore how he wanted to operate. He talked to Derek, Jim and myself ... but nobody else. He wanted a monthly review with each of us, with me as his public ambassador. Jim and the academy were to report to me, but with Jim having a dotted line to him.

Dotted lines spell confusion and can lead to disaster, in my book, as you can never really have two bosses if you want it to work. However, we agreed to it, not least because for the first time it was clear that – despite deciding against becoming chairman himself – Marcus really wanted to be heavily involved.

### The fateful day

I woke up on Monday, 17 December 2007 with a feeling of anticipation mixed with dread, after spending the weekend immersed in my notes ahead of the fateful EGM. Being chairman of our beloved Ipswich Town has always been a great privilege, but that day it felt particularly lonely. Perhaps sensing that, I was bombarded with supportive calls by all the board members and many others. Our appointment with destiny wasn't until the evening, and it was something of a welcome distraction to head out to Stowmarket, as I had promised Annie Steward that I would support her at a naming ceremony in honour of her late husband and fellow FA councillor. So Suffolk FA's headquarters is now known as 'Bill Steward House'.

When I drove to the meeting at the Corn Exchange, I couldn't find anywhere to park for at least ten minutes, which didn't help. I can't say I was especially nervous, but there was a real sense of foreboding at the momentous nature of what we were about to do.

After finding Mona, the other directors and assorted friends, I mixed with some of the shareholder fans, as I find chatting often helps ease pressure. But on my way to the stage, one of them warned me that James Wood was intent on asking why well-known football agent Ken Anderson was not being entertained as a serious contender to acquire the club.

James is a stockbroker, and a great friend of Lawrie Lewis, who was one of our larger investors. He had somehow attached himself to Ken Anderson, and after about 20 minutes of me going through formalities and taking some fairly benign questions, James did indeed rise to speak. He clearly thought he was being clever, but I could see what was happening so let him get on with his pontification, as he slagged the club off as 'a basket case'.

I thanked him for his question and referred to his client as 'the football agent', knowing that the connotations would be understood by everybody in the room. I explained to the audience that James had wanted a six per cent introductory fee, and then asked why his investor hadn't rung me directly, if indeed he had been so keen.

The chair of the Supporters' Trust then asked why I had cut James Wood short. I replied that he'd had his time, and asked James if he had anything else to add … and he didn't. It was soon clear to the whole room where James was heading, and it smacked to me of sour grapes.

I stayed on my feet for over two hours, fielding a whole range of questions, many of them wondering who the new owner was, whether he and his team were football people and why none of them was present.

Finally, with the questions all done, I proposed a poll vote, which our auditors were in place to conduct, and my predecessor John Kerr seconded the motion with a short, supportive speech. When, after what seemed like an age, the counting was complete, I called the meeting to order and announced the result: 98.9 per cent had voted in favour! At which there was spontaneous applause.

I was hit by floods of relief, and was left exhausted by the whole experience. Perhaps it was because I was driving so slowly on my way home that I was stopped in Melton by flashing lights, and a policeman standing in the road.

'Hello, sir. Have we been drinking this evening?'

'No, officer, but if you let me go, I'd like to get home as I'm dying to have one!'

A new era had begun.

**A lucky escape**

In January I headed down to London for the first post-deal meeting with our new owner. It all felt a bit schoolboyish, being summoned to see the headmaster in his study. Jim was told to be there an hour earlier. My sixth sense told me this might have been a sign of things to come.

Around that time somebody brought along by Peter Coates and his fellow directors for the Stoke City game was Nick Hancock, who had made a joke about the name 'Sheepshanks' as a quiz question on his television show *They Think It's All Over*. Needless to say, we had a great laugh, and honours were left even with a one-all draw. Ironically, their star performer that day was Ryan Shawcross, who was on loan from Manchester United, and who we had talked about signing. But when I put the call into United's David Gill, we were told that he had already agreed a permanent transfer to Stoke. Humph!

With Marcus's financial muscle, we could now afford bigger signings, so it was a busy transfer window. We ended up resisting a bid for Alan Lee from Burnley, but finally bought midfielder David Norris for £900k after some protracted negotiation with Plymouth, and Alan Quinn from Sheffield United for £450k.

Back on the pitch, February saw an uptick on the back of the signings, with three wins in four games, but apart from that we proved unable to string any results together. Blaming one particular game for the outcome of a whole season is a pretty fruitless exercise, but the obvious candidate would be the 2-0 defeat in early April at Colchester, then at the highest they would ever be in the league pyramid.

Shortly afterwards I flew to Amsterdam with Jim Magilton and Charlie Woods. Charlie is an amusing character who had been a player and then coach under Bobby Robson, and who was now operating as chief scout. At London City Airport we were also joined by Richard Glass, an agent specialising in international transfers. Things went swimmingly at our meeting with Luuk Balkestein, an impressive figure who would have won more than just a solitary cap had he not been fighting the legendary Ruud Krol for his place in the Dutch side. He had been chief scout of Sparta Rotterdam (and is still involved at Borussia Mönchengladbach) and had excellent contacts in Northern Europe. We liked what we saw and agreed to explore working together. He also asked us to give a trial to his son, a 1.91-metre centre-half named Pim, which we duly did, and signed him.

My memories of the flight back were of miles and miles of tulip fields, and of Charlie's nonstop jokes, including one I recall about Fockers and Messerschmitts! Our player liaison officer, Wolfe Powell, an affable former schoolteacher, was there to collect us. (I was deeply saddened to hear, as I was writing this book, that Wolfe had died. He was a dear man.) We were making good time getting home from the airport, but near Brentwood I remember telling Wolfe that there seemed to be something going on ahead of us. It was a jam under a bridge – he had seen it too, and slowed down. Not long afterwards we were hit very hard from behind by a car travelling at great speed and were shunted 30 or 40 yards down the road. Wolfe did well to avoid the car ahead of us, although we did catch it and scraped along the side I was sitting on.

What followed were the kinds of confused, chaotic, quick-quick-slow moments that anybody who has been in a crash can probably identify with. Jim had hit his head against the back of my headrest. Wolfe had smashed into the airbag but, sitting next to him, I had smashed into the doorframe. That left my head pounding. Charlie had hit his knee and chin, but seemed okay physically, although he was shouting, 'The car's on fire,' as he leapt on to the verge. The car that was actually on fire was the one that had hit us, and it was now fully ablaze.

Wolfe opened his door into passing traffic, so I was shouting too, to warn him. He couldn't find his glasses, and kept on saying, 'I can't see.' My glasses had also fallen off with the impact, but I dug them out of the fragments of windscreen and gave him mine. Jim and I had both lost our phones and had to scrabble around. There was glass everywhere.

Outside, people were tending to the injured on the side of the dual carriageway. We looked at the remains of the Shogun, with the back all squashed up like a concertina. And it began to dawn on us how lucky we were to have been travelling in such a robust 4x4.

Eventually a medic showed up and put me, shaking, into a police car to keep warm. I heard a conversation on their radio about a lady who had asked six youths to stop throwing things at her house. They had threatened to stab her and burn her house down. 'Thank goodness we live in the country,' I thought to myself.

I phoned Mona, and got into an ambulance, my first time ever. I joked with Charlie that I would swap that experience for three points that weekend. Somebody called Vicky took my blood pressure and checked me over. I was okay but I was feeling very woozy.

They gave me oxygen in hospital. I had the shakes again. It was normal. Shock, they said. Charlie was alright, happily watching the Masters golf. I chatted to the family from the car in front. The father, a policeman, was driving, and was being treated. I took their details so I could invite them to something.

The wait to be seen by a doctor dragged on. Was something wrong with the queuing system? Mona arrived. Thank goodness for her. My head was still throbbing. But eventually she decided to take me home.

I slept deeply, but I was still very slow and heavy the next morning. Mark Piper, our team osteopath, was waiting to see me at the training ground. Mona told him I wasn't right, and after her own head injury, she didn't want to take any chances. I take Warfarin blood thinner, and she was worried it could be some kind of haemorrhage. So we went to A&E and saw the club doctor, David Lewis, who gave me a CAT scan. The porter, Paul, was an Ipswich fan, so we chatted away about our chances that Sunday as he wheeled me down the corridor.

Five (painless) minutes later, and I was given the good news. Concussion, but nothing too serious. I said I wanted to fulfil my speaking engagement that afternoon at RHS school, before being told very firmly that I couldn't, and that I had to take plenty of fluids. I didn't actually need to be told that, as I am always very keen on staying hydrated.

Back home, Mona came in with the local paper: 'Town Chiefs in A12 Drama.' Sky and Anglia had also latched on to the story. I got loads of messages, and I appreciated that support.

**Missing out, and the beginning of the end**
That weekend was a big one for us. The next day produced a lot of draws among our direct competitors, but it left sixth as our best possible finish – and with it the last play-off spot. Our game that Sunday was against Norwich.

With a 29,656 crowd packed in, there was certainly plenty of atmosphere, all the more so when the name of the returning Shefki was read out. The game started at a frantic pace, but just four minutes in – disaster! Ched Evans scored for them. Still, Shefki was really getting stuck into the game and we soon pulled level through an own goal. Not long before half-time, Danny Haynes – who for some reason seemed to just love playing against Norwich – grabbed what would prove to be a very deserved winner. None of this left Canary manager Glenn Roeder too happy, and he locked his team in the dressing room for an hour!

A couple of weeks later, I got to Portman Road early for the final game of the season. I wanted to thank the stewards for their hard work in the front line as club ambassadors. It was a poignant day in many ways.

The odds to make the play-offs were stacked against us. And so it proved. We did beat Hull 1-0 with an Alan Lee goal, but we needed our two rivals to lose as well. With both Palace and Wolves winning, we ended up eighth, just a point off the play-offs. It was very disappointing, but our season had just been too inconsistent at key moments, losing games that we shouldn't have. Still, Jim's teams played attractive football, and I can still hear him now, yelling, 'Quicker,' in his Ulster brogue if anybody ever dallied over a pass.

The following week, Mona and I went to the Portsmouth vs Cardiff FA Cup Final and were seated between Aston Villa's Doug Ellis and Shadow Minister for Sport Jeremy Hunt, who asked me to come over and talk through their strategy! We had a special interest in the game, as our old friend Hermann Hreiðarsson was playing for Portsmouth, who won 1-0. Two days later I went to see Marcus at his offices.

Marcus had strong views on the academy and thought we should focus on 15–16-year-olds from all over Europe and forget anyone younger. It felt as if he was showing a lack of knowledge. He may have had a point in trying to rev us up, but it was irksome to listen to his criticism, as we had developed loads of young players on a shoestring. Within a few weeks of taking over, he was getting involved in our transfers and the nuances of every possible deal. It was his right as owner, of course, but he was a controller by nature and certainly didn't have many relationships across the game. His early advisors were rumoured to be the agent Jonathan Barnett and Alan Shearer – who is said never to have liked us as a club, and supposedly once commented that the only easy game in the Premier League was playing Ipswich at home.

And that day in London, Marcus said that he preferred to operate by telling people what to do, and that I was getting in his way. The pragmatic approach was for me to recognise that things had changed, and it was his right to say what he wanted. I really was too heavily emotionally invested in it all, so it was better that I smell the coffee and move over. However, that wasn't so easy on a personal level!

Anyway, we agreed that I should move to a non-executive chairman role and leave Marcus to make the big calls. I told Jim the news as calmly as I possibly could, but he wasn't too happy. 'Chairman,' he told me, 'I want you at the training ground every week.' As it turned out, not long afterwards I was asked by Marcus's team to stay away, and not go there.

This was very hard to take, having been the one who bought the land and led the development in the first place. It felt like the beginning of the end.

## Chapter 31
# 2008/09: End of an Era

IN THE close season we lost striker Alan Lee to Crystal Palace, and my old sparring partner from those therapy sessions in the pool, Richard 'Bam Bam' Naylor, who went to Leeds. Much like the previous season, it was to prove another inconsistent campaign, and the whole season felt different, strangely hollow. In truth, it was an inescapable fact that our club now belonged to someone else. It's what has happened to nearly every club now, and we had been unable to buck the trend.

We had good attacking players such as Jon Walters, Pablo Couñago, Jon Stead, and Tommy Miller back in midfield. Furthermore, we were boosted by the arrival of Giovani dos Santos, the supremely talented young Mexican on loan from Spurs – he scored some cracking goals! But we were simply not getting the results, despite expensive investments, like midfielder David Norris. The early spring games delivered only six points from a possible 24, and attendance levels were dropping below the 20,000 mark.

However, over 28,000 packed into Portman Road on 19 April 2009 to see us beat Norwich 3-2.

A couple of days later I saw the news that Marcus had fired Jim Magilton. It didn't come as a complete shock, as I knew that Marcus wasn't happy, but coming after the previous weekend's high, it was absolutely gobsmacking. And then they announced that he had been replaced with none other than Roy Keane! When I called Marcus, he said, 'It will be fun, David, it will be high profile'. To which my retort was something like, 'It will be high profile, but I don't think it will be fun. Culturally it is not a good fit,' which is as about as polite a comment as I could manage.

It all felt very hard on Jim, and I really felt for him. He had brought great energy, insight and passion to the job, and considering his lack of experience he had done very well for us, especially at the start. Had he and I been able to continue working together, with me supporting him as the board had requested when he was appointed – and as we had done for the first 18 months – then I think he would have been very successful. Looking back, it had been getting increasingly difficult for him, and Marcus was himself an inexperienced owner.

I also thought it was a good time to agree with Marcus that he would replace me as chairman. But I did ask to stay on as a club director as that would qualify me to continue on the FA Board, which I needed so as to stay at the helm of the National Football Centre, which was a few years out from completion.

On reflection, in terms of meeting his obligations under the deal, Marcus did everything honourably and correctly, and I can say that I am proud that we got the deal done.

What happened afterwards is regrettable, but after buying the club he invested millions of pounds in players for Jim, more for Roy Keane, and more still for Paul Jewell. Marcus spent a lot of money, but unfortunately it neither worked for him, nor the club, as we flirted with relegation every year. Ironically, things only stabilised when Marcus was really limiting his investment, so what Mick McCarthy achieved with much less funding was all the more remarkable. That is not to suggest that he wasn't entirely supportive of Marcus, as Mick always behaved with enormous integrity to his chairmen, as indeed Marcus did to him.

## Bobby Robson, and what a club should be

That summer, just as we were beginning to get used to a new part of the Ipswich Town story, another chapter of our proud history came to an end. One that had been absolutely central to everything the club represented.

On 31 July 2009 we received the desperately sad news that Sir Bobby Robson had died.

Eighteen months earlier, I had been honoured to be invited to BBC's annual Sports Personality ceremony to watch Bobby receive a lifetime achievement award. It was a fantastic occasion, held in a huge auditorium full of stars from every discipline and genre, all in their finest. Lots of his great England team from the 1980s were there, as well as Newcastle titans such as Alan Shearer and, of course, his Ipswich legends: Mick Mills, Allan Hunter, George Burley, Terry Butcher, Russell Osman and Roger Osborne (but sadly no Kevin Beattie, who was unwell). Former club secretary David Rose, Jim Magilton and I were asked to represent the club that day, which was very humbling. It was already a proud and memorable occasion for us all, but when it came time for Bobby's presentation we were called up to the stage to join him. When he was announced, the entire audience of 5,000 stood to applaud ... and applaud ... and applaud! And so it went on and on and on, for I would say eight or ten minutes. And that was on live television. Finally, Bobby, who was emotional of course, was asked how he felt. I will never forget what he said: 'If only my mother and father could see me now, they would be so proud,' which brought the house down.

He was 74 at the time and being treated for cancer, and his parents must have departed 20 or so years earlier. As I said on the death of my father, it doesn't matter how long ago your parents may have left you, you can still go on trying to make them proud. As Bobby did. What a giant of a man!

In May the previous year, Bobby had been given the freedom of Ipswich at a civic reception on the 30th anniversary of our FA Cup triumph. It was a wonderful and very emotional day, with thousands crowding the route to see the open-top bus and cramming into the town square. All kinds of people turned up, even match referee Derek Nippard put in an appearance. There were some amusing comments from John Motson, a great speech from the ever-modest Mick Mills, and then goalscorer Roger Osborne, who said Arsenal keeper Pat

Jennings seemed to get a little bit closer to saving his shot every time he watched it! I was still part of the FA, so was delighted to be asked to present Bobby with a replica of the famous cup.

The following week I received a call from the great man. He was effusive in his thanks for our hospitality: 'David, you gave me one of the best weekends of my life, it takes a special club and special people to do that.' I was so moved that I wrote it down.

I was very lucky to have got to know him well, especially in his later years. His wife, Elsie, invited me to go up to see him at home about a month before he died. It was meant to be for an hour, but I ended up staying for three. Bobby just wouldn't let me go. He was in his pyjamas and dressing gown, and insisted on showing me all his archives, old programmes, newspaper articles and the numerous artefacts and trophies he had collected. I will forever treasure that day. As I do some words Bobby once said that still resonate with me, as they will with every true fan of the game:

> What is a club in any case? Not the buildings or the directors or the people who are paid to represent it. It's not the television contracts, get-out clauses, marketing departments or executive boxes. It's the noise, the passion, the feeling of belonging, the pride in your city. It's a small boy clambering up the stadium steps for the very first time, gripping his father's hand, gawping at that hallowed stretch of turf beneath him and, without being able to do a thing about it, falling in love.

When the sad news arrived, I talked it through with new CEO Simon Clegg and we decided that flags should be flown at half-mast and a wreath placed on Bobby's statue in Portman Road.

Some weeks later we went to Durham Cathedral for his memorial service. There was quite a turnout – Lineker, Charlton, Gascoigne, Venables, Shearer. Alex Ferguson gave the most wonderful eulogy, and Katherine Jenkins sang like an angel.

The fixture gods willed us to be at home to Newcastle just a few days after that, in what became a celebration of the great man by both sets of fans. 'Two clubs, one legend' was the theme. Elsie cut a ribbon to open the Bobby Robson Stand, escorted by none other than my dear assistant, Anne-Marie Williams, who supports both Newcastle and Ipswich.

In truth, he was a very modest man who might not have felt comfortable with all the adulation. Bobby would have been even more uncomfortable with our performance in the 4-0 defeat that day. 'Lady Elsie's scissors had more cutting edge' was the wry comment from *The Guardian*. 'Mick Mills, Kevin Beattie and John Wark were in the stand. Ipswich could have done with their moustaches.'

# PART SEVEN

## Chapter 32
# Meanwhile, Back at the FA

ON A rainswept night in late November 2007, England contrived to lose 3-2 at home to Croatia, and with it qualification for the forthcoming Euros. The enduring image of that match will be Steve McClaren standing on the touchline sheltering under an umbrella, 'Wally with a Brolly' as a wag from the press corps most unfortunately and unfairly christened him.

The crisp new Wembley, forged in a spirit that was supposed to have consigned debacles like this to the history books, was left echoing to a chorus of 'You'll be sacked in the morning' from those who had bothered to stay the course.

And they weren't wrong. The next day I received a call to take part in an emergency FA Board meeting. So I was again to play my part in what is frankly the only thing the FA does that most fans actually care about – choosing the England manager (or sacking the old one!).

I think it's fair to say that the other decisions had been easier. There had been Glenn Hoddle back in 1996 and his successor Kevin Keegan, both of whom had already made great contributions to England and had taken some of their creative wizardry on to the bench when they retired from playing. Indeed, Keegan had been in charge when I had stood for the FA chairmanship, and we were touted as a dream team.

McClaren's own appointment had taken a bit more consideration. Without doubt he was a top-class coach, and one of the things in his favour, apart from getting Middlesbrough to punch above their weight on the way to their first-ever trophy, was that there would be a degree of continuity – as he had held a position in the national squad set-up under Sven-Göran Eriksson. I didn't actually have anything to do with appointing Sven, who was England's first foreign manager, as my position on the FA Board only came through being a Football League representative. So when Ipswich won promotion to the Premier League in 2000, I automatically stepped down, before rejoining in 2003 after we were relegated.

I admired Sven as a very adept strategist, and got on well with him. My wife, Mona, being Swedish, helped the relationship, and he was very charming and courteous whenever he visited, often with his assistant Tord Grip. He also had a way with the women, something that puzzled Mona since – she says – he apparently had a reputation for not having the sweetest breath! Nevertheless, Sven, who is sadly no longer with us, certainly attracted plenty of stunners, not least Nancy Dell'Olio, who Mona and I got to meet on occasions. She was undeniably alluring and attractive, and came across as a bit of a man-eater.

Sven's fling with FA secretary Faria Alam would later hit the headlines, and there was a further twist when it emerged that she had also, allegedly, had an affair – including a romantic getaway to Paris – with CEO Mark Palios. I can remember an excruciatingly uncomfortable board meeting with Mark in the FA's old offices just as the news was breaking. He resigned shortly afterwards, and David Davies and Nic Coward were made joint executive directors.

Mark's departure was a shame as he was a capable and likeable man. I am glad to say he moved past the fuss surrounding Faria and would later become chairman of Tranmere Rovers, where many years earlier he had played while qualifying as an accountant. Mark made over 400 league appearances, and remarkably kept playing amateur football until the age of 58, reportedly shaking off a double cardiac arrest a few years earlier after getting elbowed in the chest!

Anyway, I can't really recall whether there were any standout candidates after Steve McClaren's departure in late 2007, as my memory of the appointment process – if indeed we could call it a process – completely overshadowed the outcome. It was an embarrassment, to my mind anyway. I was in Dubai on a business trip when I received the original call about McClaren being sacked, but the board meeting had started some time before. I was left in disbelief, and expressed my disappointment to Geoff Thompson, who held the chair, and I then asked what other business had been concluded without me. 'Oh,' said Geoff, 'we have decided to have a root and branch assessment of the England set-up.' And yes, he insisted, that would include recruitment, and FA CEO Brian Barwick would consult widely to ensure it was handled properly. 'Can you assure me that he will talk to all those who have experience in appointing managers?' I remember asking.

I shot off an email to the FA Board complaining at what had happened, and almost immediately got a note back from Michael Game, one of the representatives of the non-professional football world (traditionally known as 'the national game', presumably because 'amateur' might sound condescending). Michael, who was a good man, and always very straightforward – refreshingly so, compared to some others on the FA Board – replied simply: 'Dear David. I concur. Michael.'

Just two days after discussing the importance of applying rigour to the process, we met again, only to discover that Fabio Capello was basically a shoo-in. There was no mention of any background research, no details of who Brian had spoken to, no reasons as to why certain candidates were discarded, no character reference or due diligence, no dossier for directors to consider. It felt as if any systematic approach had been thrown out of the window, and the other directors had been completely disenfranchised. The lack of consultation left me feeling steamrollered and that a process had been abandoned, which reeked of the poor decision-making of the bad old days of the FA.

Not everyone agreed with me. A senior colleague said I was overreacting, and that these things had to be done quickly. So I then asked whether anyone had spoken to the presidents of Real Madrid or AC Milan, where Capello had been before, and if not, why not.

'Because,' they said, 'you learn everything you need to from the media and the papers.' 'Has anyone run a comparison of costs for Capello and his team with the earlier Eriksson regime?' 'No,' we were told, although we were assured that the package was competitive.

Very competitive, as it turned out, for Fabio Capello. But rather less so for the FA, who had to fork out the requisite millions. Of course, Capello was at the very top of the world game and it was a coup to secure him. But it was a massive sum at the time, especially for an organisation that was constantly pleading poverty when it came to long-term investments such as the National Football Centre. Even more so for someone who didn't speak very much English, something that had simply been brushed over - although Fabio himself would later famously claim that he only needed 100 words to manage his players.

Even so, I voted for him. This was one of those occasions where I felt obliged to go along with something for the sake of board unity.

## The need for reform at the FA

My reaction to all this was probably a reflection of my deep-seated unease at seeing the state of the FA. Although nothing should have surprised me, given the level of duplicity and backstabbing politics that permeated the organisation in those days.

Nowadays, the FA leadership is quite unrecognisably better. They have a first-class independent chair in Debbie Hewitt and an excellent CEO in Mark Bullingham, with a top-notch executive team supporting them, as well as high-calibre directors who are cognitively diverse, and – if anything – I hear almost too independent!

The change really began when former BBC Director-General Greg Dyke took over as chairman in the summer of 2013. A couple of years later, in partnership with new CEO Martin Glenn, he really set about imposing some commercial rationale. That included shedding around 200 staff – the FA had become bloated in much the same way as the Civil Service. And, as so often happens, the more people you have, the more they seek to justify their existence by creating new initiatives, all of which means that it's not just their employment costs that are weighing you down, but also the external budgets they are driving. However, in terms of knowledgeable oversight, from what I saw there were very few business brains sitting around the FA Board with either the experience or inclination to begin to deal with the issue, and those that there were too often allowed themselves to be distracted. The people representing the national game had mostly never sat on another board before, while those from the professional game were in the main obsessed with political manoeuvring and preserving their positions.

It all reminded me of something Groucho Marx said: 'Politics is the art of looking for trouble, finding it everywhere, diagnosing it incorrectly and applying the wrong remedies.' My pal David Davies later took to calling the FA the 'Palace of Varieties'!

So despite sporadic, valiant efforts from some of those in charge, the FA had all too rarely been run along sound business principles. The FA CEOs I came across were in the main good people – Adam Crozier, Mark Palios and Brian Barwick all brought good things – but by the time Brian left it had become increasingly political, and at the cost of rational commercial criteria.

There will, of course, be those who argue that the FA is not really a business, and actually more of a charity or governing body. I would respond by saying that even charities are to a large extent commercial enterprises. Cash management remains paramount, as does people leadership, and cultural alignment behind universally understood aims and objectives.

**Knight of the realm**
Before the arrival of new brooms Dyke and Glenn, the FA had been the stomping ground of football politicos, people such as Dave Richards, chairman of the Premier League – which made him an FA vice-president – and formerly of Sheffield Wednesday. It seemed as if he lost no opportunity to point score for the Premier League, or for himself and his friends. I remember being at an England match when

Dave leaned across to whisper in my ear to lobby for a mate: 'It won't do you any harm if he knows you have backed him.'

Richards was very good company and, to his credit, he did at least make no secret of his priorities. At one FA Board meeting he proclaimed that England were the '21st club in the country', and even doubled down on that stance when I challenged him: 'Hang on, Dave, don't you actually mean England should come *before* the Premier League?'

At the September 2008 meeting he argued against giving the FA Cup winners a Champions League place. I was irked in the extreme by that, and decided to weigh in, making a plea for 'the good of the game' and to 'keep the dream alive'. The national game directors all nodded their heads, but nobody said a word, and I was left to battle on alone! One thing that wasn't brought up was that Dave was also vice-president of both the FA and the FA Cup committee, so had a marked conflict of interest. That said, I suppose that was something you could say about most of us, with everybody wearing too many hats – which the arrival of more independent directors has helped rectify, albeit at the expense of some football knowledge.

Talent should be nurtured, and I can honestly say that I look to have people around me who know more than I do, particularly about specific areas. But at times, it appeared to me as though Richards actively sought to have people around him that he could influence and keep things just the way he wanted. That approach extended to diminishing others, myself included. I heard on several occasions how he had told people that what had been achieved at my company Suffolk Foods was all down to my younger brother Rick (who is indeed a brilliant man, and is now making a great success of Stokes Sauces). Rick had of course contributed massively, and we were a great team. But it was another twisting of the truth.

In my opinion this kind of pettiness and trivial empire-building did nobody any good. I remember being warned that Dave, would only vote for whatever Lord Triesman (FA chair for some of this period) did not want!

Somehow people like that seemed to flourish in the kind of highly politicised semi-public bodies like the FA, which have no clear for-profit identity or status.

Dave was knighted in 2006. For services to sport.

**The Football League**

Needless to say, the Football League was not immune to the same kind of nonsense, albeit to a lesser degree. And I have to say that it was around this time that I first began to feel a bit of fatigue with the constant meetings and the shenanigans they inevitably involved. And whereas the FA Board in around 2006 or 2007 was looking at a range of things such as the threat of a government regulator being imposed, the possibility of a women's premier league, racism, referee protection, betting, 'bungs' and the regulation of agents, by comparison a lot of the Football League sessions were simply about survival.

In the new financial climate, some of the things we found ourselves having to consider were how to stop clubs fielding under-strength line-ups in the Carling Cup (which reduced the value of the TV deal) and complaints from clubs that the £60k they got per game from Sky wasn't enough to compensate for people staying at home and watching on pay-per-view.

We started working out how to create a television market of our own, and tried to build relationships with other key broadcasters, such as Setanta, Virgin, BT and even foreign groups such as Canal+. Hanging over all of this was a growing, often unspoken, recognition that Vic Wakeling at Sky was basically the paymaster of English football.

The board at that time was led by former Conservative politician, the late Brian Mawhinney. A very committed Christian, Brian was justly proud of having introduced better governance and a new fit and proper persons test as a filter to try to get the right people involved in the game, and to ensure we excluded the wrong ones.

During the Capello selection calamity, Mawhinney actually boycotted the second meeting in protest at how the first one had been run. I suppose you could say it was a principled stance, but Dave Richards joined him, and I think as much as anything else Brian had become used to working without restrictions, and in my opinion simply wasn't used to being told what to do. I can still hear him saying, in his Ulster drawl, 'I have been bounced, and I don't do being bounced!'

I got to know Brian over the years and we got on well for the most part; however, I always felt that in his case ego was never far away. In fact, I may have rather scotched his retirement, as at one meeting he put it to the board that he would stand down providing he was made lifelong president! He went round a speechless room until finally coming to me to ask my opinion. Very politely, but rather firmly, I told him, 'Brian, forgive me, I always thought that honours like that are bestowed rather than negotiated.' So we succeeded in putting that one to bed. I recall in the end we did make Brian president for a year or two but with a strict time limit. But he never forgave me, nor I think Ian Ritchie, the other independent director, who shared my view.

# Chapter 33
# Branching Out

IN THE summer of 2008, and only a few months after the Marcus Evans purchase, I was very surprised to receive a call from Peter Hill-Wood, asking me to come along and meet some of the other Arsenal directors, as they had identified me as a possible new CEO! We had a very friendly chat, and they persuaded me to return for a final interview with their full board, which I duly did.

I was told it was between me and one other candidate. That other candidate turned out to be Ivan Gazidis. And he won. Ivan is a great operator, and had a strong track record in the US, which I think may well have swayed American owner Stan Kroenke. Still, the invitation came out of the blue, and I was delighted to have been asked.

My only hesitancy at the outset was that, as a one-club man, I wasn't sure I could ever work for another side. So although I was tempted by what was a huge opportunity, I was just not sure I could do it. So I never really went for it wholeheartedly, a reticence that may well have been picked up by the Arsenal board. However, probably because of the long-standing affiliation of the Cobbolds and the Hill-Woods, Arsenal will always be my second club.

**Banking and biotech – work outside football**
With the direction of travel as regards ITFC becoming clearer every day at that stage, I took on a few external consultancies in addition to my FA responsibilities. One of those was with Aziz Tejpar at

Environmental Biotech, where he and his wife Riz had built up an impressive nationwide drainage clearing business.

I was also approached by Coutts Bank to become a 'local chairman' to help them build their business in East Anglia. I really enjoyed doing that, supporting and mentoring the exceptional Mark Noble, and they also asked me to help Ian Turland with their already impressive sports portfolio nationally. That meant co-hosting numerous very convivial networking lunches for leading lights from the sporting world, held in the directors' private dining room at their head office in the Strand. I took a modest retainer, but refused any commission as I wanted to be able to look everyone in the eye and say I would not be paid extra if they opened an account.

Meanwhile, David Bingham, the former ITFC head physio (and the man who had got me into the routine of early morning swimming), asked me to come on board at IPRS as a consultant for the new medical triage business he had started, which was going great guns. Added to that was a consultancy company called Alexander Ross that I started with Ben Hatton, David Davies, Joanna Burns and Mike Blood, which looked to capitalise on our wide-ranging commercial, legal and leadership experience in the football world. Setting up the Premier League in the UAE was one of the projects we were hired to support, as was a project for Lesotho, and we also took a stake in Jimmy Worrall's Leaders in Sport conference group. Leaders turned out to be a great success, and we didn't sell our shares until several years later.

## Suffolk Community Foundation

This growing portfolio of professional work (I needed to earn something!) came in addition to my charity commitment at the Suffolk Community Foundation, which was perfecting its narrative to:

1. outsource local giving to thousands of small charities in Suffolk that were doing amazing things, but often fell under the radar;

2. connect local causes that were in need with local donors that care;
3. encourage Suffolk companies to support the causes that matter to their workforce, customers and suppliers.

This would later distil into 'Supporting pressing local needs that otherwise struggle for funding by connecting them with local donors who share a passion for Suffolk'.

One of the things we worked on from the outset was to separate core funds from donations for charitable giving, so as to demonstrate our control over costs. With a majority of trustees from the east of the county, including me, we made an effort to do more in the west. Tim Tollemache agreed to co-host a launch event in Bury St Edmunds for us to engage people there, in an event that included all the MPs from the county. We also discussed a Walk for Suffolk, and a drive to meet the area's corporate players, by working through the Chamber of Commerce and the Institute of Directors, as well as the business editor of the *East Anglian Daily Times*.

In early 2008 I had a fascinating and very instructive meeting with Michael Brophy, who had chaired the Charity Aid Foundation. He asked whether every one of our trustees was able to answer clearly and articulately exactly *what* we did and *why* we were there, the point being that it was a complex value proposition and everyone has to be driven to be successful, which is of course true in any area of life. My experience is that, with the best will in the world, too many people take on a trusteeship because of flattery, or the status of the position, rather than clarity about what they can actually contribute. Of course, this is within the control of the existing trustees that interview and select them. Michael emphasised the fact that David Cameron was very vocal in encouraging social enterprise at a grassroots level, particularly citing interaction with local councils. When prime minister he would even invite me to become a patron of the National Citizen Service that grew out of his big society concept.

By 2008, in our third year, our endowments had grown to £2.5 million, and we had distributed grants of £250,000 to a hundred causes, with the plan for 2009 to increase that to £750,000 and 250 local causes. At the time of writing, thanks to the brilliance of the staff and trustees, both past and present, those numbers have grown exponentially. Over the course of our existence, we have made 10,900 grants totalling over £43 million to 3,346 different local charities and community groups. I was recently honoured to be made a life patron of the foundation. What a fabulous concept and an inspirational charity!

## Leading England's World Cup bid

Not long after the approach from Arsenal, another opportunity emerged after I had a meeting with Labour peer David Triesman, the first independent chair of the Football Association, at which he suggested I put my name forward to lead our bid to host England's 2018 World Cup. I was interested, of course, but I told him that I was committed to creating the National Football Centre, and that I didn't want to take it any further unless they were pretty sure they wanted me. However, he insisted, so I went through the interview process with Nolan Partners – I knew Paul Nolan as he had headed recruitment at the FA. I got to the final stage, only to discover I wouldn't get the nod and that instead it was going to former Man Utd executive Andy Anson. He was a good chap, but I soon discovered that he was a close friend of one of my colleagues on the board.

I was upset about that, not least because one of my strengths has always been building friendships with foreigners and international audiences such as the World Cup evaluation panel. When Ipswich played in Europe I always made sure I had learnt enough to make the welcome speech in the opponents' language, and at least show I had made an effort. I am a firm believer in what Nelson Mandela said on the subject: 'If you talk to a man in a language he understands, that goes to his head. If you talk to him in his language, that goes to his heart.'

It's fair to say that, historically, the FA, and English football in general, had been guilty of taking a rather insular, dismissive approach to the international game. After all, we didn't even take part in the first three World Cups, and it took losing to the American part-timers in 1950, and a Wembley drubbing handed out by Ferenc Puskás and company for us even to begin waking up to the fact that we were not everything we thought we were.

Our chances of winning the World Cup bid – if they ever realistically existed – had essentially disappeared when David Triesman was recorded making suggestions of impropriety in relation to both refereeing and the selection process for the upcoming tournaments. 'To FIFA's electors Triesman's remarks will have confirmed the English tendency towards condescension and arrogance and its addiction to tribalism,' remarked *The Observer*. I still have a copy of the fax from Wilma Ritter, secretary of the FIFA Ethics Committee (which must have been an interesting job), giving a deadline for clarifications on what Triesman had said. It was harsh on David, but symptomatic of the world we live in. If the media sniff anything, you get your comeuppance.

The fuss when we fell at the first hurdle after only getting two votes, after six had supposedly been promised to us, looked like sour grapes and merely served to further reduce the likelihood of England hosting the planet's largest sporting spectacle.

It was an embarrassing fiasco. And what really stuck in my craw was the way in which Prince William – our future king! – and Prime Minister David Cameron were brought in as a desperate last-gasp measure to save a hopeless campaign. While neither could ever possibly comment on it, I can only imagine how they saw things.

With hindsight, I am glad I had no association with the whole sorry saga, and yet by the same token, had I been leading it, I think a lot of that nonsense could have been avoided. That said, with Sepp Blatter holding court at FIFA, it's unlikely that the end result would have been any different.

So the 2018 World Cup went to Russia, and it later emerged that the computers used for the bid had been leased, and the hard drives later destroyed.

Then the 2022 tournament went to Qatar, where Blatter's replacement now resides. Gianni Infantino clearly likes that part of the world, as personal business there – accompanying Donald Trump, no less – meant he was late turning up for the 2025 FIFA Congress, which he was supposed to chair.

**CEO of the Football Association**
When Brian Barwick stepped down in January 2009, I was also asked to put my hat in the ring as CEO of the FA. Needless to say, I had plenty of experience of the FA, so could shape what I put forward about myself to what I saw as the need for change. I made copious notes about my style as a leader and engager of people, the way I try to drive continuous improvement and a high-performance culture, and build cohesive organisations that nurture collaborative relationships at home and abroad.

My concerns were at what I saw as 'mission creep' as departments grew and forever looked to justify themselves, together with a habit of reordering rather than asking for fresh tenders from a range of suppliers. And with a consultant culture that frankly felt a bit lazy, we were failing to grasp the huge opportunity we had to recreate a dynamic brand image in tune with our ethos.

My beliefs align with what I hold to be the seven principles of public life: Selflessness, Integrity, Objectivity, Accountability, Openness, Honesty and Leadership.

Needless to say, I did not get picked. Looking back, I was probably viewed more as a chairman than an executive by that stage, and a few months later Ian Watmore was appointed. By then I was increasingly full on at St George's Park, so wasn't too disappointed.

**Sharing a seat at the top**
I was a beneficiary, of sorts, from the sting that had led to Triesman's downfall. That came just two months after the departure of Ian Watmore, an excellent CEO who sadly only lasted nine months. He was desperately frustrated at his inability to hold sway over

the committee culture and vested interests at the FA, in particular the Machiavellian characters from the Premier League who were constantly manipulating matters around the board table.

An emergency meeting of the board decided that Geoff Thompson would take over as chair of the World Cup bid, Barry Bright would head the FA Council, and Roger Burden and I would become joint FA chairmen, with Roger chairing the board for the first year. The move was not entirely expected, as *The Guardian* pointed out:

> The decision to appoint Sheepshanks ... in favour of Sir Dave Richards is a surprise. [Richards] might have expected that recognition of his seniority. However, Richards is as divisive a figure as Triesman has been and would not have enjoyed universal support from the amateur game. By contrast Sheepshanks ... has broader appeal.

After things had settled down and we surveyed the situation, it became clear that, in the aftermath of the Wembley build (which came with the complication of having delivered a very poor pitch), the finances were still very stretched.

Meeting with the senior executives, in particular commercial director Stuart Turner, also showed that there was a real disconnect between them and the board. It turned out that most of them never saw the board members, or even knew who most of them were!

I was also concerned that there was a lack of stated targets, weekly reviews and so on, and that the business development side was being run separately from sales. It certainly didn't feel as if the FA was very business orientated. Given my background, I was itching to get in there and assist.

I remember arguing with the management team at the time when they said they felt leadership at the FA was all about process and systems. I disagreed and asserted (and still do to this day) that it's about clarity of vision and purpose, getting the right bums on seats and wrong bums off them, and getting the whole team aligned, with everybody knowing the roles they play. Culture and values that were easy to remember had to be agreed on, which everybody involved was proud to own. In my book, only then do we need good systems.

At the end of June, the FA Board met again and decided that having co-chairmen was not a workable model. David Gill suggested Roger Burden should take the position, and that I should stand back, which I did. Privately I felt miffed, as they had clearly discussed it all in advance. The world had changed, and I now know that my background was an issue for some of the people involved. But there is a code of ethics that I have always tried to live by, something along the lines of 'try to do to others as you would be done by'.

By the end of the year, there had been another change, and David Bernstein was appointed. He was the man that made the most sporting of speeches as chairman of Manchester City, who we had just relegated, congratulating us on qualifying for Europe.

David opened his first meeting by saying that he wanted the FA to get back to basics, and that our business had to start at home. That meant stopping spending money we really didn't have on things like international aid, which was music to my ears, and a message that might now have even finally reached Westminster.

**Premier League chairmanship**
I have to say that, as far back as 2009, I had come to the conclusion that the great offices of state would not be coming my way. So when a few years later another opportunity came at me from left field, I was really taken aback. It was all completely unexpected and unsolicited, but in 2013 I was asked by Chelsea chairman Bruce Buck, who also headed the PL Nominations Committee, whether I would be interested in interviewing for the chairmanship of the Premier League, as – he said – I was his favoured candidate. Without that reassurance, I don't think I would have proceeded. So I made some enquiries, including talking to their CEO (and my close friend) Richard Scudamore, who was characteristically meticulous in staying strictly neutral on the issue. I took the application seriously and made

an exhaustive checklist of the questions I could expect, practising my replies in front of the mirror and then with Mona at home.

I had been on the wrong end of press leaks before, including when David Triesman had asked me to stand for CEO of the World Cup bid, so happily they arranged to have the interview at the headhunters' offices.

It went well, but suffice to say I came second! Apparently the panel took the view that I was perhaps too close to Richard. I was close, of course, but made no secret of the fact, nor that we had done exactly the same for the Football League as their chair and CEO 15 years earlier, when it had worked incredibly well.

I was disappointed, as I would have really enjoyed working with Richard again. However, when your face doesn't fit, then I have learnt that you can't take it personally, and have to move on.

## UK Community Foundations

Happily, another important role was in the offing, as I was appointed to chair the national board of UK Community Foundations (UKCF), where there was a big challenge ahead. As soon as I arrived, CEO Stephen Hammersley resigned, assuring me that it was nothing to do with me. While he did stay on for a few months, it created an added onus on me to reorganise and galvanise the London office. There were 46 foundations (now 47) in the country and I, along with the eight-strong team, had to represent them, raise their national profile and funding, encourage best practice and help share innovation. Fortunately, I was eventually able to appoint an excellent new CEO in Fabian French. During my tenure we managed to bring the organisation together, and win a major government-matched funding scheme for community foundation grants – which were a template for what was to come.

I did the job for just under six years, my permitted term of office, and believe that I left the organisation in much better shape than I found it. I recently attended their 50th anniversary celebrations, and it was wonderful to hear that community foundations had now passed the £2 billion mark for grants made across the UK.

The efficacy of place-based philanthropy is now much better understood in Westminster, as reflected by the announcement made at the celebration that the government had agreed a new £500 million matched funding support for young children and family causes, as part of a new Better Futures Fund. That was extremely gratifying, as I have long been an advocate of this kind of public/private investment partnership, and it's something I had worked on extensively, having been helped in this by Tim Kiddell, a senior private secretary in the Prime Minister's Office (and coincidentally also a Tractor Boy).

# PART EIGHT

## Chapter 34
# The National Football Centre: A Long-Postponed Necessity

I HOPE that what we achieved at the National Football Centre is something that will live on long after I am gone. Being asked to lead the creation of a permanent training and educational home for England was as exciting as it was challenging, and an opportunity for which I am immensely grateful. I was never going to play for my country, so the honour of building something for England was as near as I was ever going to get.

To head up any national project is huge, but what was at stake for the game only increased the importance of getting it right. So the design, construction and launch of the cutting-edge facility that we named 'St George's Park' was in many ways the culmination of my career, utilising as it did many of the skills I had acquired in both business and football. I will forever credit the entire group that supported me for their invaluable contributions. It was a huge team effort.

At the outset my starting point was, as it is with any new venture, large or small, to begin with the end in mind. That meant having to decide what we were trying to achieve, work out what we wanted the facility to do, and to establish what success actually looked like.

There were many answers to those questions. But one aim stood out above the rest – we really needed to find a way to arrest the cycle of underachievement and create an environment that would catalyse success, raising the standard of our England teams to the point where we could consistently challenge for major honours.

This wasn't just something that suddenly came to me when I got the job to lead the project. It had been a constant theme with me for years. Indeed, the first point of my manifesto back in the 1999 FA chairmanship campaign said just that, as well as spelling out a lot of what I felt the facility would need to deliver:

> To build a winning Club England of which the whole nation will be proud and that will act as a shining beacon to improve the popularity and accessibility of football. For Club England to be WINNERS we must adopt a vigorous approach to technical improvement. A strategy that starts with youth and progresses through all age groups for men and women.
>
> A co-ordinated approach is required nationally for every aspect of Player and Coaching Development: technique, fitness, lifestyle, psychology and nutrition ... an Institute of Football should be founded and equipped with all the appropriate facilities and mentors: the aim to promote excellence and continuous improvement throughout the game ... sharing of techniques ... the realisation of the full potential of a much larger number of high-quality home-grown players will result ... [with] continued support and encouragement for the Charter for Quality and everything that it encompasses.

### Getting left behind – the need for change

As the century drew to a close, the feeling that there had to be a radical change in approach in the English game, and the national side in particular, had been growing almost as long as I could remember. It seemed as if we were being overtaken in terms of skill, tactics, attitude, coaching, fitness, physiotherapy, career management and just about every other department that could be named. There were penalties, sendings-off and Gazza's tears and then his outstretched boot on the way, of course, but at the end of the day we had become all too used to being overshadowed by Germany. Italy were always there too, and then France rose to superpower status by taking the World Cup and followed it up at the Euro 2000 championships, before becoming a fixture at the business end of big tournaments.

Not that long before, the French had actually felt much the same way about things on their own side of the Channel. Yes, Michel Platini's side had become continental champions in 1984, but they had mostly punched below their weight. Or at least their potential weight. So, driven by their federation chief, in 1988 they set up a national academy system centred upon a new facility at Clairefontaine, near Paris. And it was there that Thierry Henry and several of the winners of the game's ultimate prize honed their skills, and indeed where the squad stayed during their successful home campaign a decade later.

The French system actually ended up turning out so many good players that quite a few couldn't find a place in the national squad and ended up playing for the African countries from which they were descended.

Italy had opened their own set-up near Florence (known as the 'university of football') back in the late 1950s, and while Germany didn't have a similar focal point, they did have an excellent sports university in Cologne. In the 1990s, their systems worked, but ours – despite the growing power of the Premier League – clearly didn't.

Fabio Capello, who became England manager while the facility was being planned, was once asked why Italian managers were so good. 'We study at Coverciano, after that, it's like being a professor. In England you need more professors of the game.'

Before 2012, the England teams had led a peripatetic life, with different age groups living out of a metaphorical suitcase, training at various facilities around the country. I remember Stuart Pearce complaining at the lack of connectivity as his U21s did their sessions in the north-east, while the senior team was in London, using The Grove and Arsenal's practice ground. Prior to that the FA and the PFA were still reliant on two somewhat outdated facilities, the first being the multisport Bisham Abbey, which was used for national squad training sessions. The other was Lilleshall Hall, where the best youngsters were coached. But, as the success of the Premier League drove budgets (and transfer fees) ever upward, that was fast being overtaken by the academies being opened by clubs everywhere. Club and country were almost in competition.

**A stuttering start, and a revolt**

It was actually not until practically the new millennium, and with 1966 fast becoming ancient history, that the FA actually got down to doing something about the problem. One of the chief drivers in getting the ball rolling was FA technical director Howard Wilkinson. Interestingly, Wilkinson, manager of the Leeds side that won the last league title prior to the arrival of the Premier League, had taken a degree as his playing career was winding down. That was in the 1970s when there were very, very few graduates in the professional game (Liverpool winger Steve Heighway is one that comes to mind). And Wilkinson's degree was in education, so it was no surprise that he became a proponent of continual learning, and coaching in its broadest possible sense. Indeed, it was Howard who had designed the Charter for Quality, which the Ipswich academy had signed up to in my day. The long-standing chairman of the LMA, Howard was a wise owl, and I would later enlist his help on the FA Learning Board, where he opened several doors for us.

In 2001, Wilkinson had been instrumental in getting the FA to invest £2 million to buy 350 acres near Burton upon Trent. The site was formerly Byrkley Park, the country seat (and stud farm) of the Bass family, and although the stately home itself had long gone by that time, the setting of the park and the majestic grounds were quite stunning. We were even eventually able to use some of the remaining stone balustrading to create a memorial garden under a giant cedar tree, with a statue of Arthur Wharton, who had been the first-ever black professional footballer, in the late 1800s.

The timing of the purchase could hardly have been worse. A series of financial and legal difficulties delayed the demolition of the old Wembley Stadium until well after Ipswich's play-off triumph, and it quickly became clear that there was going to be a very significant budgetary shortfall in the development of the new ground. Faced with that, the FA felt it just didn't have the cash for the National Football Centre, and the project was mothballed. So the financial rigour (helped by a reputation as hard bargainers!) that my board of directors and project team brought to the development process when we finally got the go-ahead was one of the things I am most proud about.

But we very nearly never got to that stage at all. For a time the whole concept of a national centre seemed to be under threat. Most of the pitches had been laid, and there was still a management board of sorts in place, but for a while the possibility of a sale had hung over the whole project. Things took an abrupt turn in 2007, at the Connaught Rooms near Covent Garden, at a meeting of the FA Council – which brings together a hundred or so individuals from all walks of football life. The Council, known as 'the blazers', ended up in open rebellion against the FA Board, demanding action to prevent the English game getting left further behind.

A lot of credit for this is also due to Andrew Halstead, who is now a lay canon at Birmingham Cathedral, but was then the FA's director of operations. Andrew had the courage to take a stand and support the move, and even take on the board at the risk of making life uncomfortable for himself back at the office. His intervention galvanised the FA councillors in the room, who swayed the directors into conducting a proper review of the situation, and – I would say – pricked their conscience into finally pulling their finger out. Sometimes you need moments like that to get some action out of an organisation in which it's easier to say *no* than *yes*, and to stick with the status quo.

At our next FA Board meeting following the review, the case for the project had strong and articulate support from Stuart Pearce, who was then caretaker manager of England. Also on board was Sir Trevor Brooking, the former – and very elegant – West Ham and England midfielder, who had become FA director of football. I was very much in favour and equally keen to stress the importance of ensuring that the complex would also become the focus of coach education and referee training.

That would, of course, be in addition to being the home of all the England teams, an idea that some had initially been against because it was a nearly three-hour drive to Wembley, and would mean going down the day before matches – which I thought was a minor issue in the larger scheme of things. And there were parts of the media, most especially the *Daily Mail*'s Charlie Sale, who goaded me to have the National Football Centre built inside the M25, which was actually unrealistic on cost grounds. They thought that Burton was inaccessible (code for 'not close to London'), whereas I argued that, far from being in the middle of nowhere, it was actually in the middle of England. I liked to say it was 'England centric, not London centric', and that was my mantra.

**The team comes together**
The decision was taken to stay at Burton (which we owned), and a few months later an entirely new National Football Centre board was appointed, which I was asked to lead. I am still tremendously grateful to the FA Board, and chairman David Triesman and CEO Ian Watmore in particular, for giving me that opportunity. Sitting alongside me were Barry Bright from the amateur game in Kent, Frank McArdle (a local FA councillor, and more importantly CEO of South Derbyshire District Council), and former Sunderland chairman Sir Bob Murray, who became the chancellor of Leeds Beckett University at around the time the build was completed. Also on our team were Sir Trevor and, importantly, Alex Horne, a very brilliant financial brain who would later become general secretary at the FA – which was good news for us in terms of the influence we needed to get things done. We were joined by the FA's Alistair Maclean, who became our lead internal project manager, a role he fulfilled wonderfully well.

The new board assembled for the first time at the end of November 2008, and we were accompanied that day by Danielle Every, who played a critical 'interphase' role, and became increasingly important as the subsidiary company she ran – and which I chaired – FA Learning (which was responsible for developing coach education and qualifications), gradually merged into the broader National Football Centre concept. Dani went on to take up senior positions at Pentathlon GB and British Cycling, and is now Chief Operating Officer at the refereeing administrators' group PGMOL (Professional Game Match Officials), who also run the VAR system. She was invaluable throughout the whole planning, construction and delivery process, so please don't be too hard on her when you start screaming at the television after another debatable VAR decision!

The great banking crisis of 2008 would be followed by years of austerity. So one thing the FA Board made clear from the start was that we would have to raise our own funds, and just as importantly create a self-financing business model. That meant building an 'enabling development' – something that wouldn't normally be permitted by planning policy, but is allowed so as to secure the long-term future of a heritage asset, with the initial idea being that we would build a residential complex on the peripheries of the site as a cash generator. At one stage we were looking at getting £5.1 million for building 42 houses. But gradually that came to look less attractive, and we would actually go on to consider creating a business park focusing on sports sciences, technology research, equipment and so on. Or possibly an educational outpost or satellite for a university or business school. But gradually it became clear that a hotel, marketed as a destination in itself, would be the best option, and that is what we pursued.

The whole process was complicated by the fact that we had an unusually wide range of stakeholders to consider, so I made it a policy that we would always share our thoughts and engage with the various parties in a consultative style. That approach worked out much better than simply telling people what we were going to do, and we ensured that they all felt involved every step of the way.

A priority was the need to reach out and engage locally with Staffordshire Council and their planning department in Burton upon Trent. In addition we had to liaise with both Natural England (a governmental advisory body) and the National Forest – which a few years earlier had planted 200 square miles of new woodland in disused industrial sites in the region. As CEO of South Derbyshire Council, Frank McArdle's knowledge of the issues was exceptional, so on his advice I also met with Staffordshire Wildlife Trust and the Woodland Trust among others. There was an unspoken quid pro quo in all this, of course, so we also had to emphasise the wider ecological benefits that we had to offer; for example, returning some of the agricultural land that we owned around the site back to pasture.

### Overhauling the professional coaching system

One of my great concerns at the National Football Centre was that we should produce not just England teams to win trophies, but also create a system to train coaches who could generate continuing excellence. From the outset I was chair of both the new facility and also FA Learning, which had a remit to provide an educational platform for football coaches, administrators and players. Over the time I was in charge, we drew the entities ever closer until they merged. We were determined that the facility wasn't just going to be a few buildings and some pitches. It had to represent a whole new way of looking at things.

Our understanding of what had to be done undoubtedly evolved as we progressed. But it was clear from the outset that one of the key issues the English game faced, but which was often ignored and even dodged, involved certification. The PowerPoint presentations I gave as I toured the country to drum up support included a comparison with our direct competitors – Spain, France, Italy and Germany. People sitting at the back of the room would have really struggled to spot the miniscule red bar for England in a graph that showed we produced only ten per cent of the number of UEFA B coaches that the others did (on average), 16 per cent of UEFA A coaches and 12 per cent of UEFA Pro coaches. There was, as the adjoining text put it, 'an overwhelming need for a new generation of more qualified coaches from grassroots to elite levels teaching across all age groups and genders'. And we needed *both* quality and quantity.

A massive influx of new money was then washing over the Premier League and by extension the English game generally. But in 2008/09, total player wages across all the professional clubs represented nearly 1,500 times the amount spent on educating coaches.

Another slide in the presentation I used to give was headed by one of my favourite phrases: 'Starting with the end in mind ...' and had the following bullet points of what we were looking to deliver:

- more home-grown managers and coaches leading England and Premier League sides
- structured international team development for a winning Club England
- careers in coaching and all other disciplines in football increasingly respected through meaningful qualifications
- age-specific coaching regarded as a profession
- pipeline for a new generation of coaches.

The 'meaningful qualifications' from the third item was an especially important issue, as it became increasingly clear that no one in England had ever actually failed the Pro Licence test! What is more, the approach was far too tokenistic – I can remember getting a call from Ged Roddy, who is now a technical director at FIFA, and was then at the Premier League. His words left an impression, and I wrote down exactly what he told me: 'We need a strong FA that is delivering coach education effectively. If National Football Centre coach education is delivered effectively, this will only serve to help Premier League Academies.'

Ged also said he thought we had to break away from a system that treated coaching qualifications as if they were like passing a driving test, which was a sentiment that I shared strongly. So a lot of people would 'get their badge' and think that was all there was to it. That attitude clearly had to change, and CPD (continuous professional development) and lifelong learning had to become the way forward.

Then there was the issue of the content and intensity of the programmes. I discovered that the leading European countries had courses for their next generation of managers that lasted 40 days or more, but we felt we could get by with only 13. By contrast, the Germans spent an amazing 73 days learning the skills. Plus, they and the others all spread the learning over a year or two and all incorporated pedagogy – the art of teaching and understanding how pupils learn. Our football was 'living in the comfort zone', as Jim Hicks of the PFA described it. He worked at PFA Coaching, which was set up by their long-standing CEO, Gordon Taylor, after our failure to qualify for the 1994 World Cup. Jim confirmed what I was hearing – that the testing for the FA's Level 5 FA UEFA Pro Licence was woefully inadequate, being very shallow on content and lacking any accountability or verification. He went on to contrast what we were doing with the Malcolm Gladwell and Matthew Syed approach, which says 10,000 hours is the minimum commitment to excel in something. The mere mention of Matthew was a confirmation that Jim and I were definitely on the same page!

**Introducing some critical friends**

As mentioned earlier, another great influence on me was Frank Dick, the former UK Athletics man and coach of the legendary Daley Thompson, who suggested we create an advisory group of what he called 'critical friends'. Some of the luminaries we discussed were McLaren F1 boss Ron Dennis, Dave Parnaby from Middlesbrough, Howard Wilkinson, and Dave Brailsford, the man who had taken British cycling to the very top. We talked it through, and Frank helped me bring together the first group with a brilliant surgeon specialising in liver cancer (whose name escapes me!), Gareth Southgate, our new CEO Julie Harrington, and former rugby star Group Captain Chris Moore, who commanded RAF Leeming. As well as Frank, we also had Dan Ashworth, the FA director of elite development, and me.

The idea was to consider what high performance meant in other walks of life to give new perspectives on our approach to football, and we did the same sort of thing later with the TAB technical group that advised the England management team.

We were also wrestling with questions over course content, what the length and cost of the courses should be, who would attend, how candidates might be failed(!), if there would be a refresher requirement, and what the continuous learning opportunities and mandatory qualifications would be. Nothing was off the table.

There was also talk among us of developing an accreditation on the lines of an ISO (or British Standards Institute) type of system, of the sort we had done at Ipswich Town and in my food businesses. Broken down into various subsections, one of the aims of this was to enable clubs to properly evaluate the return on investment from their academies. This proved to be the genesis of the Elite Player Performance Plan (known as EPPP), and was the brainchild of Ged Roddy.

Ged had previously helped create a degree-based football programme at Bath University, with the aim of producing more rounded players, so we saw eye to eye, as I liked to think of the National Football Centre as being the 'Oxbridge of football' – a term that Gareth Southgate would also adopt.

Gareth thought we had some good content, but also shared the view that the course was too short and in need of a revamp. I heard much the same from former Scotland midfielder Paul Lambert, who had spent a season at Borussia Dortmund and was the first UK manager that I knew who had done his coach education in Germany, where he studied alongside a certain Jürgen Klopp.

Paul was then managing Norwich, so we met in secret – in a private room that Coutts lent me in their local office – in case people got the wrong idea. Local fans would have gone mad if I had been seen talking to the enemy.

You also had to be careful about internal politics. There was the ever-present need to continually sell our case to the FA Board, and we had to be particularly careful about treading on the toes of people with overlapping remits, such as Trevor Brooking's Technical Department. Trevor, a legend in the game, should be particularly congratulated for pushing to bring Gareth Southgate in as the U21 manager. But you can't make an omelette without breaking eggs, and some people were inevitably not going to be happy about what we were trying to do. Especially since it was immediately clear that there would be no point in simply moving the same underperformers and status quo merchants into the new facilities in Burton upon Trent and thinking that anything would be different.

We needed to apply a completely new approach, and adopt a growth mindset. After my visits to see what all our competitors were doing, and my subsequent complaints about it, our Level 5 Pro Licence was massively revamped and became a 30-day-plus course. And improvements are still being made. We never pretended that there was a magic bullet for immediate success. Until recently there were only two English managers in the Premier League, and I am very disappointed that it has taken us so long to get our own elite coach education up to the level of other nations.

Soon after arriving at the FA, chairman Greg Dyke issued a rallying call that we should aim to win the World Cup by 2022. It was ambitious stuff, and there was nothing wrong with that (except that we didn't). Not long before, I had gone on record as saying that the new facility would mean England would win a major championship by 2026, and as the clock ticks down I feel obliged to stick with that! We have come mighty close with the men, and gloriously won the Euros twice with the Lionesses under the brilliant Sarina Wiegman. But I think it's going to take us another five to ten years before we have significant numbers of top home-grown coaches running Premier League clubs. Indeed, I said at the time that this would be a generational thing to achieve.

But I was convinced, and still am, that we were putting something together that would be the first critical step in advancing the American model of respect for coaches as teachers, mentors and leaders, rather than just trainers and tacticians. That is a fundamental cultural change, and not just a tap that can be turned on and off. It requires a long-term commitment and a concerted effort among all the game's stakeholder.

The facility aimed to be, as I was quoted saying in 2012, 'a place to build on strengths and challenge underachievement ... an educational hub ... [for] developing a new generation of young players who are not only technically adept, but are also decision-makers. We achieve that by investing in the teachers. It will take time for them to grow up and deliver on a world stage.'

*Escorting the then Prince Charles as he is presented with his Tractor Boy colours by BAM BAM (Richard Naylor), Gareth McAuley, David Wright and Moritz Volz, December 2008*

*Close rapport with Jim Magilton at the Annual LMA Dinner, London, March 2008*

*A famous cricket match among the gentlemen of the football press in Trinidad in late May 2008 ahead of England beating our hosts 3-0 in the match that counts! Henry Winter, Charlie Sale, Brian Woolnough and Michael Hart are prominent*

*A handshake with Lord Mawhinney Football League/FourFourTwo Awards*

*Having a Caribbean soft drink on an FA tour, with two of my favourite people I met in football – Peter Coates and Terry Robinson, 2009*

*With Alan Smith (brilliant SGP architect) looking at the large-scale model of St George's Park before it was built, 2010*

*Talking on stage with the delightful Gérard Houllier at the Soccerex Manchester event in 2012*

*Hard hats off! Showing some gentlemen of the national football press the full-size indoor pitch under construction at St George's Park*

*Aerial view in 2011 of St George's Park under construction by Bowmer and Kirkland, demonstrating the sheer enormity of the site. The buildings alone are approximately 500 metres from one end of the Hilton Hotel complex on the left to the end of the indoor pitch on the right*

*An up-to-date aerial view of the full-size Sir Alf Ramsey indoor pitch today and the Sir Bobby Charlton elite pitch outside it, built to replicate Wembley dimensions and reserved for the senior England Men's and Women's teams' training* (Credit: Spark Media)

*A view from the east over one of the other 14 elite outdoor pitches looking toward the 228-bedroom Hilton Hotel* (Credit: Spark Media)

*An early morning view of the whole building complex, hotel, banqueting and conference facilities, indoor pitches and the FA's Football Centre* (Credit: Spark Media)

*Prince William and Princess Catherine meet Mona, FA CEO Alex Horne and me on arrival to open St George's Park, October 2012* (Credit: FA)

*Sitting with the senior St George's Park FA team who played such big roles. (L to R) – Mel Millner, Mark Donnelly, Sir Trevor Brooking, Julie Harrington, Alex Horne, Alistair Maclean*

*Unveiling the statue of Arthur Wharton, the first black professional player*

*At my CBE award, summer 2013. Mona, Sophie and Tom with me on a joyful day at Buckingham Palace*

*Farewell photograph after chairing my final FA meeting of the Professional Advisory Group in April 2025. L to R: Lee Carsley, Thomas Tuchel, Mark Bullingham, Sarina Wiegman, Jobi McAnuff, (Lord) Michael Barber, David Sheepshanks, Col. Lucy Giles, John McDermott, Anthony Barry, Paul Cleal, Kevin Sinfield, Damian Hughes and Arjan Veurink*

*Celebrating the presentation of replicas of the old First Division championship trophy (1962), the FA Cup (1978) and UEFA Cup (1981) with assembled stars from the 70s including Mick Mills, George Burley, John Wark, Mick Lambert, Bryan Hamilton and more recently Mick Stockwell, Simon Milton, James Scowcroft, Adam Tanner, Matt Holland and Carlos Edwards, present and past chairmen Mark Ashton and I were also joined by archivists Liz and Tim Edwards, COO Luke Werhun and CFO Tom Ball, November 2025*

## Chapter 35
# Designing the Dream

IT HAD fairly quickly become apparent that the start made on the National Football Centre project in 2003 was distinctly unambitious and not at all what we were looking for. So we said thank you and goodbye to the incumbents, looked at a range of suitable new architects and came up with a shortlist of three.

The KSS practice were working on the Spurs training ground at the time, and had a whole host of sport-related work in their portfolio, including the Bolton Academy and Brighton's superb Amex stadium.

It was a similar story for HOK and Rod Sheard, an Australian who I knew well, having been one of the architects we had used both at Ipswich and at Wembley for the FA. Then there was Wimbledon, the London Olympics, Arsenal's Emirates Stadium, the Melbourne Olympic Park ... they had an amazing track record.

So these were guys at the very top of their game.

The third contender was the much smaller Red Box Design from Newcastle, which was owned and run by the utterly brilliant Alan Smith. We immediately clicked and felt genuine empathy with Alan, who just seemed to 'get it' right from the off, and quickly identified with some of our key issues, especially the need to 'future-proof' our design. That was some compensation for the fact that Red Box didn't have quite the same depth of experience as the other two. Although they had done exceptional work on the new Sunderland ground for our National Football Centre director, Bob Murray, who had introduced them to us.

In the end we invited all three to quote.

We decided to appoint Red Box, and shortly afterwards Alan Smith and Bob Murray asked our board members along to visit the Stadium of Light, before a working dinner in Newcastle. It was an evening I will never forget, despite the copious amounts of white wine Alan poured me to get my imagination flowing. He took the seat opposite, and cleverly only pretended to drink himself, while proceeding to quiz me on my vision for the project, and take notes.

The next day Alan had it all down pat. But he said he wouldn't put pen to paper and wouldn't draw a single line until everyone had agreed on our values. And this, in my book, was mission critical. We all had to be aligned.

In much the same way as the great business guru Peter Drucker talked about how 'culture eats strategy for breakfast', Alan was saying that any design is pointless unless you have determined what your project, and the development itself, will stand for. 'Think before ink!' as he liked to put it. Alan was full of one-liners. Another I remember is: 'Good design will always be good design, and not just a fashion!'

So began an extensive consultation process both internally at the FA and externally among the many other stakeholders in the game. This soon extended into asking what the National Football Centre meant to them, and what facilities they thought should be included.

Some of the most important stakeholders of all were the FA technical and coaching team. Alan and I met with them in early January 2009, and many times subsequently, all of which was well marshalled by Dani Every. And – much like what had happened when I took over at Ipswich – we teased out of them our shared objectives, ones that possibly had just been lurking in their subconscious up till then.

We were even able to leave the room with a wish list:

- To provide an inspirational training home for all 22 England teams;
- To provide an inspirational centre for coach education;

- To facilitate a holistic career path in coaching and other football careers;
- To provide a satellite for delivering higher and further education models;
- To create a leading centre of sports medicine and sports science (research, diagnostics, treatment); and
- To provide both a national and international destination for coaches, players, officials and administrators/leaders to meet and share learning and experiences.

Alongside these we defined our four guiding principles, the first of which was to operate a centre that was both relevant, and of service, to the whole English football family. The second was to focus on becoming a driving force behind encouraging and facilitating CPD at all levels in the game. The third was to develop the practical and experiential (rather than academic) aspects of coaching. And the fourth was to retain control over our awards and certification system.

So there was an emphasis on what was real, rather than just theoretical. But the National Football Centre itself didn't yet exist, nor even a concept of what it should actually look like, or how it would function. We were creating it from scratch. There was no blueprint or existing template. At least, not in England.

I decided the time had come to see what our competitors had been up to, and what we could learn from them.

**The continental way: what the competition were doing**
The first stop was Clairefontaine, where former Liverpool boss Gérard Houllier could not have been more helpful. He was a wonderful host, and insisted that Alan Smith and I sat down for a traditional French lunch, with not one but two bottles of Beaujolais! As we were breaking baguette together, I asked him what he would do differently if he were starting again. Gérard said there were too many ancillary buildings around the site, and indeed it did feel a bit like a maze; however, his main advice was to turn to our advantage

the fact that we were the last of the major European nations to set out on a project like this. We could learn from everybody else and set a new benchmark.

Anyway, we left with a big hug from Gérard, who I nearly forgave for inflicting the final nail in our coffin against Ipswich almost ten years earlier!

Next stop, Italy.

Before getting on the plane to Florence, I was reminded of the words of Andy Roxburgh, the former Scotland manager, who was by then technical director at UEFA (and who, interestingly, also had a brief but successful career as a schoolteacher): 'Italy won the World Cup by design, not by chance.'

So we set out for a land famous for design, and with Fabio Capello's number two, Franco Baldini, as an expert guide. Although practically anywhere on earth would struggle to match Coverciano's location in the rolling Tuscan hills, they had much the same facilities as we were planning to build, albeit ones dating from many years earlier. There was a hotel and pitches, obviously, but also lecture halls, a swimming pool, library and medical facilities. And, being Italy, a top-class restaurant of course.

The only thing that Franco, a keen golfer, thought they lacked was a nine-hole course to keep the players entertained. We did actually meet with the top guys (Sandy Jones and Rob Maxfield) at the PGA, the Professional Golfers' Association, to see whether we could create a realistic, fundable business plan for building a golf course around the National Football Centre park. I really wanted to pull it off and, my goodness, we tried. But in the end we had to face reality, and decided it just wasn't what our focus should be, or within our budget.

Other visits included Zeist, the Dutch national centre, and some very instructive days at the Spanish Federation's training centre, the Real Madrid academy and La Masia in Barcelona. Seeing a wall packed with photos of the incredible world-beaters that have emerged from that famous former farmhouse – Messi, Xavi and Iniesta in particular – really brought home one of their messages to us: remember that champions come in all shapes and sizes, and you should try to create a pipeline of talent, rather than a production line of carbon-copy players.

In fact, once we opened, Barcelona, who then had Luis Enrique at the helm, were one of the first of many big clubs to come and do their pre-season training at St George's Park.

## A safe space to meet the enemy

You may well be wondering why competitors would so readily give you the keys to their castle and be so candid about what they were doing. Obviously we already had established links with Gérard and Franco, but the real answer is that I was determined that we should go in a spirit of openness and mutual transparency. It was 'I'll show you mine if you show me yours' kind of stuff, which – judging from the way conference speakers often open up about their companies – is actually more common in the business world than you might imagine. A spirit of reciprocity was our maxim. Essentially it was a matter of saying that we might want to beat you on the pitch, but it will help us all if we share what we are learning about player development.

Since then we have had visitors from all over the world. Indeed, we welcomed numerous national associations while still in the construction phase, including a group from the DFB, who run the game in Germany. They left us with a distinctly envious look. Our return visit to Cologne, at the German Sport University, opened up a whole new world of learning, and the science of pedagogy – then a completely new word to us, but a concept that played a big part in their programme. They may not have had a centre like ours, but they were way ahead of us in their thinking and in developing coaches who knew how to nurture young players as individuals, not as one-size-fits-all units.

Something else the Germans clearly understood, as did everyone else frankly, was that experiential peer-group learning is every bit as important as lectures. Just being together with other like-minded people acts as a catalyst, and we became intent on creating an environment at the National Football Centre in which players, coaches, administrators, referees, groundsmen and others felt relaxed enough to open up and share their experiences. I wanted it to be a safe space to meet the enemy.

**Other sports**

Any lingering notion of an arrogant FA held by people in other sports was something we wanted to banish. This was to be a new era.

So, to change perceptions, I embarked on an extensive series of meetings around the country (often in the excellent company of architect Alan Smith) to meet with those involved in running all kinds of different sports, including visits to the tennis centre at Roehampton, cricket centre at Loughborough, and the elite hockey unit at Bisham Abbey. We would also end up talking to people from the netball, basketball and badminton worlds about usage of the indoor hall, which could easily be converted from football or futsal. Discussions over futsal actually took up an inordinate amount of our time, as there was a court only half an hour away, and the need to create our own – with the sprung floor it required – was not immediately clear. But in the end we went for it.

In addition to the three-plus-hour journey to Burton from home, normally done twice a week, my diary of the time gives an indication of the miles I must have clocked up. In just one month in 2009 there were visits to BBC Enterprises, the FA Management Team, PGMOL (referees), the English Institute of Sport, the Midland local government office, the Football League Club meeting, Umbro and Nike, UEFA head office in Switzerland, and finally the Professional Game Board and the National Game Board (which are both part of the FA).

One of those meetings, at the English Institute of Sport, or EIS, was with former Irish full-back Conor O'Shea, who is now at the Rugby Football Union. He was very supportive, and advised us to ensure we created something that would still be fit for purpose several decades down the line. Perhaps the most valuable insight he had was to cement my own thinking that this was an opportunity to build a one-stop shop for coach education and sports science/medicine, all on one site. Quite apart from the practical benefits in terms of logistics, we were sure that kind of environment would create chemistry and cross-pollination of ideas across disciplines – in much the same way as teams of different ages and genders can share ideas and learn from each other. Conor also told me that the England rugby people were considering building their own facility, and might even want to invest in ours, as they were strapped for cash.

That wasn't to happen; however, both codes would eventually make use of our campus, and although the rugby league people didn't last very long, we continued to see a fair bit of the union boys. That included hosting both Ireland and Argentina during the 2015 World Cup, while we welcomed the England squad several times during Stuart Lancaster's time in charge. The avuncular and delightful Bill Beaumont came to see us, and I even got to see a young Owen Farrell practising his kicking on the magnificent full-sized indoor pitch. I had seen plenty of rather basic indoor facilities going around Scandinavia, where the weather means they are practically obligatory, and had always wanted our covered pitch to be something of a statement. And I think we succeeded in that.

The England indoor hockey team used the smaller hall – which was easy to convert from indoor football or futsal – before we had to put a stop to it because of the damage being done to the surface. The same space was used in the run-up to the 2014 Glasgow Commonwealth Games – another organisation we got on very well with – to store the material used by the various teams, and for a few weeks it was piled high with all kinds of kit. They then duly appeared, though not always the athletes themselves, to pick their things up, and some of them stayed on and used the facilities.

The England cricket team used to come for seminars and weekend training camps, while on other occasions there were pan-sport national coaching seminars, and I was often invited along as guest speaker.

One of the last initiatives to come on board was training company Michael Johnson Performance, run of course by the athlete and broadcaster himself, who won an astounding four consecutive world 400-metre titles. He is also a delightful man, who I was thrilled to get to know. He had developed a company that was working with schools in the US and around the UK, but in the end Michael couldn't deliver the necessary financial assurances or monetise the initiative. All of this sounds sadly familiar, since I am very sorry to see that Michael's project to inject more interest into the international athletics circuit is itself struggling.

On the subject of speed, I met Ron Dennis at the wedding of mutual friend Selina Tollemache, and he invited me to the McLaren headquarters. Dani and I went along and were blown away by the sheer scale of what it takes to put two cars on the Formula One grid. Something like 200 engineers alone! Their relentless pursuit of 'there is always a better way' or 'how can we shave a fraction of a second off the time needed to change a wheel' were all object lessons for us in our game.

No stone went unturned in our pursuit of contacts across the board. I went to see the British Olympic Association, and even spent time talking with rider-turned-broadcaster Brough Scott, who introduced me to the Injured Jockeys Fund. I went down to meet them at Lambourn, including the indefatigable Rachel (Lady) Oaksey, with the discussion inevitably focusing on our proposed medical and rehab centre, and how we could support them.

One of the most important things to emerge from my contact with the equine world came about rather tangentially. One of our visitors in November 2011 was Tony Kelly, CEO of locally based Northern Racing (owners of ten courses, shortly to merge with Arena Leisure), who brought a colleague, their operations director Julie Harrington, along for the 'hard hat' site tour that I used to lead several times a week. I remember being very struck by this bright and inquisitive lady. Little did I know that the very same Julie Harrington would apply for our MD position a few weeks later. Her application was excellent, and it was an extremely hard decision between her and our own Dani Every – a much-liked and admired member of the team who, as already noted, went on to ever-greater things. However, Julie's wider leadership experience and skills were plain for all to see, and her appointment was a unanimous decision by the panel.

I was assiduous in meeting people across the sporting spectrum, to stimulate ideas and also in engaging potential commercial partners or customers. Financing was an ever-present concern, especially given both the cost overruns at the new Wembley and the fact that we were going through the aftermath of the 2008 financial crash.

**Hotels**

Once it had been decided that our primary enabling development would be a hotel, finding the right partner became of paramount importance, as it would be financed using a mechanism called 'sale and leaseback'. This would require a long-term operating agreement of bankable repute. The first firms to declare an interest were Marriott, Hilton and De Vere – who had been involved in the original 2003 project.

With limited knowledge of the hotel business, we soon found ourselves having to learn about terms like RevPar (revenue per available room) and other hospitality sector jargon. So we also met with Dan Anderson of Locum Consulting, and international consultant Marc Finney. They were both incredibly helpful and became key parts of our team as we looked at a range of different business models, with the aim always to produce somewhere that would actually attract visitors, and not simply be a place people had to stay while on a training camp.

Eventually we chose Hilton, largely because they convinced us that we would not just be a small tadpole in their ocean. They seemed to fully buy into our whole concept and wanted to make it a properly bespoke destination hotel. And so it proved to be.

To help build atmosphere, and create that unique, destination feel, we reached out to all kinds of people from across the extended

FA family, and with their invaluable help were able to put together a fabulous collection of artwork and pictures to decorate the surroundings. The FA's international relations and heritage specialist Jane Bateman, who now also helps administer the Sir Bobby Charlton Foundation, was a superstar in assisting with all of this. The works honoured numerous important figures in the English game. And we even named various function and guest rooms after them.

The initial list of managers (and apologies for any omissions here) was Robson, Clough, Revie, Paisley, Ramsey, Venables, Howe, Sexton, Greenwood, Winterbottom, Hope Powell and Herbert Chapman, while the players I can remember starting off with were Charlton (x2), Moore, Peters, Greaves, Banks, Shilton, Rooney, Lineker and Mo Marley. Wayne Rooney, for example, would be given the room named after him when he came, and the possibility of guests being able to stay there themselves added real cachet to the whole experience. It was just the kind of thing we were looking for! In much the same way, nowadays people want to come and stay where Harry Kane and his team-mates sleep.

I struck up a very good relationship with the family of England's first-ever manager, Sir Walter Winterbottom, and we held a special ceremony to unveil a bust of him at St George's Park, with his son-in-law Graham Norse and family.

As the grand opening of the whole facility drew closer, in summer 2012 we did some trial runs in the hotel, with discounted rates. By then we had gone through various value-engineering debates, cost driven it has to be said, over whether to go with three- or four-piece bathroom suites. I think bath tubs are important and was dead against cutting them out of the larger rooms and just leaving a shower. The baths actually ended up being one of the distinguishing features between the premium Hilton and slightly less exclusive Hampton brand (I would call them 4.5 and 3.5 stars respectively, but they would kill me for saying so!). The idea was to be able to cater to both the senior team/business market, and also the more budget side of things for youth sides, coach education courses and so on.

As it turned out, after a couple of years Hilton found that running two receptions and two booking systems to comply with their brand standards proved just too expensive and cumbersome. So everything was merged into a Hilton brand with a single check-in, and the smaller rooms were simply called Hilton Compact and sold at a cheaper rate.

This flexibility was an example of how cooperative and what great partners Hilton had been (and, I am sure, still are). The charismatic Nick Smart at the start, and later Stephen Cassidy, were pivotal in helping us create a genuinely constructive relationship that enabled this unique arrangement to work. I applaud them. Together with Holly Murdoch at our end and their hotel manager Greg Crawford, they went a long way towards ensuring the relationship worked on the ground.

The hotel contract enabled us to sign a sale and leaseback deal that generated just shy of £50 million, the lion's share of the money we needed. It was a 30-year funding agreement because we had a contract with Hilton, and the FA's covenant (derived from its financial stability) was considered rock solid.

**Healthcare**

Healthcare and rehab work was an area that I was extremely keen to incorporate into our plan, and another significant potential income stream. It was also a string in our bow when it came to attracting customers to the facility, including the hotel. We started by identifying eight major medical providers: BUPA, BMI, Spire Healthcare, HCA, Nuffield, Ramsey, London Clinic and Circle Health. I think we met first with BMI, who certainly made a compelling case, and talked about making the complex state of the art in every way, which certainly resonated with us. I recall thinking afterwards that the challenge was how to monetise it, how to actually make it pay!

In the following weeks and months we also met with Circle, who were leading private hospital operators at the time. Their founder Ali Parsa and his team made the point that 95 per cent of all injuries are non-surgical.

These early discussions helped us to more clearly define what we were looking for in any potential partner. Top of the list was that they had to create a one-stop solution, that came with a multidisciplinary approach to complex injuries, and the full range of best-practice methods. Next was the need to provide the protocols, programmes and clinical support for residential rehabilitation. And finally we wanted to create a football-orientated sports science unit, with objective assessment and speed/agility/strength/stamina/suppleness testing. All of this meant we were aiming to deliver not just rehab, but also prehab.

Also in the running were IPRS, run by former ITFC physio Dave Bingham (I had been a consultant for the firm for a short period, so had to declare an interest). Interestingly, they had developed into a specialist triage company and had a national network of PRISM centres registered with the CQC (Care Quality Commission), so there was a ready-made network for us to plug into. Their suggestion was that we share revenues, but the whole idea needed more flesh on the bone ... as did everything that was being proposed at that stage.

We then met with Aspetar from Qatar, part of the highly impressive Aspire project that was run by a likeable Australian, Wayde Clews. We were also assisted by an Iraqi, the affable and very efficient Mushtaq Al Waeli, who was closely allied with the Qataris. This was well before the Qatar World Cup, of course, and the country's profile was considerably lower. But we all felt we could learn a lot from what they were doing there, as we were still trying to invent the wheel, whereas they had already developed a world-class facility. They were particularly interested in collaborating on screening and research, an area where they could provide the expertise. They even drew a virtuous research circle to illustrate their approach (above right).

Naturally, we also thought we might be able to get them to invest, and I liked the idea of research expertise giving us an edge on any other establishment in UK – but we really had to nail our differentiating proposition.

That investment didn't materialise, and instead our choice was to go with Circle Health, despite some early doubts about their financial

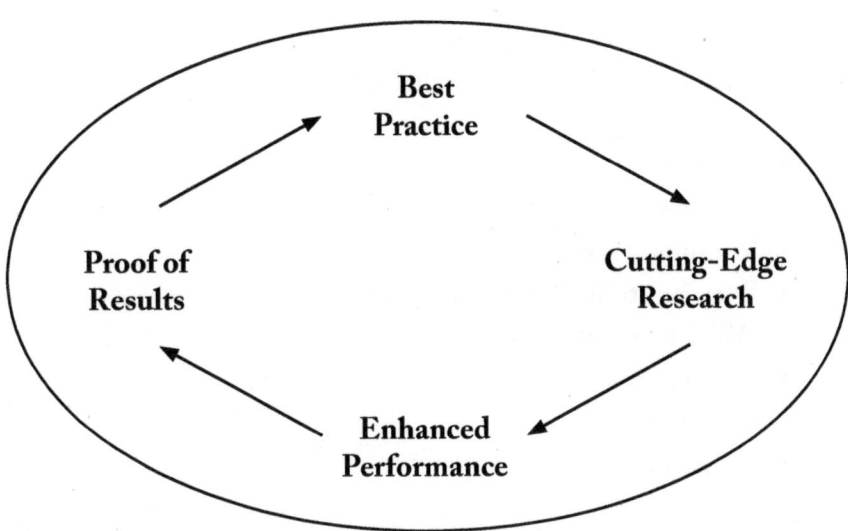

strength. So we agreed that we would need a covenant from their backers if we were to proceed. As it turned out, by July 2011 it became clear that things had taken a downturn for Circle, who were no longer able to fund what we had planned. That was a blow for both sides, as they had given us some very useful input. However, we had plans B and C, and we asked the specialist consultants Colliers to help us move on.

In the end we went for Spire Healthcare, for whom Elizabeth Potter was tireless in her efforts to make it work. They had 37 hospitals in the UK, as well as five 'Perform' centres that came with the strapline 'Perform for Sport, Perform for Life, Perform for Work'. They were presenting together with Pure Sports Medicine, a London-based specialist clinic working out of three locations, with 27 per cent of their turnover coming from elite athletes. They told us that there were nearly 30 million injuries nationally a year from sport and recreation, ten million of which affected people's work, seven million of whom had private healthcare insurance. So we had a big market to aim for! They talked about there being a real imbalance between the huge amounts spent on football players and the lack of funds devoted to their care and fitness (which is not quite so true today).

We ran through all the facilities and expertise we would ideally want in our sports injury clinic:

- Strength and conditioning
- Diagnostics, prehab and rehabilitation
- Nutrition
- Psychology
- Podiatry
- Running track
- Exercise studio/Pilates and boxing
- Weight room fully kitted out
- Aquatherapy
- Cryotherapy
- Sports massage

Spire's idea was for the National Football Centre to offer the ultimate corporate retreat and to be a focus for referrals across the UK. The fact that they already had a hospital 30 minutes away at Little Aston was a bonus. It was perfect timing for them, and frankly the withdrawal of Circle – sad as it was – worked for us as well. We agreed that the biggest risk would be being able to drive enough corporate clients to reach break-even as quickly as possible.

Anyway, we proceeded and, thanks to some expert advice from Mike Davison and Aussie Tim Wright, made sure that Spire's 'Perform' clinic was there as part of the set-up on opening day. It became an integral part of our business at the facility for the first five years, bringing in numerous patients and athletes from different sports and walks of life. And this was not just to the unit itself, but also to the hotel. There was also good synergy with the FA Medical Department, which was under the new leadership of Dr Charlotte Cowie.

We were also fortunate to strike a brilliant deal with Phil Horton and Technogym to kit out the phenomenal new gym that we had deliberately sited overlooking the number one Wembley replica pitch. This was a ploy that I had learnt from a visit to Monaco's training ground, where they had a similar set-up. The psychology behind it was that injured or rehabilitating players would look out on to the pitch, see their team-mates and want to recover quicker.

I had developed a good rapport with Spire CEO Rob Roger and his senior team. However, sadly, some time after I had ceased being involved on a day-to-day basis, Spire decided that they just couldn't make it work financially, and closed the unit. It was a great pity. Somehow the fire went out. However, the facilities have now been reconfigured to accommodate the FA's expanding presence on site, including in sports science and analytics.

**Christening our baby**
One of the most crucial days in the entire project came on 4 November 2009, when in a discussion about what to call the National Football Centre project, Bob Murray – in his own calm, quiet way – suddenly piped up and asked, 'What does anyone think about St George's Park?'

The room went silent, but that was then followed almost immediately by excitement. I loved it, I think we all did. It was an inspired moment from Bob.

In January 2010 we held a press conference to announce our new name. I still maintain it was one of the best decisions we took. And to think that not long before we had even talked about selling the naming rights!

**Military-type training**
I was keen to have an outdoor course, akin to what I had seen being so effective at Sandhurst and other locations, where they teach people to solve problems under time pressure on an obstacle course. Howard Wilkinson, Trevor Brooking and Gareth Southgate all joined us on our visits to Sandhurst and Westbury (home of army officer selection, which would later be run by Colonel Lucy Giles). Afterwards we came up with some takeaways, starting with the obvious value not just of experiential peer-group time, but also of doing exercises and practical tests – making it not just a matter of listening to lectures. We also talked about how important selection was in recruitment, and the fact that it's the leader that sets the culture of the group. In everyday language I would define culture as 'this is how we do things around here, and this is why'.

I tracked down Jerome Mayhew (who is now an MP), the owner of zipwire firm Go Ape!, who are based in East Anglia. But there was no traction in having one of their adventure scenario sites, mainly aimed at children it has to be said, at St George's Park. That meant my best chance was looking to be Grahame Robb, who I have a lot of time for despite being a Canary! I had seen his set-up at the BMW Hotel near Reading, where they ran an assault course and various programmes involving 'command and leadership' tasks using outdoor apparatus.

It looked like just the kind of thing we wanted, so Grahame came over and took us through his business and how he thought it could work at St George's Park. We soon appreciated that they were much more than an outdoor training provider, and actually ran international courses in South Africa and the US, and had contracts with big players in the UK, including BMW, KPMG and HSBC. He wanted to use our facilities to hold their national conference shortly after we opened, which was great news. As was the fact that, once Grahame had come on board, 70 per cent of people attending their courses stayed in the hotel.

Still on a military theme, I also spent time talking with Dr Andrew Franklyn-Miller, who had worked with the Melbourne Storm rugby league outfit before coming back to work at Headley Court, the specialist centre for badly injured soldiers. Many of them had lost limbs in Iraq and Afghanistan, and meeting them was a humbling experience, both shocking and inspirational in equal measure. The late Duke of Westminster was a massive supporter, and was in fact in the process of funding a new centre at Stanford Hall, which was not that far away from us. I was naturally keen to see if we could do any rehabilitation work for them, so I went to meet the duke at his London office. But it turned out that there wasn't really an opportunity for us there, mainly because his enormous generosity had already ensured that the new site was extremely well resourced.

**Universities**
Given the importance we attached to the educational nature of the coaching scheme that was at the heart of the project, it made complete

sense to forge ties with universities. We talked to Leeds, Birmingham, Warwick and the Open University to name but a few, and also with business schools such as Oxford's Saïd, Judge at Cambridge and LBS. Clive Woodward, the World Cup-winning rugby coach, lent us a hand throughout and was keen to get Sebastian Coe engaged. Seb was chancellor of his alma mater Loughborough, but when I met him he explained that they had already gone down the Olympic Park route in terms of satellites.

The whole process meant that I met a lot of fascinating people, and either directly or subliminally I could feel a constant drip of new ideas germinating. That was a compensation, as in the end we developed some excellent relationships with the academic world, affiliations even, but no business partners among the universities, and certainly no injection of capital.

On the advice of our local board member, Frank McArdle, we approached Dawn Ward, the principal of Burton and South Derbyshire College, the further education centre where Frank was a governor, and they pledged a very welcome £1 million towards an educational partnership. Throughout the process we really tried hard to fully engage with the surrounding community, including putting on presentations in village halls and other nearby venues, the highlight being one held at Burton Albion's Pirelli Stadium. To cap it all, Albion owner Ben Robinson and I were made Fellows of the College, and marched around the streets in full regalia. We also made a point of retaining our arrangement for Burton Albion to use our new facilities as their training ground.

But other local funding failed to materialise. Nothing came of my meeting with the Duchy of Lancaster, in whose domain we were located, and we were also turned down by AWM, Advantage West Midlands, the government funding body for the Birmingham area. They basically told us that there wasn't any money left. They were very apologetic, said they liked our plan and would recommend it, etc. Even so, humph!

For a while we got excited about the possibility of Tesco joining forces with us, perhaps using St George's Park as a training hub. I met with their Peta Hay, and they really liked the Academy Leadership Programme, but location was an issue for them, and nothing came of it. The same was true of McDonald's, a long-standing FA sponsor.

And it was a similar story when I called the Premier League teams: Arsenal, West Ham, Stoke, Newcastle, Manchester United, Wolves, Chelsea and others all said it sounded great, and confirmed their backing. Verbal backing, that is, and nothing more. Everyone on the FA Board was openly supportive when we succeeded, but – and while I can't prove – at the critical moments I had the feeling that some of the Premier League clubs saw us as a threat or competitor to their academies and were secretly waiting for us to fail.

I am proud of the number of groundbreaking initiatives that we explored, and there was certainly no lack of trying or experimenting. Not all were going to work, of course, but the added hoop that I always had to jump through was that we were a governing body, or part of one, and not an entrepreneurial business, so the FA didn't necessarily view things with the same excitement as I did.

## Chapter 36
# Costs ... and Values

IN THE summer of 2010 we had a dodgy moment when we found that we were £8 million short of what we needed to build the project.

The building quotes had just come in, the best being from Bowmer and Kirkland at £76.5 million – considerably over what we had in our plan. And to cap it all, not a single commercial opportunity had come through. We had somebody delegated to us from the main FA commercial arm, but we all had the nagging feeling that we were always coming second in their priorities, at a time when we were intent on demonstrating new revenue opportunities.

They were not easy days. We spent a lot of time going through the tender documents line by line, to 'value engineer' the specification. We also considered the options for sponsorship deals on raw materials, or getting cheaper financing options, and then we started talking about fixed-price tenders, hotel funding, managing consultants ... we looked at everything. We simply had no option. Monday 23 August 2010 became 'Challenge the Business Plan and All Its Assumptions' day, and at the end of it we reckoned we could get everything done for £69 million, which was nearly there. Alex Horne was the financial gatekeeper (and later Mark Donnelly) who kept us on the straight and narrow.

Being hard-up can make you lose perspective. And as the months went by we came to realise there was a real danger that we were trying to cut costs beyond what was consistent with building a world-class facility.

Mark Richards from project managers Turner and Townsend insisted that we had a top project that we could deliver for around £80 million, and urged us to have the courage of our convictions: 'A Rolls-Royce with a matt finish will be self-defeating' was how he put it. The message was 'let's get it built and let it sell itself'!

So that is what we did.

**Other sources of capital**

In October 2010 we did finally identify some new sources of capital. In what sounds like the corporate equivalent of finding 50 quid sitting in an old suit pocket (though it was an awful lot more than that), the trustees concluded that £3 million in a largely redundant FA trust could be repurposed to us. And it also looked as if the Football Foundation would probably be providing half a million towards the community pitches.

Meanwhile the League Managers Association had confirmed that they wanted to move their offices to our site. That would bring rent, but no capital. But just adding to the critical mass of proper football people in the game's new home was a real boost, and so the LMA's Richard Bevan became the first major football stakeholder to pledge support. Something I appreciated no end. And soon after, following my pleas to CEO Gordon Taylor, the PFA agreed to invest £1 million in a new library facility, and were also considering renting a satellite office at St George's Park.

Around the same time we found that Umbro, our England shirt producers, could be channelling a multimillion figure our way! That was amazing news. They were then owned by Nike, and although Umbro was actually sold while the complex was being built, Nike went on and rebranded all the stuff around the park.

The dominoes were finally beginning to fall.

**BT**

At my meeting with Chris Townsend from LOCOG, the London Olympics off-shoot that had raised an impressive £680 million (but couldn't really do anything concrete for us), I learnt that their main sponsor, BT, was very keen on football. Frank Dick had worked with the company for years, so through him I managed to track down Nigel Stagg, the CEO of BT Wholesale. We talked through the possibilities of doing some kind of contra-deal, with them supplying not only our IT/communications infrastructure but also Wembley's. When things finally came through it was for around £2 million, and was a fantastic deal for both the FA in general and us in particular, with the possibility of that amount growing considerably further with the Wembley contract.

**Westminster**

One of the most important relationships I nurtured during my time on the project, and still treasure, was with Hugh Robertson, who is now Sir Hugh after serving as chair of the British Olympic Association. When we first met he was the Shadow Minister of Sport, and I immediately discovered that the FA had not been in touch with him or anybody in the Conservative Party for five months. In fact, and especially given the number of Labour supporters in the FA ranks, it was not a generally happy relationship with what was becoming increasingly likely to be the new government — and did indeed become just that in the spring of 2010.

Hugh told me he felt it was important that any party in power should get behind a project as important as ours, and that he would support our cause. And, despite austerity policies and widespread cuts, he kept his word. Hugh stayed rock solid, and when we had to account for our budget to the FA Board, I was able to tell them that the new administration had promised us £6 million. To the visible surprise of the assembled!

Hugh was adamant throughout that he didn't want to get too involved with our issues, and that the government wanted to help sport, not run it. 'You've got to Olympify it,' he told me. And from that day on 'legacy' would become a watchword for us. So anyone getting involved was helping build something that would benefit people for years to come. Much as they were doing for London's 2012 extravaganza.

The government funding actually came through Sport England, who were initially very sceptical and gave me a rough ride over what the community benefit would be – the answer was the pitches for local grassroots schemes and schools usage. And there was another wrinkle on the way when they demanded their pound of flesh by insisting that we ensure public access to the whole site. Accessibility was indeed one of our values, but there is no way we could tear down the fences and allow a free-for-all, especially when some of the most famous people in the country would be training there. It would be mob rule. It took some negotiation, but we eventually resolved that.

Something similar relating to the accommodation side of things was flagged by Michelle Farrer, the director of team operations for the England set-up. She pointed out that undesirables (especially undesirables armed with telephoto lenses and reporters' notebooks!) might be able to book hotel rooms when the team was in residence. So, while it wasn't the case on day one, the FA do now lock down the whole complex during senior player training camps.

**Stepping down, and stepping up!**
In April 2011, I announced that I would step down from the Football League and FA boards (and indeed Ipswich Town too) to concentrate on St George's Park. I have to say that being able to focus all my energy on something that had become so all-consuming, rather than waste it on political infighting, was a real relief. I still had a burning passion to get it right, a desire that had, if anything, grown as we progressed. By contrast, I increasingly struggled to feel the same intensity of purpose about tiresome administrative (i.e. political) issues down in London. I was touched at the time by a very kind message Barry Bright, the Kent FA man, sent me: 'Your dignity alongside your professionalism impresses me ... I know that St George's Park will be a success under your leadership.'

The truth is that since 2009 I had seen my role as being to stay on the main FA Board long enough to get the vote through to build St George's Park. The same to a large degree is true of what happened at Ipswich, where I had to stay as a director to keep my place at the FA.

But all that was behind me now. Yes, I had felt the need to compromise, but not to the extent that I ever felt that I *had been* compromised. And there's a big difference between the two.

## Breaking ground

The day of 31 January 2011 was a big one for us, as we assembled on site to 'break ground'. The Bowmer and Kirkland guys had brought along a symbolic, shiny silver spade for the ceremony. We plunged it into the earth to many cheers and camera flashes.

This is it, this is real, I had to tell myself. After all the travails, we were actually building the much-maligned National Football Centre.

By then it was firmly St George's Park, of course, and we had brought on Turner and Townsend as project managers, and they had an excellent relationship with Bowmer and Kirkland, our builders.

There was a lot to build, and a whole range of things that required attention. All the myriad of consultants played their part. Everything from laundry facilities, a media area, the lecture theatre, games and leisure rooms for the downtime when players stay there, the library, a computer room (those were the days!), weights areas, gymnasium, swimming pool, hydrotherapy pools ... they all needed decisions made in one way or another. As did the goalkeeping areas, sand pits, sand rehabilitation lanes, sweat boxes, bleep test zones and the perimeter trail.

Then came the indoor pitches, and small-sided synthetic pitches for skills training, but also for partially sighted and blind teams. We should recall at this point that this was a facility not just for Wayne Rooney and co. but for all 26 of England's men's and women's teams. And that includes the cerebral palsy and wheelchair sides. Being inclusive and embracing as possible was a priority with us from the start, as was making sure we injected positive energy throughout.

When it came to the outdoor pitches, we had to redo all those laid eight years previously – which along with the roadways and floodlights were all that was still in place from the initial project. A great deal of thought went into producing a replica of the Wembley playing surface, and to ensure the consistency, camber and general feel of all the pitches.

To lead the way in looking after our new domain, I chose none other than our old friend, former Ipswich groundsman Alan Ferguson. One might speculate that he had grown tired of trying to get the latest expensive new kit out of Marcus Evans and his finance people, but the truth is that the St George's Park job was clearly a once-in-a-lifetime opportunity. Hard to manage or not, he was the best groundsman in the country, I wanted him there and I knew I could rely on him to deliver.

Not everything got into the final plan, of course. A lot of people had wanted a hypobaric chamber, for example, which replicates the kind of low oxygen environments you might find climbing in the Himalayas, and apparently does wonders for endurance. That would have to wait, but I did win my battle for the $500,000 funding for the American underwater treadmill. That put us at the very forefront of hydrotherapy in the country, and it was one of only eight then in existence in the UK.

There was one set of stakeholders that really set us back, and they were not middle-aged men sitting around a boardroom table (though they did look a bit like dinosaurs!). But they were the terror of building crews all around the country. Yes, like many others before us, we had fallen foul of the greater crested newt! It had fairly quickly become apparent that we had these six-inch critters on our patch, and would need to take the appropriate measures to rehouse them and keep the environmentalists quiet. All of that would end up delaying us by more than three months.

There were also protected trees that we had to navigate around. And then we had an issue with Severn Trent and our water supplies, as a survey was needed on our weir, which had seen better days. Doug Ellis, the notorious chairman of Aston Villa and heavyweight FA influencer, came over to visit one day and was so impressed by what we had done that he offered to stock the pond by the weir with 200 trout. The trouble is that the water was shallow and needed dredging and we just didn't have the budget to do it. By the time we could afford to drain it and repair the weir, dear Doug was sadly not just 'deadly' but actually dead. So we never got our trout!

Although he definitely had quite an ego, Doug was often unfairly maligned, and was actually a generous philanthropist for various causes in the West Midlands. I was greatly amused the time he told me about when he went to Buckingham Palace to receive an award, whether it was his OBE or knighthood I don't recall. What I do remember is the delight on his face when describing how he had presented a signed copy of his autobiography to the Queen! History does not record Her Majesty's reaction to the addition of *Deadly Doug: Behind the Scenes at Aston Villa FC* to the royal collection.

Handling the St George's Park project was a bit like running a football club and learning to take wins and defeats in your stride, treating those twin imposters the same. We learnt to expect that there would be pluses and minuses along the way. An example of this was when the Environment Agency people informed us in early March 2011 that our plan didn't cover foul water. That would cost us another £850,000.

Fortunately, that bitter pill was very much sweetened by the news that very day that the UEFA HatTrick fund might be able to help us with no less than £3 million. And the same week we identified two new deals, one with NPower and the other with TOPPS for a total of £425,000 per annum for four years, which was all very welcome.

## Final tweaks

As we drew nearer to practical completion, the big-ticket items were mainly in hand, but again there was a plethora of small details to deal with. Whether it was the provision of a multi-faith room and final consultations on what that needed to include, or the layout of jogging trails and footpaths, a play area for kids, retail merchandising, stocking the library, or putting up 'where am I?' signage ... I must again pay tribute to Ali Maclean, who did a masterful job as in-house project manager, and kept on top of all this detail quite brilliantly.

I should also reserve special praise for our MD, Julie Harrington, whose extraordinary operational skills came to the fore as we got nearer to opening. There was no template whatsoever, or a manual as to how to run a national football centre of such colossal size. But she created one, refined it and made it work. Inevitably there were some odd early hiccups, but she did it quite brilliantly, so much so that later she was promoted to become operations director for the whole FA, before going on to run British Cycling and then British Horseracing.

As a dedicated early morning swimmer, something that particularly caught my attention was the fact that the full-height windows along the sides made the pool feel a bit too public. The Red Box team came up with a genius idea: they had the lower level glass panels cut with engraved bamboo reed patterns. It looked great, and meant you could see out, but nobody could look in.

Another issue that had to be nipped in the bud was that people had started calling it 'St George's'! We certainly weren't having that, and insisted on the proper name.

St George's Park was to have a soft launch date in mid-August, and then the big day, the grand opening on 9 October 2012.

**A royal opening**
Any royal visit comes with a fair degree of protocol, and once the FA Board agreed that we were to ask Prince William, etiquette meant inviting him through the Lord Lieutenant of Staffordshire. The next step was booking an inspection date. We were fortunate that our recce was conducted by Jamie Lowther-Pinkerton, a former equerry to the Queen Mother who, like me, was a deputy lieutenant of Suffolk. He was rather taken aback at quite how enormous the site was, and concluded that we would need at least two hours to do it justice.

I cannot overstate the importance of the constant encouragement we have had from Prince William. His support for all the England teams, both men's and women's, right across the age and disability spectrum, has been immense ever since he took over as FA president. He joined us for St George's Park's tenth anniversary celebrations, and he has come up to meet both men's and women's senior teams and the Under-21s to wish them well before they embarked for every Euro and World Cup campaign. And he has regularly been present to cheer them on at big tournament matches, wherever they were played. That is a real commitment in what is already a very busy schedule, and I know it means a lot to players, managers, coaches and officials.

For the opening, the Duke and Duchess of Cambridge did us proud, planting a commemorative pin oak tree outside the hotel. The duke even playfully admonished me for being 'corny' when I told him we had chosen William and Catherine roses for the Memorial Garden. They were very diligent in spending two hours touring the facilities, meeting the players and many of the team who had built it. There was even an amusing interaction between Ashley Cole – who was in the ice bath – and Princess Catherine.

So it was really a day to be treasured to have William and Catherine with us. We had built St George's Park in 17 months. It was on time and came in at £83.7 million construction cost against a budget of £82.5 million, adding to the original cost of land and pitches, leaving us all in at £105 million. And though I say it myself, we had got superb value.

It had been a real team effort, and everybody in England's football family is indebted to the people that made it happen. Although I have already named quite a few of them, several other people involved in the project are included in the acknowledgements section at the end.

While the values that the FA now state are slightly different, I would say that all seven of the ones that we started to identify along with Alan Smith in that restaurant in Newcastle are very much embodied at St George's Park:

- *Accessible* – to everyone
- *Aspirational* – football careers all start with a dream
- *Educational* – we hope everyone who comes will leave having learnt something
- *Rewarding* – everyone will be able to reflect positively on what they gained in their visit

- *Stimulating* – a stimulating environment, surroundings and people
- *Sustainable* – a place that can renew and refresh
- *Symbolic* – of the environment and the culture of the FA

Had we ever added another value, then that could – or should – have been 'adapative', or perhaps even 'evolving'. It was, after all, an inability or refusal to move with the times that had made the creation of the facility so crucial in the first place. So I am pleased to say that the current leadership team are today considering further enhancements, and what St George's Park 2.0 should look like.

Looking back, there are four areas where I would have loved to have done more, and that might yet still merit consideration in the future. The first is that there could be greater, and more visible, collaboration with universities, colleges and business schools, something that would also contribute to the continuous learning philosophy. Secondly, and despite the fact that it didn't work out for Spire, I remain convinced that there are synergies between healthcare and the performance and coaching environment. Thirdly, on the commercial side of things, I would say there is plenty of scope, and physical space, to create a sports technology park that would reinforce the 'destination' factor in the appeal of the overall package.

Finally, but most importantly, I believe that we are really missing an opportunity to help the young people setting out on a football career by not offering a 'skills for life' programme. This, possibly offered in partnership with educational providers, would put greater emphasis on a learning culture, and could include invaluable assistance in negotiating a way around the pitfalls that can beset even the most successful careers. For example, research suggests – shockingly – that as many as 40 per cent of players get into financial difficulty, or even go bankrupt, within five years of retiring from the game. We ask them to have old heads on young shoulders when playing, but too often these off-the-pitch issues are overlooked.

Above all, when looking to future-proof our mothership, the importance of competitor analysis and knowing what initiatives other countries are implementing will be a critical factor. And, like us, they are going to have to look far and wide and be open to a whole range of viewpoints and ideas.

**CBE: an unexpected honour**

I came home one evening in late November 2012 to find a very official-looking envelope from Buckingham Palace, and an excited Mona handing it to me. With my heart racing I soon discovered that I had been appointed CBE for services to sport and local charity. It was utterly thrilling, and as anyone who has received an honour will tell you, the worst thing is keeping quiet about it for a whole month, as you are required to do, until the New Year's announcement. I, of course, realise that this was also a recognition for everyone who had helped along the way, particularly at St George's Park and the Suffolk Community Foundation, and the citation reads 'for services to football and local charity'.

The investiture wasn't until May the following year, but it was an utterly glorious occasion. I was accompanied to the palace by Mona, Sophie and Tom, where I was delighted to receive the honour from Her Majesty Queen Elizabeth II. Among others to be honoured that day was the very talented violinist Nicola Benedetti.

Around the same time, and actually just around the corner from the Palace, I found myself honoured in a quite different way and this time by football royalty! I was walking down Jermyn Street when I heard a broad Scottish voice hailing me ('David! David!') from the other side of the road. I looked up and it was Sir Alex Ferguson! He came over, we embraced and chatted for a few minutes before each going on our way. Bear in mind that I had met Sir Alex many times over the preceding 20 years or so, and in the early days he must have had doubts concerning our very different journeys, at least that was how I felt. But this was the first time he had been so overtly warm towards me.

It meant a great deal to me. I rang Mona up excitedly and told her I had finally made it! I felt that I had finally earned my spurs, and been accepted as a worthy football person by the greatest manager of our time!

**Legacy**

At the beginning of this section I mentioned the importance of legacy, and St George's Park's primary aim – to get England teams winning. You would have to say the balance in recent years has been distinctly positive and, aside from what the two senior and U21 teams have achieved, there have been numerous successes at U17 and U19 level, and I remain convinced that we will win both a men's and a women's World Cup soon.

England training camps certainly look very different from what they did before St George's Park existed. Dan Ashworth did invaluable work in establishing what the 'England DNA' looked like, and in identifying the attributes that he, Gareth Southgate and others wanted to see in our top players. Gareth should also be praised for having fostered a real sense of fellowship among the squad members, and in building off-the-pitch friendships that were in such contrast to the atmosphere during the so-called 'golden' (but nevertheless underachieving) generation – which failed to live up to its potential in part because inter-club rivalries were allowed to corrode the team spirit.

One of the greatest benefits of having a concentrated national training centre is the 'rub-off' effect. Like, for example, when different-aged players train next to each other, giving the senior team coaches the option of inviting over U21 or even U19 players to join their sessions. There is real value to bouncing ideas off one another and interacting and sharing experiences, whether it be among players, coaches, physios or even data analysts.

I loved the story of Raheem Sterling when he was an England star, going to play FIFA with some of the U17 squad in the hotel. I am sure loads of that kind of thing happens, and you can only imagine how the youngsters feel when they get to meet their idols, and what they pick up in an informal, social environment.

And that is what St George's Park has enabled: people coming together, creating friendships in a learning and sharing environment, as well as improving their skills. It's the power of experiential, peer-group learning at work and – as I was about to experience – that is a magic that can be worked in business as well as sport.

# PART NINE

## Chapter 37
# Manager, Chairman ... and Now Coach

WHEN MARTIN Glenn took over as CEO at the FA in 2015, he and chairman Greg Dyke set out on a series of much-needed cost-cutting measures.

Martin is a first-class operator, with experience at the top of PepsiCo and United Biscuits, and the rationale behind the cuts at St George's Park was clear – the facility had been built and launched successfully, and it was felt that it no longer needed the same high-level attention.

What I was disappointed by, however, was what I saw as a rash decision to cut the St George's Park board without properly understanding its role or, indeed, its cost – which was insignificant. It wasn't out of any sense of self-preservation, but rather because I feared that – without its board stewards – St George's Park would lose some of its identity and the beating heart that we had worked so hard to create, and might simply fade into becoming another FA department where the emotional bond with what we had brought to life wouldn't be the same.

Martin agreed to meet me at the facility, and listened attentively as I spelled out the values we had embraced so passionately. It's a reflection of quite how committed – obsessed even – I had become in my support for the project that the whole story took two hours. But my heartfelt account clearly hit the mark, as at the end he admitted he hadn't fully appreciated the situation, and simply couldn't let me go. Even better, he paid me the ultimate compliment – and one I have never forgotten – of saying he wanted me to be 'the guardian of the St George's Park vision'! There was no job brief as such, but it was a nice thing to say that I really appreciated.

A little while later we agreed that I would set up a think tank to challenge internal thinking and, needless to say, I was excited at the prospect. But it would only meet three or four times a year. So, aged 63, and full of energy, I would need to look for something more.

One day, I saw an advertisement in the *Sunday Times* from the Vistage Group, who were looking for experienced senior business operators to chair their 'leadership peer groups'. That sounded like me, so I rang up and arranged to visit their head office in Southampton.

It quickly became clear that it would be a lot harder work than I had at first thought. I would need to go back to school and do their two-week course, where my Vistage coach was Steve McNulty. He taught me a lot! But I would then also have to find at least 15 local business leaders ready to pay Vistage north of £1k per month to have me as their coach/mentor. So my value proposition had better be good!

Curiously, as I started casting my net around East Anglia and London for suitable candidates, the people who I thought might sign up said 'no', while I found willing subjects where I had least expected to.

My pitch improved as I practised it. It focused on the loneliness of being at the top of an organisation and the value of having someone to turn to, who could challenge their thinking in an independent, non-judgemental and confidential manner. The proposition was essentially: 'How would it feel to sit among a trustworthy, growth-orientated peer group of business leaders from different sectors, who you could bounce ideas off, or who could confirm that you are on the right track, or not?' Affirmation is so valuable when we are out there in the heat of the moment.

This approach resonated, and continues to. Vistage has about a hundred coaches around the UK and many thousands more in the US, Canada, Australia and Europe. There are dozens of coaching firms out there, and I would recommend nearly any of them, although ultimately it comes down to how good your own particular coach is. But I am biased and do think the Vistage model is rather different to the others, and is definitely the one I prefer. It places a premium on peer-group learning, where we encourage participants to share something they are wrestling with and then invite the group to help them sort it out. We start with questioning to properly understand the problem and then deep-dive into it. It's a very powerful tool and, crucially, is experiential and deals with real 'live' issues. Confidentiality is a key feature of the whole process, of course, so what is said in the room stays in the room.

The second element of the Vistage model is that for most meetings (but not all), we have a whole array of brilliant workshop speakers who typically present interactive sessions for about three hours at the monthly or bi-monthly group sessions. As the host, I choose them to speak on whatever subject is most topical or useful to the group, with Marcus Child and Brad Waldron being among many of them who are right at the top of their game.

The material ranges across all aspects of leadership, team building, goal-setting, making values relevant, conflict management, negotiation skills, time management, managing up (and down!), effective public speaking and presentation skills. They are interactive sessions, so there is lots of 'discuss in pairs ... what do you think about ...?' And the aim is to make them fun.

The third element is the 1:1 coaching that they then get with me. This is really the glue that holds everything together. I have developed a very simple two-page template, the first part of which concentrates on what they would like to be clearer about in 90 minutes' time, while the second is their own 'One Page Plan'. That covers the following one and three-year periods, an exercise we call 1/3/5. It means putting down one three-year vision, three annual goals that move you nearer to that three-year target, and then five quarterly 'rocks' (a concept taken from a book called *Traction* by Gino Wickman, and from the Reclaro model developed by Geordie, Pete Wilkinson).

Too many people complicate things, so I aim for simplicity above everything else, and encourage participants to come up with a shortlist of things that really matter, often limited to three priorities that are memorable, and the actions that really 'move the dial'.

As I have got older I have learnt the wisdom of asking better questions and the importance of 'understanding before being understood'. That is from Stephen Covey's utterly brilliant *Seven Habits of Highly Effective People* that I mentioned earlier, my other favourite habit being 'beginning with the end in mind'. I have also acquired a golden rule, which is that any 1:1 meeting or appraisal has to start with something positive, before we take a closer look at the issues of the day.

When first meeting a new client, I want to assess their mindset and their curiosity. After asking what makes them tick, I start off by telling them that while I have plenty of experience in several different areas, and may offer advice, I am by no means an oracle, and I certainly don't have all the answers. I am there to ask them questions to help clarify their thinking, rather than telling them what to think. In fact, in my own mind I still have 'L' plates on, and am convinced that I will go on learning until the day that I drop and – hopefully – so will they. For me, every day is a learning day. I always try to give them some examples of that, like how I have only just discovered that you could email content to your Kindle!

I tell them about Frank Dick, whose effect on me has been profound, and whose mantra is that a learning mindset is a winning mindset. Frank imbued in me the 'take the risk of winning' approach – as opposed to the paralysis that accompanies fear of failure. I also tell the story of how Satya Nadella, when starting out as Microsoft CEO, told his leadership team that the big issue was that too many of them were know-it-alls, and that the only way the company was going to get back on the front foot was if they all became learn-it-alls. I love that story and find it resonates with a lot of people I work with. It's a matter of finding how to encourage your team to embrace a learning culture. So in selecting clients, I am probing for their curiosity and openness, their zest to learn.

That is something that our young manager, Kieran McKenna, has done brilliantly at Ipswich Town. He will not have anyone in the building – whether it be players, coaches or support team – who does not want to commit to improving. Indeed, players are already choosing Ipswich because they know Kieran will help them get better. It's simply a new take on the older, established kaizen, marginal gains or continuous improvement models, but I am convinced it will pay dividends in the end.

I succeeded in filling three Vistage groups quite quickly, with between 15 and 20 members each. I have been fortunate enough to coach about 150 people over the years, probably a third of them women, with most people in their 40s or 50s, but with some still yet to turn 30, and others over 60. Many of them were established leaders, while others were up and coming. I have been very lucky to do it – for me it was almost like becoming a non-executive director to each of them as individuals. And, while I do challenge them all ('carefrontationally', as I like to put it), many have become great friends. Typically members stay with us in a group for three to five years; however, I have had a few who stay for nearly ten. I do less nowadays, but still get a buzz from working with numerous selected private clients.

As I mentioned at the outset, I wish I'd had a coach when I was setting out in business. Or had simply met Frank Dick earlier. You have to choose very carefully, but I do recommend that all leaders find themselves a coach or mentor if they don't already have one. Contrary to what many might say, I think the increasingly impersonal AI and robotic world will actually increase the need for coaching.

### The Churchill Fellowship

At around the same time as I was beginning my next chapter as a leadership coach, I was invited to become a trustee of the extraordinary Winston Churchill Memorial Trust, which now uses the name 'The Churchill Fellowship'. The organisation has a remarkably low profile considering the outstanding work it does, especially in funding visits for 120–150 people every year to learn from world experts in a wide range of fields. The demand for places is huge, with a record 1,700 requests received this year from applicants ranging in age from 18 to over 70.

There have been 6,000 of these fellowships awarded since their inception in 1965. It's a wonderful charity, a community of changemakers who champion global solutions to today's social and educational challenges. And I love the fact that, unusually for a charity, it supports individuals rather than groups.

I am still involved with the cause, as – after finishing an enjoyable seven-year term as trustee – I was lured back by CEO Julia Weston and chairman Jeremy Soames, Winston's grandson. This was to chair their 60th anniversary 'activate' appeal, which is looking to raise £10 million for a type of incubator fund to enable fellows to implement and scale up their ideas. At the time of writing, our quest to 'enable changemakers to start changing things' is well over halfway to its target.

One of the most extraordinary things I find about this hidden gem of a charity is that there are Churchill Fellows everywhere in public life, ranging from academics to reformed offenders, as well as more high-profile alumnae such as Paralympian Dame Tanni Grey-Thompson and 1972 Olympic pentathlon champion Dame Mary Peters.

One of my favourite quotes from the great man himself perfectly illustrates the satisfaction that comes with the wonder of philanthropy: 'What's the use of living if it be not to strive for noble causes, and to make this muddled world a better world for those who will live in it after we are gone?'

## Argent Related

In 2016, I was approached by a close friend, Rob Townshend, one of the country's leading landscape architects, about one of his clients, Argent Related. They wanted to engage with someone knowledgeable in the world of sport who could help them with their major new construction project in north London. Argent had already developed a tremendous reputation for their novel and imaginative development of King's Cross and, together with their US partners Related, had won the contract to develop Brent Cross South, which is the area immediately between the A1 and the beginning of the M1.

I met with Richard Meier and Hannah Grealish to hear that they wanted to place various sports and recreational activities at the heart of the development, with a special emphasis on community engagement and even social prescribing; areas that I was familiar with through my work with community foundations and various football trusts. They had a big, bold vision for what they could design, reflecting the request of the Leader of Barnet Council, Richard Cornelius: 'It is important to this council that we create a living, thriving neighbourhood with a real sense of place. We want to create a new town centre that will set the standard for developing successful new neighbourhoods in London.'

Over the following years, I introduced Argent to an extensive array of governing bodies and sports institutions to explore what could be created on site. As well as the FA and the national netball, rowing, boxing, swimming and hockey associations, we talked to UK Sport, the NBA, Tottenham Hotspur, Go Karting, Middlesex University, Loughborough University, St Mary's College in Twickenham, the British Olympic Association, Sport England (Charles Johnson was particularly helpful), and Go Ape.

Although Richard Meier left us to pursue his own business venture, by 2019 we had been joined by Heath Harvey – who I had recommended and had previously run Club Wembley and all the corporate hospitality for the FA. Heath did a tremendous job and we developed a radical blueprint for both indoor and outdoor multisport facilities at Brent Cross. We were also assisted by David Portas and his excellent team. However, after four years, Covid struck and, tragically, Argent Related had to retrench, with the majority of our endeavours either being canned or put on long-term hold, including my contract with them. Of course, times were very uncertain and the building industry was hit hard, not just our project. But it was a crying shame. I loved working with Argent Related.

## Picking up the TAB: building the FA Technical Advisory Board

Soon after setting out with Vistage, I shared the peer-group model with Martin Glenn and floated the concept of doing something similar at St George's Park. Martin liked the idea and, after we had discussed a few names, he gave me carte blanche to set up the TAB (Technical Advisory Board – which sounds a bit grandiose, but the FA love titles!). So I started contacting people from high-performance worlds who we thought could add special value. The first group I enlisted comprised:

- Sir Dave Brailsford – formerly of British Cycling (where he became known for the 'marginal gains' approach), then at Team Sky and now at the extended Ineos sports group
- Stuart Lancaster – former England, Leinster and Racing 92 rugby coach, now with Connacht
- Manoj Badale – co-founder of the hugely successful tech 'venture builder' firm Blenheim Chalcot and owner of the Rajasthan Royals from cricket's Indian Premier League (IPL)
- Lord Barber – educationalist, cabinet advisor and McKinsey consultant who started Delivery Associates (proponents of *deliverology*, 'a practical, adaptable set of tools for turning big goals into real outcomes') and chairman of Somerset County Cricket Club
- Colonel Lucy Giles – the first female College Commander at Sandhurst, and former president of the Army Officer Selection Board
- Baroness Sue Campbell – former chair of UK Sport, CEO of the Youth Sport Trust and the FA's Head of Women's Football, recently appointed as the head of UK Netball
- Matthew Syed – four-time British table tennis champion, exceptional thought leader, journalist and author of *Bounce, Black Box Thinking, Rebel Ideas* and other books

- Graham Le Saux – former Chelsea, Blackburn and England player
- Dame Katherine Grainger – Olympic rowing champion, chair of UK Sport and now the first-ever woman to lead the British Olympic Association

In Matthew's case, I had simply read *Bounce* and been inspired, but I didn't know most of them, so it was exciting to meet them all. I would say that the three Ms – Manoj, Matthew and Michael – have three of the most incisive, yet complementary, minds that I have ever encountered. Every single member of our board contributed valuably and – although there was no fee involved – they all wanted to come along, and, having experienced it, simply wanted to hear and be inspired by each others' ideas.

We started out in 2016, coinciding with Martin's appointment of Gareth Southgate as England manager. What a decision that was, coming on the back of the demise of Sam Allardyce.

The way it worked was that either Gareth, or occasionally another senior leader at the FA, would begin the meeting by proposing an issue with a short introduction or a few slides. I used to chair the meetings with a light touch, steering the members to ask clarifying questions first, before coming in with their own ideas. It was utterly compelling – not surprisingly given the brilliance and diversity of the assembled minds – and I loved every minute of it.

One of the best meetings I recall was when Gareth asked how he could deliver a training camp during the Russia World Cup that would be most conducive to a happy and winning team. Gareth, it should be noted, is quite untypical as a football leader in being prepared to really open himself up, and indulges in what FA technical director John McDermott called 'brutally honest self-reflection'. Combined with 'incredible intuition … a strong moral compass and insatiable work ethic', John says this makes people 'want to follow [Gareth], have his back and be frightened not to let him down!'

It was a brilliant session. So many good ideas came out of it, including a blueprint for handling both traditional and social media, the first time that had been done. Michael Barber pitched in with an excellent compendium on Russia for players and coaches alike, which included a short history, and sections on the culture, music, the arts, etc.

Needless to say, Gareth wasn't under any obligation to use all the suggestions. We only kept brief notes, but didn't circulate minutes, working on the basis of strict confidentiality. Sections of the media did, however, manage to get wind of the composition of the group, and set about lambasting the concept because we only had one footballer, demanding to know what the rest of us knew about the game, which completely missed the point. As Matthew Syed later wrote when discussing our approach in his book *Rebel Ideas*, this was all a matter of cognitive diversity. It was the very opposite of the 'group think' that has for so long plagued sport and indeed organisations right across the spectrum.

This was a collection of high-performance leaders in other sports, business, education and the armed services who were not there to tell the England manager what to do, but rather to challenge and broaden his thinking from a range of perspectives. We ran sessions on all sorts of other subjects for Gareth, who thoroughly embraced the concept, as later did Sarina Wiegman (who I can say, having got to know her, is a remarkable lady). We also did a session on diversity, ethnicity and inclusion, and the meetings – while becoming less frequent – continued right up until the end of Gareth's tenure. It's a measure of what great leaders Gareth and Sarina are – as is new man Thomas Tuchel, and indeed technical director John McDermott and U21 coach Lee Carsley – that they can open themselves up to embrace and learn from such 'carefrontational' and critical thinking without being defensive.

## From TAB to PAG

In early 2024, Mark Bullingham, who had been in post for some years as CEO of the FA, called me to say that he wanted to create a revamped TAB, which would now be known as the Professional Advisory Group (PAG), as a subsidiary of the FA Board. He wanted to have a board member to chair it and put forward Jobi McAnuff, which was a shrewd appointment. A broadcaster and former player, Jobi was open about his lack of experience in that kind of role, so Mark asked me to help him by chairing the first four meetings, while mentoring Jobi to take over. It worked incredibly well. I finished in April 2025, when they gave me a lovely send-off, and I hear that Jobi is now taking it from strength to strength.

We retained Michael Barber, Lucy Giles and Manoj Badale from the old TAB group and added new blood in Kevin Sinfield from the rugby world (league and union) and author and podcaster Damian Hughes, both of whom brought excellent insight.

I have been impressed by the new approach. My admiration for Gareth Southgate is well known, and I think his contribution to the FA, St George's Park and England has been immense. So I was desperately sad when we lost the final of the Euros in Germany, having watched the match with the rest of the England fans (and getting soaked in beer when we scored) as the newly elected Labour government seemed to have taken a disproportionate number of the FA's allocation of seats!

There is no doubt that Thomas Tuchel brings a new perspective and acuity to the job. We can – and should – debate the fact that we have not appointed an English coach, but the fact of the matter is that the cupboard is bare. There are quite simply not enough candidates of the right calibre available. So, despite my devotion to St George's Park and what it stands for, I am strongly in favour of the move – quite simply, you pick the best winner you can. Thomas knows our domestic game, and it helps that his very skilled assistant, Anthony Barry, is English.

Anthony is quite open about his obsessive attention to detail, an obsession that led him to analyse over 16,000 throw-ins for the dissertation on his UEFA Pro Licence course. Concerned about his presentation skills before delivering those findings, Anthony reportedly tried his pitch out on literally one of the toughest audiences around, and went to a prison! Now that is what Frank Dick would call a true 'mountain person'. Not surprisingly, he finished top, earning not only the admiration of classmate Frank Lampard, but also a seat on the Chelsea bench, where he was the only coach kept on at the changing of the guard when Thomas arrived.

A friendship was born, and the rest is history ... and hopefully the best part of it is yet to be written by the 'Team England' group, and the 'brotherhood that everybody wants to be part of' that the two of them are trying to create.

'It's a constant process to have this problem/solution-finding mentality ... and to make the complex clear,' Anthony says. 'Everything starts with a dream, but dreams won't get it done ... how do we do it, day by day, step by step?'

I couldn't have put it better myself!

### A Caribbean cricket interlude

Although I have spent nearly four decades working in football, as noted hundreds of pages (and over six decades) back, cricket was actually my first love.

Ironically, one of my favourite cricket memories came about because of my involvement in football. In the summer of 2008, I was picked as one of three FA representatives to accompany the England team for their first-ever game in Trinidad. I flew out in very good company, with long-standing friends Peter Coates (Stoke City and bet365) and Terry Robinson, originally known as 'Terry from Bury', but who was at that point with Sheffield United and was subsequently at Ferencváros in Hungary.

Upon arrival in Port of Spain, we had a chat with Fabio Capello, an imposing character who had a touch of severity around his smile that left you – and particularly his players – a little uncertain where you stood with him. He also called his squad members by their surnames, thereby avoiding the familiarity that had so characterised previous regimes.

After breakfast the next day, we went off to watch the practice session and met with the infamous Jack Warner, president of CONCACAF, who was very much the big cheese in that part of the football world. Surrounded by a phalanx of pressmen and photographers, he was absolutely in his element. This was his moment.

It's debatable whether the whole event would ever have happened if the FA had not been so keen to win over one of FIFA's most prominent power brokers. But some good did come of it, as the visit included coaching sessions for local kids with David Beckham, Steven Gerrard, Rio Ferdinand and David James. They were brilliant, and it was great to see some of our big guns being nominated by Capello for the clinics, which drew thousands of spectators and ended with a lovely image of Beckham high-fiving his group.

The event was held at the Marvin Lee Stadium, the home ground of Jack's own team, the amusingly named Joe Public FC. The club folded a few years later, as I imagine did much of Warner's empire, when he was banned for life from football activities by FIFA.

The next day I was invited by Henry Winter, who I know well, on a boat trip down the coast, along with a veritable *Who's Who* of the gentlemen of the press, including Martin Samuel, Charlie Sale, Matt Lawton, Oliver Kay, Brian Woolnough, Michael Hart and 'laptop' Martin Lipton. I had known a lot of them for years through my league and FA roles and, although I always had to watch my step, we generally got on very well. It was a bit of a booze cruise, and turned out to be lots of fun.

We anchored, grabbed a bat and made our way through the undergrowth to a beach facing Venezuela. But to our horror it was high tide. Not to be denied, stumps were placed on the waterline, and the bowlers and fielders plunged into the sea with tennis balls, to be joined in the game by various local kids.

We were then told of a nearby garden that would be ideal, so we relocated and played an impromptu match in the shade of the palm trees. Charlie Sale was my captain and an able wicketkeeper, from where he directed operations. We could each bat for a maximum of two overs, and also had to bowl one over.

Our team won by fair means (and foul!), and Henry was the star of the show with some lusty hitting. At the conclusion of a jolly afternoon, we chugged back to harbour in the alcoholic haze of a Caribbean sunset; it had been a perfect day, and I had enjoyed chatting and getting to know everyone on the trip.

Next day, David Beckham captained England to a 3-0 victory. We were given a police escort to the airport after the match and had a very plush charter flight home with 50 first-class seats. Most of the players lived in the north, so we landed in Manchester and then flew on to Luton. It was quite a trip.

**Somerset CCC, and the IPL**

I am a long-standing member of the MCC, and became a follower of Somerset back in the days of Viv Richards, Joel Garner and Ian Botham. What I love about Somerset is that they have a lot in common with my beloved Ipswich. They are a rural club with great values, who have, for the main part, punched above their weight.

My passion for the game is high, so imagine my reaction when Michael Barber asked me to set up an advisory board for the county, where he is chairman. We have been going for a couple of years now, and what a pleasure it is, meeting two to three times a year in support of Michael, CEO Jamie Cox and their team of coaches. Our non-exec group includes Frank Dick, Colonel Lucy Giles, *Test Match Special* pundit Vic Marks and author Peter Frankopan. We also invite a guest expert, the latest being Damian Hughes, to the meetings, along with director of cricket Andy Hurry and coach Jason Kerr.

To compete with the big boys, Somerset have to do things more cleverly, quickly and be cuter and wiser. They have a great youth pathway, blooding numerous future England players. Our little committee supports their brilliant leadership team with some 'out-of-the-box' type challenges and thinking. I love it! And we consistently challenge for honours, winning the T20 Blast again this past year.

I also support Manoj Badale and his Rajasthan Royals, having enjoyed five trips to India to watch them in recent years, including an extraordinary occasion in April 2025 when 14-year-old Vaibhav Suryavanshi hit a 35-ball century That was an amazing night, and in fact all the IPL games are really exhilarating, as they have turned the whole event into an utterly compelling experience. Last year, I went to Bengaluru to watch the Royals play the Royal Challengers, or RCB, Virat Kohli's team. The Chinnaswamy Stadium was absolutely jumping, with a disc jockey blasting out music and a light show bouncing off the stands – nothing at all like the cricket we know back home.

So, as they say in the pink city of Jaipur, *Halla Bol*!

# PART TEN

*Nothing in this world can take the place of persistence. Talent will not; nothing is more common than unsuccessful men with talent. Genius will not; unrewarded genius is almost a proverb. Education will not; the world is full of educated derelicts. Persistence and determination alone are omnipotent. The slogan 'Press On!' has solved and always will solve the problems of the human race.*

Calvin Coolidge, US President 1923–1929

## Chapter 38
# Reflections

I RECALL sitting down with my mentor Frank Dick many years ago and hearing him speak about the 80-year-old in his proverbial rocking chair, surrounded by grandchildren asking him questions about his career, and whether he had any regrets.

The key, of course, is to try to live one's life intentionally, with positivity and purpose, and without regrets. Things don't always work out the way we want at the time; however, almost invariably we get another chance. We take some and miss out on others.

Personally, I have always believed in 'turning every stone' to see what lies beneath, and to explore every opportunity.

I might always wonder how I would have got on as chairman of the FA, which was a role I was passionate about. I certainly believe I had the attributes to do it well, but I know that, by the time I was acting co-chairman in 2010, my face didn't fit for a few of my colleagues, labelled a privileged old Etonian as I was.

Equally, I occasionally wonder what might have happened had I chosen a life in politics. At the time I think I might have enjoyed it, as many aspects of public life have brought out the best in me, and the moment when that doorway of intriguing possibilities stood open to me was certainly a crossroads in my life. In the end I didn't take that step. And looking at it today, with the intrigue and invasion into the lives of politicians in the social media age, I feel sure that I made the right decision.

I am a supreme believer in meritocracy, with an 'equal opportunity' mantra running through my veins throughout a life in entrepreneurial business, football and charity. I am proud of my achievements and the plethora of wonderful friends I have made from every walk of life throughout the journey, because a fabulous journey it has been ... and continues to be.

I have enjoyed some wonderful blessings, and successes along the way, most of all in meeting Mona (we have been married 47 years! Imagine her reserves of patience!) and having Sophie and Tom, our two brilliant, much-loved, and now grown-up children.

What was achieved at Ipswich Town, the Football League, St George's Park, the Suffolk and UK Community Foundations and the Churchill Fellowship rank as the big pluses, along with Vistage coaching and the peer/rebel ideas groups that I have loved doing with the FA and Somerset CCC. I am thrilled that I did finally get to do something in cricket as well, and that Manoj paid me the compliment of allowing me to be an honorary member of the Royals. I have also been privileged to have served Suffolk as a deputy lieutenant for 20 years, as the county is dear to my heart and in my blood.

Disappointments? Yes, I came second in a few job interviews, which I am sure others won on merit. That said, doing that well in a large field for top positions feels like a plus to me. If you never try, you will never know. And I am also a bit of a fatalist ... it's a matter of what is meant to be.

That is something I especially feel because heading up St George's Park turned out to be so much more worthwhile than those other roles, and there is something lasting to show for all the effort we put in. I am really proud of the fact that we were placemakers, although we had made clear at the outset that places alone do not win things, people do. But our dream was to create the environment for the national sides – both men and women – to flourish: a catalyst for learning, self-improvement and, ultimately, to excel.

Indeed, the first objective in building the facility was to lay the foundation from which winning England teams could emerge, and I think we can say that it's working well, with the new reality reflected in recent honours:

| | | |
|---|---|---|
| 2024 | Men's Senior Euros | Runners-up |
| 2020 | Men's Senior Euros | Runners-up |
| 2025 | Men's U21 Euros | Winners |
| 2023 | Men's U21 Euros | Winners |
| 2025 | Women's Senior Euros | Winners |
| 2022 | Women's Senior Euros | Winners |

The area that remains work in progress at St George's Park is coach education. Our aspiration, and that of others around us, that we could create the 'Oxford and Cambridge' of coach education has not yet materialised. Indeed, the landscape has changed, with many leading clubs introducing their own learning opportunities and objectives for their staff. That is the way of the future; however, UEFA gives individual national associations the opportunity to control the final coaching and management qualifications. While we have made many improvements, in my view there is still plenty of scope to learn from our European peers and set our standards even higher than theirs. And that is my sincere hope. Very good courses are run by the Scottish, Welsh and Irish FAs, and some young coaches opt for these for several factors, including accessibility and cost. So we have plenty of competition to spur us on.

What I would really like to see is the St George's Park/English qualification being held up as the very best you can get, a gold standard for clubs, and one that includes, for example, meaningful refresher courses after graduation.

As for Ipswich Town, it was an immense privilege to serve and lead our club in the years that I did. Through highs and lows, thick and thin, it's like a contract for life! In my head I have kicked just about every ball for nearly 40 years, and still do when I watch. There was plenty of agony with the way things contrived to thwart us, especially in the play-offs, and then the absolute ecstasy of winning promotion at Wembley and the joy of seeing our beloved Ipswich Town back on the big stage again.

But then more agony. Real agony. With relegation and everything that followed it, which left a pain that still hangs over me. Still, we managed to turn things around, to hand over a club that was refinanced, and what was ultimately a much more professional organisation throughout. The stadium and academy infrastructure was much improved, of course, but more importantly I would like to think that I had overseen a change in culture, leaving everyone aligned and working together as a proud and competitive team.

## Ipswich Town today

So what about our Ipswich of today? Well, WOW! It's so utterly different to what it was. Financially transformed, with investment on a scale that simply wasn't available 15–20 years ago, enabling all us fans to dream bigger and bolder than ever.

Importantly, the game has also been transformed culturally. The attitude towards fitness and skills training, work ethic, lifestyle, etc. is all much improved when compared with my day, not just at Ipswich, but throughout the top echelons of the game. Many players are even teetotal nowadays, so there are no problems like on the England cricket team's recent Ashes tour. It's worth noting that over 70 per cent of the squad members in Premier League for the 2025/26 season are foreign nationals, so the multicultural influence is enormous.

With all the money and investment in the transfer market come expectation and added pressure to deliver. Kieran McKenna on the pitch and Mark Ashton off it have masterminded four years of extraordinary growth and achievement, and they deserve all the praise that has come their way. However, the Premier League rather found us out in much the same way as it did 20 years earlier. The big difference is that the club is now so well funded that relegation, while a big disappointment, was not the disaster that it used to be. It's a time to retrench, learn our lessons and go again, hopefully stronger, wiser and better.

I have huge admiration for what has been achieved and I back Mark, Kieran and their teams to the hilt. I am a fan, like most of you reading this. I love going to the games and get just as excited as I did 50 years ago.

At long last Mark has recreated the community scheme – this time as the Ipswich Foundation – that we worked so hard to build up. Kids are proud to wear Ipswich shirts again and the mood in the town and the county is bright. That mood is a precious commodity, though, and one to be treasured, as we all know it can never be taken for granted.

Looking forward, the massive investment in the first team, training ground, academy and women's team all bode well for the future. In my day I thought we had every chance to challenge at the top end of the Premier League (as indeed we did, briefly), in much the same way as Brighton, Crystal Palace, Brentford and Bournemouth have shown is possible of late. But when I was at the helm, we were undone by a lack of resources to cover us when things didn't go right on the pitch.

Not this time, and I think Mark is eyeing something much bigger. With the backing of the American investors, Mark has both the resources and the will to realise those dreams.

I have passed the baton: he is now the Man on a Mission!

### UPPA TOWEN!

*Courage is a big word and it covers a multitude of accomplishments, be they mental or physical. Courage is more than just being able to get up after a buffeting on the field of play. Courage is also the ability to get up when things are getting you down, to get up and fight back, never to know defeat, let alone accept it. To have principles, be they fitness or morality, and stick to them. To do what you know you've got to do not because it's the popular thing to do, but because it's the right thing to do. Courage is skill, plus dedication, plus fitness, plus honesty, plus fearlessness. Courage is a big word, but it is one which should be hung above our bed if we are really serious about being professional and being a credit to the game and ourselves.*

—Attributed to Bill Shankly

# Acknowledgements

I WOULD like to close with a heartfelt 'thank you' to the team of very special people who have helped guide and challenge me, and sharpen my writing, during the long journey that creating this book became. It has certainly been a labour of love, starting as I did back in 2019, even before Covid. Combining writing with an active working life didn't come naturally, and I have suffered regular bouts of writer's block. My PA, Anne-Marie Williams, has been wonderful throughout, despite having been really put through the mill, typing and retyping what must have seemed like endless corrections. A lot of the original manuscript was handwritten, and she is the only one that can read my writing (and that quite often includes me!).

Latterly, last summer I was introduced to the brilliant Richard Bastin, who accepted the challenge of galvanising me to complete what was a three-quarters-written book. Just as importantly, he has edited it, cutting out much of the waffle and ensured that you, hopefully, have had an enjoyable and informative book to read. Thank you, Richard, you have been patient and a fabulous catalyst and supporter to helping me get this done.

Special thanks are also due to Neil Prentice (a diehard ITFC fan and author/compiler of wonderful books on George Burley and John Wark) for his support, and his expert commercial and creative input in particular. I also want to thank the similarly ardent Seán Salter (known locally as the 'Renegade Statman') for his eagle eye in checking all the Ipswich Town facts, and in compiling the season summaries. A number of the photos were taken by Warren Page, who

I have always enjoyed watching at work over the years and is really one of the best in the business.

I am indebted to David Luxton for introducing me to Paul and Jane Camillin and the team at Pitch Publishing, including Duncan Olner, whose creative genius can be seen on the cover, and Ivan Butler, who provided additional editorial prowess, and also super-attentive typesetter Gary Nickolls.

Other dear friends who have read and checked all or part of the text and whose judgement I have, as always, valued greatly include Henry Winter, Matthew Syed, Damian Hughes, David Davies, Julie Harrington, Jane Bateman and Chris Horne. It goes without saying that any errors or omissions are my fault, not theirs.

I have worked with, and for, many different organisations and people in my career, a number of whom have featured in my story; however, there is a wide cast who deserve special thanks (some of whom are sadly no longer with us):

**Family:** Mona, my wife and best friend of 50 years, Sophie and Paul, Tom and Liv.

**Our special home team:** Anne-Marie Williams, Karen Coady, Kay Potter, Jenny Westley-Richards, Sue Kimber, Lucas Hatch and Paul Smith, Lawrence, Chris Cubitt and Sally Taxi.

**Starfish (1980–1989) and Suffolk Foods (1990–2004)** would not have worked as well as they did without the unswerving support of my dear brother, Rick, to whom I am forever grateful. A lot of special people helped build those companies, but at Starfish I particularly valued the contributions of Gavin Cornall, Simon Muse and Sandra Firman when we first set up in 1981 in St Margaret's Green, Ipswich. While among the many at Suffolk Foods I especially remember Linda Moore, Barbara Whatley and the incomparable Tim Mack, not forgetting my future sister-in-law Anni Sheepshanks.

**Ipswich Town Football Club:** the privilege of working with three managers as exceptional, each in their own way, as George Burley, Joe Royle and Jim Magilton is something I will always cherish.

Huge credit is also due to all the directors I served with: Patrick Cobbold (who invited me on to the board), Harold Smith, Murray Sangster, Ken Brightwell, John Kerridge, John Kerr, Philip Hope-Cobbold and club secretary David Rose – sadly, none of whom are alive any longer. Those happily still among us include Richard Moore, Roger Finbow, Richard (Lord) Ryder, Kevin Beeston, Holly Bellingham, Peter Cohen, as well as CEO Derek Bowden, who came in and was a rock of support for me at an incredibly difficult time, finance director Anna Hughes, as well as commercial director Paul Clouting and his successor Andrew Goulborn.

I would especially like to thank Mike Noye, Pat Godbold, Alesha Gooderham, Terry Baxter, Mark Andrews, Bryan Klug, Charlie Woods, Dave Williams, Trevor Kirton ('Wheels'), Clair Westlake, Richard Powell, Ronnie Lamb, Sally Webb, Andy Crump, Rosie Richardson, Sally Williams, Jo Shevlin, Helen Broughton, Sue Crowe, Christine Last, Colin Hammond, the legendary Pat Godbold and the voice of Ipswich Town – our wonderful receptionist Edwina Sesto. They were an integral part of what we achieved, but the truth is that thanks are due to many, many more people who are simply too numerous to mention.

Among the players, we owe a debt to Bryan Hamilton, Simon Milton and later Matt Holland, among others, who took over the organisation of reunion dinners from Pat (which I can say from experience are a lot of fun and very well attended).

**Football League:** David Dent, Andy Williamson, Glynis Firth were the Holy Trinity and a guiding light for me when I was at the helm, but thanks must also go to former journalist Dennis Signy, and to Richard Masters (who would later move to the Premier League), Stewart Reagan and Andy Knee – who successively took on the near-impossible role of championship director, which is a truly thankless task. And, of course, there is Richard Scudamore, who was such a brilliant chief executive, and became a great friend, as did numerous special people who served on the board with me, including Theo Paphitis, Terry Robinson, Barry Hearn and Ian Ritchie.

**The Football Association:** from back in the early days I should mention Deputy CEO Pat Smith and Finance Director Mark Day (who have been friends ever since – and are now Tractor Boy converts!), as well as David Davies and Nic Coward. On the board and committees the names of David Dein and FA councillors Barry Taylor, Mark Arthur, Peter Coates, Terry Robinson, Rupert Lowe and John Elsom are ones that stand out from the many I enjoyed working with, while later it was good to get to know Greg Dyke and work with the very professional CEOs, Martin Glenn and Mark Bullingham.

**Wembley Board:** it was extraordinary to watch architects of the calibre of Lord Foster and Rod Sheard at work at close hand during my two years (1998–2000) helping to create the new Wembley Stadium. I sat alongside many interesting people in the role, including Ken Bates (who should be credited for his vision), CEO Michael Cunnah and, notably, Ian Peacock, the former head of Dunlop Slazenger, and a giant in both the golf and tennis worlds. He is one of the kindest and most courteous men I have ever met, and both he and his wife Philippa became close friends, and devoted Ipswich fans.

**FA Learning:** Sir Trevor Brooking, Dani Every, Jamie Houchen, Chris Saunders, John Little, Frank Dick and Howard Wilkinson were all fundamental to what we achieved at what proved to be an essential precursor to the St George's Park project.

**St George's Park:** I owe a debt of gratitude to the late David Triesman, Ian Watmore and the entire FA Board for entrusting me with the task. Alex Horne, Ali Maclean, Danielle Every and Jane Bateman were immense from day one, as were our board of Sir Bob Murray, Frank McArdle, Barry Bright and Sir Trevor Brooking, while it was a gold star moment when we found Julie Harrington, who was supported as MD by the incomparable Holly Murdoch and Sylvia Blackshaw. The early backing from Richard Bevan at the League Managers Association was a major and much appreciated factor in getting the ball rolling. Special praise should also be reserved for architect Alan Smith, whose design is as inspirational as it is enduring, with credit also due to his colleague Barry Farrar and to the whole project team. I also want to thank Sir Gareth Southgate, who was resolute in his support and belief in the importance of St George's Park from day one, as was technical director Dan Ashurst and later John McDermott.

**The FA Technical Advisory Board:** the support of Martin Glenn, Sir Trevor Brooking and Sir Gareth Southgate was invaluable in setting up the TAB in 2016, when it was a groundbreaking concept. Sir Dave Brailsford, Stuart Lancaster, Manoj Badale, Michael Barber, Col. Lucy Giles, Baroness Sue Campbell, Matthew Syed, Graeme Le Saux, Dame Katherine Grainger all joined me on the board.

**The FA Professional Advisory Group:** this became just as important thanks to the huge contribution made by Mark Bullingham, Jobi McAnuff, John McDermott, Paul Cleal, Thomas Tuchel, Sarina Wiegman, Lee Carsley and Anthony Barry in the TAB's reconstitution as the PAG in 2024. We were joined by Manoj Badale, Michael (Lord) Barber, Col. Lucy Giles, Damian Hughes and Kevin Sinfield, and I can honestly say that none of what we did would have been possible without this pantheon of brilliant and inspired leaders who brought so much energy and wisdom to our meetings at both groups.

**Suffolk Community Foundation:** I worked alongside Simon Loftus, Clare Euston, David Barclay, Claire Horsley, Fi Mahony, Canon Graham Hedger, Richard Middleton and Clare Howes and many others to help set up the foundation, and the first executives, Stephen Singleton, Judi Newman and Mandy Aziz, then took it on; it was a truly rewarding experience, and a charity that I am very proud to see flourishing today under the leadership of George Vestey and Hannah Bloom.

**UK Community Foundations:** Matthew Bowcock encouraged me to get involved, and it was great to have Stephen Hammersley there for his early guidance. Later, finding Fabian French was one of the best things I have done, and he became an excellent chief executive. Tim Kiddell in No. 10 was a huge supporter, as was Cath Dovey, while Gay Huey-Evans did a wonderful job in chairing Beacon Philanthropy.

**The Churchill Fellowship:** immense thanks are due to chairman and dear friend Jeremy Soames, who encouraged me to become a trustee, my fellow trustees, CEO Julia Weston, and also Claire Dakin, Valerie Humphrey and Cat Smith who helped and guided me with the Activate appeal for their 60th anniversary.

**Debate Mate:** I loved contributing to this extraordinary charity that teaches self-confidence, literacy, fluency and so much more through learning the art of debating. It works through schools, often in deprived areas, and is also active in the business world. My thanks are due to their indefatigable and inspirational founder Margaret McCabe, as well as Scarlett McCabe and Jess Dix.

**Vistage:** I have been very fortunate, later in life, to find Vistage and the uplifting world of leadership coaching, so thanks is owed to my coaches Steve McNulty and Tony Price, Cat Cawley (a classmate from my induction process), and wonderful staff Sam Oddie, Karen Price, Karen Butcher, as well as our leader in the US, Sam Reese. We never disclose who takes part in Vistage groups; however, it wouldn't have happened without the fabulous members who joined my various groups over the past ten years: so mega thank yous to all the Alliums, Diamonds and Disruptors – you know who you are, and your friendship and trust has been immense and will always be treasured.

I have worked with several other organisations that I haven't managed to include in the main story of the book, but who I want to thank:

**Twenty First Group:** I was thrilled to become an early investor and supporter of this pioneering company, who are leaders in sports data and predictive intelligence, so my thanks go to Compton Hellyer for bringing me on board and to the brilliant team led by Blake Wooster.

**Environmental Biotech:** thanks to Aziz and Riz Tejpar for inviting me into their family business.

**Coutts Bank:** Michael Norfolk, Michael Morley, Ian Turland, Harry Keogh, Joanna Thornell, Dylan Williams and Mark Noble and their many colleagues have my full appreciation for their assistance and kindness.

**IPRS:** thanks to Dave Bingham and later Martyn Jackson.

**Video Platform:** the extraordinarily clever Graham Baines invited me to assist in promoting this visionary company that produces next-generation meme games, placing groups of friends directly inside the games, with themes that range from politics to sport, and from news to celebrities.

**Onside Law:** I enjoyed working with Jamie Singer, Oli Hunt, Chris Walsh, Simon Thorpe and Compton Hellyer (again) in the formative years of what has become one of the country's pre-eminent sports law firms.

**Argent Related:** I am indebted to Rob Townshend for recommending me, and to Richard Meier and Hannah Grealish, and director Nick Searl who signed me up, as well as Heath Harvey who came from the FA to lead our efforts on Brent Cross.

**Alexander Ross:** I had a lot of fun with my partners David Davies, Ben Hatton, Joanna Burns and Mike Blood – it could have been so successful in another world!

**Somerset County Cricket Club:** I am grateful to Michael Barber (who was elevated to the peerage while I was writing this book) for inviting me to help, and also to Jamie Cox, Andy Hurry, Jason Kerr, Matt Drakely and Erin Osborne. We have been pushing back the boundaries and punching above our weight with the inspired help of Vic Marks, Frank Dick, Lucy Giles and Peter Frankopan.

**The Professional Golfers' Association (PGA) Advisory Group:** Between 2017 and 2021 I led a small advisory group for the PGA, at the request of chief executive Rob Maxfield. It was much like what we had done with football and latterly cricket, and joining us were Manoj Badale, Chris Sullivan and Jonathan (Lord) Marland. This was enjoyable and interesting work, done pro bono.

**Humotion GMBH:** Johannes Rosenmueller, who invented 'smart track' technology, brought me on board to help promote his company, which captures advanced data with installations at athletics facilities and training grounds across the world.

**Weatherbys Bank:** I recently joined this exceptional private bank and have enjoyed supporting them, so my thanks and appreciation are very much due to Nick Gornall and his team.

# Appendix
# Statistics while Chairman at ITFC

| Season | Manager | League | League Position | FA Cup (round) | League Cup (round) | UEFA CUP (round) | Anglo-Italian Cup | Top Scorer | Ave. Home League Attendance |
|---|---|---|---|---|---|---|---|---|---|
| 95/96 | George Burley | 1st Division | 7 | 5th | 2nd | - | English SF | Alex Mathie & Ian Marshall (19) | 12,588 |
| 96/97 | George Burley | 1st Division | 4 | 3rd | QF | - | - | Paul Mason (15) | 12,024 |
| 97/98 | George Burley | 1st Division | 5 | 4th | QF | - | - | David Johnson (22) | 14,893 |
| 98/99 | George Burley | 1st Division | 3 | 4th | 2nd | - | - | David Johnson & James Scowcroft (14) | 16,963 |
| 99/00 | George Burley | 1st Division | 3 | 3rd | 2nd | - | - | David Johnson (23) | 18,524 |
| 00/01 | George Burley | Premier League | 5 | 4th | 5th | - | - | Marcus Stewart (21) | 22,532 |
| 01/02 | George Burley | Premier League | 18 | 4th | 4th | 3rd | - | Marcus Bent & Marcus Stewart (10) | 24,425 |
| 02/03 | George Burley / Joe Royle | 1st Division | 7 | 4th | 4th | 2nd | - | Pablo Counago (20) | 25,455 |
| 03/04 | Joe Royle | 1st Division | 5 | 4th | 2nd | - | - | Darren Bent (16) | 24,520 |
| 04/05 | Joe Royle | Championship | 3 | 3rd | 2nd | - | - | Shefki Kuqi (20) | 25,651 |
| 05/06 | Joe Royle | Championship | 15 | 3rd | 1st | - | - | Nicky Forster (7) | 24,253 |
| 06/07 | Jim Magilton | Championship | 14 | 5th | 1st | - | - | Alan Lee (17) | 22,445 |
| 07/08 | Jim Magilton | Championship | 8 | 3rd | 1st | - | - | Jonathan Walters (13) | 21,935 |
| 08/09 | Jim Magilton / Roy Keane | Championship | 9 | 4th | 3rd | - | - | Jonathan Stead (13) | 20,961 |